C000177023

THE COMPLETE BOOK OF THE
UNEXPLAINED

THE COMPLETE BOOK OF THE
UNEXPLAINED

A THRILLING EXPLORATION OF THE EARTH'S MOST BAFFLING MYSTERIES

Lucy Doncaster, Karen Farrington and Andrew Holland

ARCTURUS

Arcturus Publishing Limited
26/27 Bickels Yard
151–153 Bermondsey Street
London SE1 3HA

Published in association with
foulsham
W. Foulsham & Co. Ltd,
The Publishing House, Bennetts Close, Cippenham,
Slough, Berkshire SL1 5AP, England

ISBN: 978-0-572-03397-2

This edition printed in 2007
Copyright © 2007 Arcturus Publishing Limited

All rights reserved

The Copyright Act prohibits (subject to certain very limited
exceptions) the making of copies of any copyright work or of a
substantial part of such a work, including the making of copies by
photocopying or similar process. Written permission to make a copy
or copies must therefore normally be obtained from the publisher in
advance. It is advisable also to consult the publisher if in any doubt
as to the legality of any copying which is to be undertaken.

British Library Cataloguing-in-Publication Data: a catalogue
record for this book is available from the British Library

Printed in China

Authors: Lucy Doncaster, Karen Farrington and Andrew Holland
Editor: Ella Fern
Design: Repro India

Picture credits: Arcturus 90, 100; Phyllis Budinger 97; Corbis 5, 6, 10, 12, 15, 31, 33, 39, 41, 47, 54, 57, 59, 60, 73, 74, 84, 88, 104, 119, 132, 134, 136, 147, 162, 218, 221, 223, 230, 247, 250, 267, 269, 274; Hulton/Getty front cover, 16, 17, 18, 20, 22, 27, 29, 37, 44, 45, 50, 51, 69, 75, 78, 81, 93, 94, 107, 108, 111, 113, 117, 120, 122, 126, 128, 130, 138, 141, 142, 143, 145, 153, 155, 156, 158, 160, 167, 169, 171, 173, 175, 179, 187, 190, 191, 192, 194, 196, 198, 201, 209, 215, 217, 234, 236, 241, 243, 246, 251, 253, 255, 258, 260, 261, 263, 265, 275, 277, 280, 282, 283, 284, 289, 292, 294, 297, 298, 299, 301, 303; Mary Evans 7, 25, 65, 98, 103, 164, 183, 225, 256; Rex Features 184, 203, 205; Shutterstock chapter heading images, 8, 34, 70, 114, 150, 176, 206, 224, 238, 270, 286.

CONTENTS

THE ENIGMAS OF SPACE

GHOSTLY ENCOUNTERS

SEERS AND ORACLES

PARANORMAL POWERS

Curses and Witchcraft

Sorcery is an age-old obsession. Humans seem irresistibly drawn to using supernatural powers against each other — whether it be in the form of issuing curses against places or people, or brewing up poisonous concoctions to seal the fate of another. The prospect that someone can manipulate natural or supernatural forces to their own ends is a frightening one, but when the practice of such ritual magic has been condemned, it has led to cruel and unjust punishment that seems to be the work of the Devil himself.

THE POWER OF CURSES

Can the utterance of a few malicious words really change someone's destiny? Those who believe in the power of a curse are convinced that catastrophe will follow in its wake. And sometimes ensuing mishaps and disasters are so bizarre and numerous that all the evidence points to a jinx.

Perhaps the most infamous curse of all was one that protected the tomb of King Tutankhamen. When Egyptologist Howard Carter discovered the tomb in 1922, it was the culmination of a career spent scouring the desert for riches. The honour of opening the inner door, revealing the treasures of the king in all their splendour, fell to Lord Carnarvon (financier of the expedition) on 17 February 1923. Within weeks after that fateful day Carnarvon was dead, apparently from an infected mosquito bite. The bite mark on his cheek was said to resemble one borne by the boy king himself.

When Carnarvon died, the lights in Cairo flickered and failed, while miles away at home his dog fell into a fit and passed away. Tales of other

> The bite mark on his cheek was said to resemble one borne by the boy king himself.

expedition members dying suddenly abounded. Even the pilots who transported the royal artefacts as cargo apparently met unexpected deaths. For several years the string of ill fortune continued, as museum curators associated with the exhibition of Tutankhamen's treasures keeled over.

The curse that protected the tomb was written in hieroglyphics on a clay tablet. When deciphered, it read: 'Death will slay with its wings whoever disturbs the peace of the Pharaoh.'

Lord Carnarvon and Howard Carter with Carnarvon's daughter, Lady Evelyn Herbert, at the entrance to the tomb of King Tutankhamen.

Yet, despite careful cataloguing of all the tomb's contents, the dire warning has vanished. Perhaps it never existed in the first place, being the product of some sun-affected imagination. However, there is another explanation. Carter may well have hidden the tablet bearing the curse to prevent a walk-out by superstitious local workers, on whom he was reliant for his work.

Cynics have poured scorn over the curse claims, pointing out that mosquito bites were and still are frequently fatal. They say that the lights in Cairo often blacked out, and that the story of the death of Carnarvon's dog is only anecdotal. Much

'Death will slay with its wings whoever disturbs the peace of the Pharaoh.'

has recently been made of the theory that the tomb contained lethal spores that afflicted those who went inside, giving weight to the sceptics' argument. Yet when Carter died a decade later it was from natural causes. The debate on the curse continues.

Belief in curses stretches back into the mists of time. Ancient verbal curses may seem comical today, but in the past they would strike terror into the heart: 'May the seven terriers of hell sit on the spool of your breast and bark in at your soul-case,' says an old Irish curse. 'She should have stones and not children,' according to a Yiddish one.

In the past people have made a profitable business out of issuing curses. The philosopher Plato (427–347BC) wrote in *The Republic*, 'If anyone wishes to injure an enemy; for a small fee they (sorcerers) will bring harm on good or bad alike, binding the gods to serve their purposes by spells and curses.'

Curses are a common Biblical theme, perhaps the most famous being issued by God against Adam and Eve in the Garden of Eden.

A wrathful god appears to have orchestrated fearful vengeance after a priceless diamond was plundered from a temple in Mandala, Burma in the seventeenth century. Originally mined in India, it was a fabulous violet-coloured specimen of the very highest quality.

No one knows what happened to the thief, but it fell into the possession of a French trader, Jean-Baptiste Tavernier. Tavernier sold the diamond to French king Louis XIV, who had it made into a heart before giving it to his mistress Madame de Montespan. Shortly afterwards she was publicly disgraced in a black magic scandal. The luckless trader Tavernier met a grisly end on a trip to Russia and dogs were discovered gnawing on his bones.

The gem remained in the royal collection, and it was worn by Marie Antoinette before she was beheaded in the French Revolution. In the chaos that enveloped Paris in the aftermath of the Revolution, the diamond was stolen and its whereabouts were unknown for some three decades. Could it be that the curse of the Hope Diamond had finally lost its power?

The diamond turned up in the 1830s, in the possession of Dutch diamond cutter Wilhelm Fals. Its exquisite beauty bewitched his son Hendrick, and the hapless boy ultimately committed suicide.

The dangerous gem was then bought by the banker Henry Philip Hope, who gave it his name, but suffered no harm from it. Afterwards, though, the curse appears to have gained some momentum. It was bequeathed to a relative, Lord Francis Hope, whose marriage collapsed.

By 1904 a certain Jacques Colot was the owner, until he lost his mind and committed suicide. Russian nobleman Prince Kanilovsky presented it to his lover, whom he later shot and killed before being bludgeoned to death himself. Diamond dealer Habib Bey drowned and Greek merchant Simon Montharides plunged to his death with his wife and child when their carriage went over a cliff top. The diamond then went to the Ottoman ruler, Abdul Hamid III, shortly before an uprising usurped the Sultanate. His favourite wife, often seen wearing the jewel, was stabbed to death.

Evelyn Walsh McLean, who bought the Hope Diamond from jewellery impresario Pierre Cartier for $180,000.

Evelyn had received numerous warnings about the curse of the Hope diamond.

The last ill-fated owner was wealthy Evelyn Walsh McLean. Within a year of purchasing the diamond from jewellery impresario Pierre Cartier for $180,000, her son Vinson was killed in a car accident. Her husband Ned began drinking, left her for another woman and finally lost his mind. Then, in 1946, their daughter took an overdose of sleeping pills. After Evelyn died in 1947 the gem finally went into the Smithsonian Institute in Washington, a move that appears to have neutered its potency.

Evelyn had received numerous warnings about the curse of the Hope Diamond, many in unsolicited letters from strangers. But she maintained that the bad luck attached to its ownership was pure chance. 'What tragedies have befallen me might have occurred had I never seen or touched the Hope Diamond. My observations have persuaded me that tragedies, for anyone who lives, are not escapable.'

From treading the sacred corridors of Tutankhamen's tomb, to plundering the exquisite jewels of Burma, many of the most potent curses seem to be released when humans tread too far into forbidden territory. And where some curses seem to lose potency over time, others retain their venom, wreaking havoc down generations…

HAITIAN ZOMBIES

We think of zombies as the dreadful creatures with a taste for human flesh that we see in films. These are, of course, the products of fertile imaginations and talented make-up artists in film studios. Yet there is evidence to show that zombies really do exist. Sapped of their personalities, probably by a cocktail of drugs, they are lowly slaves rendered incapable of independent action.

The phenomenon of zombies is associated with the voodoo faith in Haiti, and there are several well-documented examples, including that of Clairvius Narcisse.

Clairvius Narcisse died at the Albert Schweitzer Hospital in Haiti in 1962. After his death had been certified, he was buried. Eighteen years later, Clairvius himself turned up at his sister's house, very much alive, and able to recount stories from their childhood that only he could know. He told how his brothers had been angry about his refusal to sell family land, and how they had sought revenge by ordering his zombification.

After his burial, during which he lay conscious but inert in his coffin, Clairvius was taken from the graveyard and became the subject of spells by a voodoo witch doctor (known as a bokor) that turned him into an 'empty vessel'. He was able to move, but he could not communicate properly and had lost his free will. Voodoo worshippers see a zombie as a body without a soul, and this is what he seemed to have become. For two years he worked in the fields alongside other zombies. After the death of his master he lived rough for eighteen years, returning home only when he was sure that the brothers who engineered his zombification were themselves dead.

Depictions of zombies are often the fanciful creations of film studios, but evidence suggests that they are in fact humans thrown into a zombified state by a cocktail of drugs.

Clairvius' story matched with the hospital records. His cheek bore a scar that, he said, was inflicted when a nail was driven into his coffin. So what happened to him after his 'death' in hospital?

For years the assumption was that zombies – if they existed – were literally raised from the dead through the supernatural powers of the bokor. Today it seems more likely that a poison is administered to a living victim. This poison slows down bodily functions so much that they become imperceptible and the body seems corpse-like. Following burial, the barely-breathing body is then retrieved and further drugs are given that bring about a controlled recovery. So while the victim might regain physical strength, his mind remains feeble and his memory is all but erased.

Much of the mystery was revealed by anthropologist Dr E. Wade Davis, who, following extensive research, assured the world: 'Zombiism actually exists. There are Haitians who have been raised from their graves and returned to life.' Davis analysed some of the poisons used by bokors and found toad skin and puffer fish were two of the most significant ingredients in the poison used to induce a coma. Toad venom is known as a potent painkiller, while the puffer fish contains tetrodotoxin that affects the nervous system. Thereafter, different drugs, including Jimson's Weed (a poisonous type of nightshade plant), are used to keep the victims of zombification stupefied.

Davis paid tribute to the macabre talents of the voodoo bokors: 'A witch doctor in Haiti is very skilled in administering just the right dose of poison. Too much poison will kill the victim completely and resuscitation will not be possible. Too little and the victim will not be a convincing corpse.'

Davis acknowledges that the deep religious beliefs prevailing in Haiti are vital to the process carried out by the bokor. Because people believe in zombiism, it is more likely to become a reality. The voodoo religion is intense and ritualistic, although not inevitably sinister. Broadly speaking, voodoo is a cross between native African beliefs and the Catholic faith once forced upon slaves when they were transported to destinations like Haiti. Davis believes that zombiism is carried out as a punishment and the mindset of the Haitian people permits bokors to do their worst.

'Zombiism actually exists. There are Haitians who have been raised from their graves and returned to life.'

Certainly this unquestioning and fearful faith would explain how the dictator Francois 'Papa Doc' Duvalier (1907–71) maintained his grip on the reins of power in Haiti. After coming to power in 1957, Duvalier posed as a witch doctor to encourage the belief that he possessed unearthly powers. His henchmen were called the Tonton Macoute, taking their name from the Haitian word for 'bogeymen'. The implication that transgressors would be turned into zombies – or that the Tonton Macoute were themselves zombies – loomed large. Political opponents were murdered and poverty became endemic as Duvalier inflated

his personal bank account. Only long after his death did the population realize they had been duped. But Duvalier's death did not rid them of their folk superstition, and they hauled his corpse from its grave and ritually beat it.

Some commentators remain unconvinced, and question whether zombies exist at all. One piece of research found that the vast majority of Haitians said they knew of a zombie. On further examination, however, it was always a distant cousin or friend of a friend that was the zombie rather than someone they knew well. This is also a feature of 'urban legends' in Western society, when outrageous events occur to someone known only by reputation to the storyteller.

Another theory is that the zombies are in fact people suffering from mental illness who, in the absence of an effective healthcare system, are compelled to wander the countryside begging or undertaking menial labouring jobs to survive. Bereaved relatives identify the so-called zombies as family members through the distortion of grief and because of a desire to see the dead person once more.

But the existence of zombies among Haitians is beyond question, and there is even legislation on the issue. According to the penal code it is illegal to induce a lethargic coma in another person. If proved, the perpetrator is treated in the same way as a murderer.

The toxins in puffer fish are a significant ingredient in the poisons used by bokors. A delicacy in Japan, where it is enjoyed for making taste-buds tingle, the fish has induced coma and even death in some diners.

'THE LITTLE BASTARD'

James Dean, the iconic Hollywood film star, died tragically young, at a point in his life when his acting career was going from strength to strength. Although he had starred in only a few films, he had earned himself much acclaim and a sizeable fortune. His death appeared to be the result of a terrible accident, but further probing revealed that a malevolent force may have been at work.

With his new-found riches, Dean had bought a sports car, a Porsche Spyder, one of only ninety in the world at that time. He nicknamed the car 'The Little Bastard', and had this name painted on the machine along with a racing stripe.

Dean had intended to race his beloved car himself, but sadly never had the chance. On 30 September 1955, only two weeks after buying the car, he died in it, following a head-on collision with another vehicle. The driver of the other car survived, having sustained only cuts and bruises.

In the weeks preceding his death, Dean had been seen driving his car everywhere, proudly displaying it to all of his friends, although he was surprised to find that many of them failed to share his enthusiasm for the powerful machine.

Several of them apparently felt a sense of horror when they saw the vehicle – some out of concern for the dangers that such a fast car might pose to Dean's reckless nature, others simply because of an innate sense of foreboding about the machine.

James Dean, as he appeared in the film *Giant*.

At the time, Dean would not have been aware that a number of strange happenings had already been linked with the car since its arrival at the Competition Motors showroom. Several mechanics had hurt themselves on the car shortly after it was delivered, one breaking his thumb after trapping it in one of the doors and another cutting himself as he adjusted the engine. At the time, these events seemed to be no more than accidents, but later they would be seen as part of a much larger pattern of misfortune, or even something altogether more sinister.

After the fatal crash, the car wreckage was bought for salvage by the motor mechanic George Barris, the very man who had customized the machine for Dean several weeks earlier. It was only when he began to re-use parts of the car that he started to suspect that some form of terrible curse might be attached to the vehicle, a curse that had not only claimed the life of the young film star, but was also causing numerous other disasters in the lives of those unlucky enough to have acquired a piece of the car.

The engine of 'The Little Bastard' had been largely undamaged by the crash, so Barris had reconditioned it and sold it to a racing enthusiast, Dr William F. Eschrich. One of the doctor's friends and fellow racer, Dr Carl McHenry, learned of the sale and decided to buy the transaxle of the car. Barris also sold several other vehicle parts, including the two back tyres.

In the first race in which the two doctors tested their new equipment, both men were involved in serious accidents. Dr Eschrich's car turned over after locking up on entering a bend. Fortunately he survived the crash, although he was left paralysed. Dr McHenry was not so lucky: he was killed after losing control of the car and hitting a tree.

As if this were not enough, before the week was out, the driver who had bought the two back tyres narrowly escaped death after both tyres blew out simultaneously during another race.

Learning of the multiple disasters, Barris decided that he would try to put the car to some kind of beneficial use. Accordingly, he lent the crumpled machine to the California Highway Safety Patrol for publicity purposes, thinking that Dean's fame would greatly enhance their campaign on accident prevention. Unfortunately, at that point he did not realize that the car was actually a source of accidents in itself.

The car was taken into the possession of the Highway Patrol and stored in a garage with a large number of other cars. While it was there, a mysterious fire broke out – many cars were completely destroyed and almost all incurred serious damage. Curiously, 'The Little Bastard' emerged from the fire remarkably unscathed.

A short time later, while the car was being taken to a display area for demonstration purposes, a strange accident took place. Dean's

The wreckage of 'The Little Bastard' being lifted away after James Dean's fatal crash in September 1955.

car was being transported on the back of a flat-bed truck, driven by an experienced driver named George Barhuis, when it skidded on a wet road, and the truck's rig crashed into a ditch. Barhuis was thrown from the cab by the impact, but is believed to have survived the crash. However, in a bewildering tragedy, he was then killed when the wreck of 'The Little Bastard' fell from the back of the truck and landed on top of him, crushing him to death.

Yet the litany of disasters was still not complete. On the fourth anniversary of Dean's fatal crash, a teenager in Detroit was viewing the car, which was on a large display. Without warning, the structure on which the car was resting collapsed, and the car toppled forward, crushing the boy's legs. It seems inconceivable

that, following this, the car was still put out on display to the public.

A few weeks after this accident, the car was once again being transported by truck, when it fell from the back of the vehicle, smashing into the road and causing the serious injury of yet more people.

The wreck of 'The Little Bastard' fell from the back of the truck and landed on top of him, crushing him to death.

Fortunately, the cursed car was doomed itself. Shortly after this final accident, the vehicle spontaneously fell apart while on show in New Orleans. Attempts were made to put it back together, but George Barris stepped in and arranged to have the remains of the car transported back to his garage in California. When the delivery arrived, the container was opened and, to their astonishment, the car had disappeared.

It is not known if it had been stolen by an obsessive admirer of the film star, but no trace of it has ever been found. Certainly, if anyone had been foolish enough to take the vehicle into their own possession, they would have been very fortunate to escape the curse that had randomly struck at those connected with the car.

Nevertheless, the fact that it is now missing can only add to the sense of mystery that surrounds not only this jinxed machine, but also the tragic, doomed figure of James Dean.

The grave of James Dean in Fairmount, USA, is still visited regularly by the actor's many admiring fans from all over the world, who leave quirky tributes to their hero.

THE EARLS OF MAR

The ruins of Alloa Tower in Scotland are now all that remains of a vast manor, the hereditary seat of the Erskine family, the Earls of Mar. The fate of the place was interwoven with that of the family who lived there, not just because they had lived there for generations, but because of the curse that predicted and assured the doom of the family and the seat of their power.

It is believed that this curse was uttered against the Earl of Mar by the Abbot of CambusKenneth during the sixteenth century. In destroying the Abbey at CambusKenneth, the Earl had unwittingly sealed the fate of his lineage for years to come, for many of the predicted details of the curse, although cryptic when uttered, were to come shockingly true.

It predicted that a future Erskine would later live to see his home consumed by flames while his wife burned inside it and three of his children would never see the light of day.

Remarkably, it was not unusual at that time for Scottish curses to predict suffering that would last for several generations, but this particular curse was very specific about certain matters. Most importantly, and typically for a curse of this kind, it was foretold that the Erskine family would become extinct – a fate which was the ultimate disaster for any hereditary aristocratic lineage. The curse elaborated further: before the family died out, all its estates and property would fall into the hands of strangers – again, this would have been a horrifying concept to a family of landed gentry.

At this point it might have been expected that even the Abbot's rage would have been satisfied, but the curse continued.

It predicted that a future Erskine would later live to see his home consumed by flames while his wife burned inside it and three of his children would never see the light of day. Moreover, adding further disgrace to the name of Erskine, the great hall of the family seat would be used to stable horses and a lowly weaver would work in the grand chamber of state. The curse was predicted to end only after all this had passed and an ash sapling had taken root at the top of the tower.

Although the curse must have worried the Earl of Mar, he managed to live his entire life without seeing any of the predicted events come true and, on his deathbed, he must have reflected that the family had escaped from the Abbot's wrathful utterings. In this, he was greatly mistaken.

This seems to have been a patient curse because it was a while before certain events began to show the truth behind the predictions. In 1715 a subsequent Earl of Mar declared his allegiance to James Stuart, the son of James VII of Scotland, who was known as 'the Old Pretender'. The Earl led a failed Jacobite rebellion against the crown in an attempt to install James Stuart as king. He was defeated and, in retribution, the family were stripped of their land and titles – in this way, one part of the curse had come true. Whether the Earl actually attributed this to the curse is unknown, as he might have merely viewed events as a punishment for his own actions. However, more of the predictions were to be borne out within a few generations.

Almost a century later, in 1801, it was John Francis Erskine who was unlucky enough to bear the brunt of the prophecy, and so pay the price for his ancestor's mistakes. To begin with, three of his children were born completely blind – thus, as the curse had foretold, they would 'never see the light of day'. Then Alloa Tower, all that remained of the family's former glory, was devastated by fire and Erskine's wife perished in the flames.

The main body of the curse had now come true and only the details were left to be completed. Sure enough, a troop of cavalry used the half-

A contemporary portrait of James Stuart.

ruined hall as shelter for their horses while they were moving around the country. Subsequently, a homeless weaver took up residence in the ruins of the building and plied his trade in the nearby town. In around 1820 a small ash tree was seen to have taken root in the ruins of Alloa Tower. The curse had now been fulfilled in every detail.

Of all the questions that spring to mind in this case, the first revolves around the existence of the curse. Was it ever really uttered or could it have been made up after the events to explain and justify the demise of the Erskines and serve as a useful warning to other potentially rebellious landowners? Certainly, both historical fact and local folklore indicate that the curse was true, but there is always the possibility that, rather than having the ability to bring about such terrible events, the Abbot was simply in possession of astonishing visionary powers.

Either possibility could apply in this case. Perhaps the Abbot did have the power to seal the destiny of the Erskine family through a curse, or maybe his powers of divination were comparable to those of a prophet, although this would appear to be the only instance of such a prediction from the Abbot. Whatever the truth of the matter, it seems that the mystical powers of the Abbot of CambusKenneth were so great that they are remembered to this very day.

CHIEF CORNSTALK

For many years the area of West Virginia known as Point Pleasant has been beset by a series of disasters and misfortunes. Although these could be attributed to nothing more than bad luck, some ascribe the events to the ancient curse of a betrayed Indian chief.

In order to understand the nature and power of a curse, it is necessary to know the background to the events – only then can it be judged whether there could have been sufficient cause for such a potent force of revenge. The story in this particular case dates back more than 200 years, to the 1770s, when the American frontiersmen were battling against the Native Americans in their attempts to push west, and later fighting the British for their independence.

As the American settlers found their way to the land around the Ohio River, now West Virginia, they encountered strong resistance from the Indian tribes, some of whom had joined together to form a powerful confederacy. This group of native American Indians was led by the chieftain of the Shawnee tribe, a man called Keigh-tugh-gua (Cornstalk).

A battle between the American settlers and the Indians took place in 1774, and both sides sustained heavy losses. The Indians were forced to retreat westwards as the settlers took over the land and fortified it. Cornstalk, recognizing that he would have trouble defeating such heavily armed men, decided to make peace with them.

A few years later, trouble was to erupt again, as the British began to stir up feeling against the rebellious settlers. They tried to bring as many Indians over onto their side as possible and several tribes from Cornstalk's old confederacy joined them to prepare an attack on the settlements. Cornstalk chose instead to honour his peace and he and another chief, Red Hawk of the Delaware tribe, went to the American fort to discuss the situation.

Cornstalk's young son, Ellinipisco, came to the fort,... whereupon he was also taken hostage.

On their arrival, the chieftains were taken hostage by the Americans, as it was believed that the Indians would not attack while their chiefs were being held. While in captivity, Cornstalk was well treated, and even assisted the American settlers in planning their tactics against the British. After a few days, Cornstalk's young son, Ellinipisco, came to the fort with news for his father, whereupon he was also taken hostage.

Shortly after this, events took a dramatic turn for the worse after a number of American soldiers who had gone out to hunt deer were ambushed and killed by Indians. When this was discovered, discipline inside the fort broke down and an angry mob broke into the prisoners' quarters with murder in mind. They showed no mercy to Cornstalk or his young son, who was shot before his very eyes. It was this act of murder and betrayal that prompted Cornstalk to utter his mighty curse, words that, it seems, have affected the area for hundreds of years.

A Shawnee warrior of the Chillicothe tribe.

According to legend, he declared 'I came to this fort as your friend and you murdered me. You have murdered by my side my young son. For this may the curse of the Great Spirit rest upon this land. May it be blighted by nature. May it be blighted in its hopes.'

After these tragic events had taken place, Cornstalk was afforded a proper burial, and he was interred near the fort where he had been killed. He was not allowed to rest in peace, however, since his remains were dug up and moved twice for the sake of new buildings and monuments – first in 1840, and then again in 1950. If the original act of betrayal had not been sufficient to secure the power of the curse, then the desecration of his grave surely was.

This area became known as Point Pleasant and, almost in defiance of the curse, residents decided to erect a monument in honour of the soldiers who had defeated Cornstalk in the first battle of 1774. Strangely, this monument was to be struck twice by lightning, first in 1909, delaying its unveiling ceremony, and then again in 1921, causing serious damage.

These happenings were nothing, however, compared to the catalogue of disasters that was to befall this relatively small community. In 1880 a huge fire ravaged an entire block in the centre of town, while in 1907 America's worst mining disaster was responsible for the deaths of 310 men. In 1967, the Silver Bridge disaster killed forty-six people. This coincided with strange local sightings such as lights in the sky and the regular appearance of the mysterious stalker known as 'Mothman'.

Shortly after this, in 1968 and 1970, a number of aircraft crashed in the area, killing more than 100 passengers. In 1978 a derailed freight train caused an immense spill of toxic chemicals that poisoned the land and the water basin of the area, destroying all the local wells.

It is thought that this environmental catastrophe could be the blight of nature mentioned in Cornstalk's curse, while the blighting of hope appears to have been manifest in the depressed economy of Point Pleasant.

There are many who would maintain that when disaster befalls a person or community, it is just a matter of misfortune. To suggest that it is as a result of a curse, they say, is to resort to ancient superstitions which have no place in the modern world. When, however, such a huge chain of catastrophes occurs, as has been the case with Point Pleasant, it is difficult not to admit that a curse might have been responsible after all.

THE SALEM WITCHCRAFT TRIALS

In 1692, seventy years after the arrival of the Pilgrim Fathers, Salem village in Massachusetts became the focus of a feverish witch-hunt that resulted in the death sentence for twenty residents and the imprisonment of dozens more. Salem remains a byword for Satanic hysteria to this day.

It all began as child's play. The young people of Salem, constricted by overbearing Puritanism, were agog to hear vivid stories woven by Tituba, a Carib slave brought to the community from the West Indies. The tribal ritual and magic recounted by Tituba must have seemed a world away from the existence of grinding toil led by Salem residents.

But when 9-year-old Betty Parris fell ill and could not be cured by orthodox methods, the doctor said she was bewitched. The affliction then spread to her friends, who writhed and groaned and uttered fanciful accusations against adults.

The childrens' imagination was fired not only by the tales told by Tituba, but also by the words of self-appointed Satan expert Cotton Mather, author of a recently published tome relating to the symptoms of witchcraft. Furthermore, they had been experimenting with fortune telling, and they knew their curiosity had led them into forbidden realms. The guilty children believed themselves to be bitten and pinched by devilish creatures and were soon seeing witches too.

Perhaps unsurprisingly, Tituba was swiftly arrested and faced the accusation of witchcraft. Two other women were also hauled before the authorities. One was Sarah Good, a pipe-smoking beggar, and the other was Sarah Osburne, a widow known to hold the Church in contempt. Matters might have died down following their confinement, but for the admission by Tituba, implicating the other two women, of contact

> The guilty children believed themselves to be bitten and pinched by devilish creatures.

with Satan himself. When the child accusers were brought into their company, the youngsters fell into fits – proof, if any were needed, that these women were indeed witches.

Now the zealous village dignitaries led a witch-hunt, convinced that the Devil's agents were lurking in their midst.

The first witch to hang was Bridget Bishop, in her late fifties and a tavern owner of dubious reputation. A field hand claimed to have seen Bishop's image stealing eggs and then transforming into a cat to run off with her

Four-year-old Dorcas Good was arrested after Salem children claimed to have been attacked by her spectre.

plunder. Another villager said she visited him at night in spectral form to torment him. Yet others maintained that she was responsible for numerous examples of bad luck in the community.

A short excerpt from the trial of Bridget Bishop reveals how pointless it was for supposed witches to try and prove their innocence. When she was accused of being a witch, the luckless woman replied: 'I know nothing of it...I know not what a witch is.'

'How do you know then that you are not a witch?' was the response of the prosecutor. Her continuing protests were deemed unsatisfactory in law. Following her trial she was taken to Gallows Hill on 10 June 1692 and hanged.

The plight of witch-hunt victims was heart-rending. Four-year-old Dorcas Good was arrested after Salem children claimed to have been attacked by her spectre. She spent months in jail in chains, weeping continually, and then watched her mother Sarah being carried off to the gallows.

Rebecca Nurse, devout and a pillar in the community, was found not guilty at her trial. Judge William Stoughton was so irate at the

decision that he sent the jury back to reconsider and they returned with a guilty verdict. On appeal, the state governor pardoned her, but prominent Salem men compelled him to reverse the decision. Eventually, Rebecca was excommunicated from the Church and sent to hang.

Deputy Constable John Willard was brought before the court after he refused to make further arrests. His fate was the same as the convicted witches. Another tavern owner, John Proctor, was denounced as a witch after pouring scorn on the trials. Robust in his own defence, he asked for the trial to be moved to Boston. His request was denied and he was hanged, although his pregnant wife was spared the noose.

Former minister Reverend George Burroughs, it was decided, led young girls into witchcraft. Before he was hanged he recited the Lord's Prayer, a feat supposedly impossible for a witch, and once again maintained his innocence. When the crowd hesitated, Cotton Mather himself stepped forward to remind them of the court's authority.

After Giles Corey refused to co-operate with the court he was pressed to death – pinned out in an open field with rocks piled upon his body until all life was crushed from it. This terrible punishment, probably illegal, was never used again in America.

Within a few months the lust for witch persecution in Salem was ebbing. A change in the judicial proceedings meant 'spectral evidence' was no longer accepted. Given that firm facts were in short supply, this effectively put an end to the string of convictions.

By May 1693, all prisoners awaiting trial or already convicted of witchcraft were released.

Judges and jurors alike were largely filled with remorse and made public apologies. The notable exception was William Stoughton, one of the driving forces in the campaign, who maintained that the village had been riddled with witches. He went on to become governor of Massachusetts.

However, no fewer than twenty people had lost their lives during the witch-fever, all through public execution. A further four people died in jail where conditions were foul. Two unlucky dogs were executed as witch accomplices.

The terrible events that took place in Salem in 1692–93 were the result of a small community riven with feuds. Suspicion and distrust were rife

No fewer than twenty people had lost their lives during the witch-fever, all through public execution.

amongst the villagers, and the witch-trials became an opportunity for them to settle long-standing scores.

At the time there was an unshakeable belief in the existence of witches. The dangers of Satan and his faithful crones were expounded weekly from the pulpit to the God-fearing congregation. Witchcraft was an issue often hotly debated among adults, particularly after Cotton Mather's book appeared.

But what of Tituba, at the start of all the troubles? Ironically – having confessed her guilt – she walked free, and was ultimately sold on into another community. The effects of her story-telling there remain unknown.

Some of the unlucky women of Salem, brought to trial for witchcraft. As their former friends and neighbours denounced them, they had little chance of survival against a corrupt court intent on the harshest punishment.

THE EVIL EYE

The 'evil eye' is one of the world's oldest superstitions, with many examples dating back to the time of the Ancient Egyptians. It is also one of the most unusual curses, for it can be cast only by those who themselves possess the evil eye and, remarkably, it is usually cast unintentionally. The evil eye can place a curse on almost anything, from children and livestock to crops and property.

This curse seems to have resonance with a large sector of humanity as it is known all over the world. The Scottish term for it is *droch shuil*, the Italian *mal occhio*, the Arabic *ayin harsha* and the Hebrew *ayin horeh*. Belief in its power is most concentrated around the Mediterranean and Aegean seas, but extends into Northern Europe, North Africa and the Middle East.

Those who possess the evil eye cannot simply acquire it – rather, they have to be born with it. Moreover, they may not have any malicious intent towards the object of the curse, but they can just be unlucky enough to spread misfortune with a simple glance.

Such a person was Pope Pius IX, who was said to possess the evil eye as catastrophe seemed to follow wherever he went.

Generally, however, the evil eye is possessed by women and, more specifically in Mediterranean countries, women with blue eyes. Those women unfortunate enough to fall into this category may be treated with fear and suspicion, or even as a witch in some societies, particularly if any form of misfortune befalls a community.

In many cultures, belief in the evil eye revolves around the perceived sin of envy, with the offending look depicted as being envious in its intent, although often accompanied by praise. Children brought up in such societies will be taught not to covet their neighbour's possessions or envy their success, for fear of the evil eye. The malevolent powers of the curse are believed to act upon those who possess the evil eye just as much as upon those on whom the curse is cast.

In an effort to counter such malevolence, therefore, fertility charms have commonly been worn. These charms, usually made out of horn or shell, often represent the sexual organs. If these were not available, various hand gestures could be made instead for the purposes of protection. Some of these gestures stay with us, although for most they have lost their ancient cultural connotations. For example, the middle finger that is extended from a clenched fist represents a penis, while the sign of the bull's head is a representation of the womb and fallopian tubes.

Even today, in the Mediterranean region, amulets and talismans are worn by many. The most common of these is a simple blue representation of the eye to return the stare to anyone who may issue the curse. Similarly, the eyes painted on the bows of fishing boats are intended to return the stare of the evil eye. Further east, in India, small mirrors and shiny surfaces are used to reflect the power of the evil eye back to whence it came. Strings of mirrors may be hung over or across doorways to protect the households within, and animals and vehicles are often adorned in this way.

Singer Ben Folds makes the sign of a bull's head.

Other attempts to neutralize the curse involve soiling whatever has just been praised or stared at. For example, in some cultures, it may be necessary to spit on one's own child if it is thought that it has been cursed. In other cultures, boys may be dressed as girls, to prevent the envious evil eye being cast over any highly prized sons.

Many, particularly those in modern Western society, are sceptical of the existence of the evil eye, dismissing it as unscientific. Yet it is true to say that many people speak of picking up 'bad vibes' from another person, and would confess to feeling uncomfortable when confronted with a display of envy or jealousy. Perhaps it is possible for these emotions to manifest themselves in a physical way, the power of the curse depending in effect on the belief placed in it? Whatever the explanation – whether the curse is due to nothing more than the power of superstition or whether the evil eye really does have malevolent powers – there are certainly large numbers of people all over the world today who would not take kindly to being the object of the evil eye.

THE BLACK HOPE CURSE

Some curses, like that of the evil eye, are so general that they are feared by large numbers of people or entire populations. Throughout the world, trinkets and lucky charms are often worn as a means of self-protection.

Other curses are more specific, directed at a particular person, group or place – often these individual stories become woven into the very

fabric of superstition, reinforcing the notion that such malevolent powers do, in fact, exist.

This type of personal experience was certainly the case as far as the Haney and Williams families were concerned, when they bought their brand new homes near Houston, Texas, in 1982. Moving into the neighbourhood was the culmination of their family dreams, as their houses were set in large gardens on an attractive new residential estate.

One year after the move, Sam and Judith Haney appeared to have settled well into their new home. This was all to change, however, when they decided to have a swimming pool built in their garden. Digging commenced, whereupon an elderly man living in the area knocked on their door and brought them some unsettling news.

This took the form of disembodied voices that disturbed their nightly sleep, appliances and lights spontaneously turning on and off and further unnatural noises.

He informed them that their new house was built on the site of an old African-American burial ground and that, in excavating part of the garden for the swimming pool, they were digging precisely over some of the graves. He even gave the Haneys the names of some black families who used to live in the area so that they could corroborate his story. The Haneys, however, were sceptical and continued work on their swimming pool.

After a short while, two crude coffins were unearthed, containing the remains of a man and a woman. Appalled by their discovery, the Haneys realized that the old man had been right. Once the shock had settled, they decided that it was imperative that the bodies should be returned to their resting place with a proper burial.

So they set about trying to establish the identity of the bodies. Their search culminated in the discovery of an elderly man, Jasper Norton, who had worked as a gravedigger within the former black community. He informed the Haneys that the housing estate on which they lived was indeed built on the site of a former cemetery which had been named Black Hope, and contained mainly the graves of slaves. He identified the exhumed bodies as belonging to two slaves, Charlie and Betty Thomas, who had died when he was a young man.

The Haneys continued their search, this time for descendants of the buried couple. When this proved fruitless, they decided to return the remains to the spot from which they had come. They were troubled at having disturbed a grave, and hoped that, by reburial, they could lay the whole episode to rest – as events were to reveal, however, they were very much mistaken.

Not long after they had reburied the bodies, the Haney's lives began to be affected by strange happenings. At first, this took the form of disembodied voices that disturbed their nightly sleep, but soon there were other incidents such as appliances and lights spontaneously turning on and off, further unnatural noises and the discovery of a pair of Judith Haney's shoes on the very spot where Betty Thomas lay buried.

After a while, the Haney's fear and bewilderment grew to such an extent that they confided in their neighbours, Ben and Jean Williams. To their amazement, they discovered that they were not the only family to have suffered from paranormal interventions – at least a dozen of the households had experienced some kind of unexplained activity, ranging from doors opening and closing to strange apparitions.

Like the Haneys, the Williams family also believed that they were being persecuted by a curse from beyond the grave. Although they had not themselves actually found any corpses on their land, they had been astonished to find that nothing seemed to grow in their garden, and that strange, deep holes would continually appear, forming afresh even after they had been filled in. This belief turned to outright conviction when six members of the Williams family were diagnosed with cancer in the same year – sadly, for three of them, this was fatal. As far as the Williamses were concerned, this was a direct intervention from beyond the grave.

Events took an even more tragic turn when Jean Williams decided to find out whether there were any graves in her garden, such as there were on the Haney's land. So one day she and her daughter, Tina, started to dig up the garden. After a short while, Tina collapsed. Two days later, she died from a heart attack, aged just 30 years old – an unusually young age for such an attack.

Could it be that these two families were right and that the dead had objected so strongly to the desecration of their graves that they had managed to bridge the gap between their world and ours? For the residents of the former Black Hope cemetery, there was no question. They believed that the land was cursed, and that they had activated this curse by disturbing the graves.

Events proved too much for the Haney and Williams families, who decided to sell up and move on. Whatever force had been acting upon them, whether it was the workings of their own subconscious or the 'Black Hope Curse' itself, several lives had been lost and many families had been driven from their homes in fear.

Curiously, subsequent tenants of their former homes did not report any problems at all. Had the spirits' anger been satisfied, or had the unpleasant knowledge that they lived above a graveyard just been too much for the 'cursed' families? If events had been restricted solely to the occasional strange happening within the households, then perhaps they could have been accused of paranoia. The extent of the illnesses and deaths involved, however, seem to make the case for a curse a rather convincing one.

Reverend Jesse Jackson speaking at the New York African Burial Ground which was unearthed in 1991 during a building project. It is one of the oldest Afro-American cemeteries in North America.

CURSED DYNASTIES

A family rich in fame, fortune and political power often arouses envy, but could anyone be so jealous as to invoke curses to bring a dynasty to its knees? Many people believe that the appalling misfortunes that befall a few well-known clans can only be the result of a malicious jinx.

Although no known curse has been sworn against the Kennedy family, a prominent political clan in the United States, the number of tragedies they have suffered far exceeds the average, and seems almost unnatural.

> The 46-year-old was shot in the head by an assassin as his motor cavalcade crawled through Dallas, Texas.

For Joe Kennedy, the adage that 'money can't buy happiness' must have left a sour taste. A multi-millionaire by the age of 30, and the father of nine children, Joe appeared to have the Midas touch. But although he and his wife Rose lived long, comfortable lives, their children were famously ill-starred.

In 1944 their eldest son, also called Joe, died aged 29, when the bomber aircraft he was piloting exploded above the English Channel. He was fighting in the Second World War – a war which Joe Senior had publicly advised the US against joining. His son's body was never found. His daughter Kathleen's husband, the Marquis of Hartington, died in the same year, and Kathleen herself perished in an aircraft accident aged 28, in 1948. Another daughter, Rosemary, was institutionalized in 1941.

In 1960, second son John Fitzgerald Kennedy became the thirty-fifth president of the US, fulfilling Joe Senior's dearest ambitions. But just three years later, the 46-year-old was shot in the head by an assassin as his motor cavalcade crawled through Dallas, Texas. He and his wife Jackie Kennedy had recently lost their son Patrick, who died at just two days old.

Now the political aspirations of the grieving Joe Kennedy lay with his son Robert. But within five years he was also dead, killed in Los Angeles while campaigning for presidency.

If all these deaths in the family were not hard enough to bear, the tragedy was compounded when youngest brother Teddy, a senator, was in a near-fatal car accident in 1969. His car plunged from a bridge and sank into the waterway at Chappaquiddick Island, and although he struggled to safety his passenger, Mary Jo Kopechne, 29, was drowned. Questions were raised about the reasons for the crash, and why

Teddy had been unable to rescue his passenger. It seemed the trouble would never end.

Daughters Eunice, Patricia and Jean emerged largely unscathed from these troubled times. But the curse regained momentum with the next generation of Kennedys. John Junior died in a light plane crash in 1999. One of Robert's sons, David, died of a drugs overdose in 1984, while another was killed in a skiing accident at Aspen in 1997. Meanwhile Teddy Junior, son of Edward, was struck down with cancer and had to have a leg amputated.

Joe Kennedy Senior saw only a portion of the disasters that fate had in store for his family. He died in 1969, aged 81. Were his children the pawns of a cursed fate, or were they simply the victims of aberrant behaviour or poor judgement? Perhaps the real victim of the string of tragedies was Rose, who lived until the age of 104, scarred by the misfortunes that piled upon her children and grandchildren.

Joe and Rose Kennedy, unaware of the calamities that were to befall their children, pose for a family portrait (with eight of their nine offspring) in 1934.

The royal family that rules the small principality of Monaco has often hit the headlines through a succession of calamities. In 1956, a union between Monaco's Prince Rainier III and Hollywood film beauty Grace Kelly seemed to augur well for the dynasty. Together they had three children and were the picture of happiness.

Unfortunately, all that ended in 1982, when a car driven by Princess Grace with her daughter Stephanie a passenger plunged down a cliff. Grace was immediately killed, aged just 52, while 17-year-old Stephanie suffered neck injuries and was emotionally scarred.

After this tragic incident, the ties that bound the close-knit family began to unravel. Stephanie had a succession of doomed relationships – she even ran away with the circus in pursuit of love. Her sister Caroline's first marriage ended after two tumultuous years, and she eventually found happiness with Italian businessman Stefano Casiraghi and had three children. But they were still infants at the time of Stefano's tragic death in a powerboat crash in 1990.

Prince Albert II of Monaco, who inherited the throne when Prince Rainier died in 2005, has shown a marked reluctance to marry and produce an heir. Perhaps he is mindful of the curse reputedly laid upon the family when one of his ancestors, Prince Rainier I, kidnapped and raped a witch. Her revenge was to curse the family with the words: 'Never will a Grimaldi find true happiness in marriage'.

And if that were not sufficient, there is talk of another curse laid in 1297, the year the first Grimaldi, Francesco the Spiteful, conquered the world's second smallest state. After he tricked his way into a fortress by dressing as a monk, he was cursed by its defeated defenders.

Problems have beset the Craven family in England since seventeenth-century baron William Craven made a servant girl pregnant and refused to wed her. She used her Romany heritage to summon a curse that seems to have had lasting effects.

Brandon Lee was shot by a gun that should have contained blanks, but was in fact inexplicably loaded with live bullets.

Since then, the family history has been fraught with calamity. The eighth Earl, Simon Craven, died in a car crash in 1990. He had inherited the title from his older brother Thomas who, morbidly obsessed with the curse and depressed following a drugs incident, shot himself aged 26. Their father, the sixth Earl, had died of leukaemia aged 47. His father had drowned after falling from a boat following a party. Indeed, from the creation of the peerage in 1801, none of the incumbents have reached the age of 60. Could the curse of the servant girl all those years ago really still have the power to cause so many untimely deaths?

The efficacy of curses is often psychological, and has much to do with the victim's state of mind. If someone feels like a victim, in many cases they will become one. Indeed, in many parts of the world, an effigy speared with pins, such as a voodoo doll, is still a powerful and disturbing symbol of a curse. This practice has long been used in India, Iran, Egypt, Africa and Europe to provoke profound fear in the intended victim.

This psychological aspect of curses seems to have sealed the fate of kung fu fighter Bruce Lee, who achieved international stardom with his films. Yet his success could not shield him from his dreadful personal conviction that demons were lying in wait for him. His greatest fear was that the curse he believed was intended for him would pass to his offspring.

In 1973, Lee collapsed in convulsions on a film set. Within two months, aged 32, he died after apparently suffering a brain haemorrhage. His son Brandon grew up in the same mould as his father, loving kung fu and fearing its spiritual powers. In 1993, aged just 27, he was killed following a film stunt calamity. Lee was shot by a gun that should have contained blanks, but was in fact inexplicably loaded with live bullets.

Logically, it seems impossible that supernatural forces could emanate from oaths uttered centuries ago, or from dolls pierced with pins, to blight the lives of a dynasty. Yet curses, like superstitions, have a habit of proving themselves.

Bruce Lee in the 1973 martial arts classic *Enter the Dragon*. His talent as a martial artist combined with his acting skills to ensure box office success.

Uncanny Nature

From the unexplored depths of the great oceans to the impenetrable jungles of Africa and South America, our planet still holds many secrets. Awesome, unexplained weather phenomena have traditionally been rejected as the fevered imaginings of witnesses. And reports of colossal serpentine creatures lurking in lakes, prehistoric monsters and terrifying beasts have often been dismissed as folklore and fantasy. Recently, however, conjecture about some of the mind-boggling life forms that inhabit the furthest reaches of our planet is at last getting scientific confirmation. Cryptozoology — the study of unknown species — is a burgeoning branch of science.

MONSTER WAVES

The notion of giant waves higher than ten storey buildings looming up from the earth's oceans was once dismissed as the fantasy of melodramatic sailors. Now science has stepped in to prove that not only do rogue waves naturally occur, they are even fairly commonplace.

The sight of a voluminous wall of water inspires awe and terror. Mighty ships that seem invincible on shore look miniature and vulnerable when dwarfed by such a vast amount of water, rearing into the air. Many have simply been swamped and sunk, leaving little trace of their existence.

In 1995 the luxury liner Queen Elizabeth II encountered a 30 m wave during a voyage across the North Atlantic. Captain Ronald Warwick said: 'It looked as if we were going into the white cliffs of Dover.' Waves like these are not tsunamis, the wave surges caused by underwater earthquakes. No one knows why the rogue waves, measuring some 25–30 m, happen or where they are going to occur next.

Film footage of the phenomenon is rare and sailors' stories were generally thought to be exaggerated. But in 2000, when it was calculated that severe weather had sent 200 supertankers and container ships exceeding 200 m in length to the sea floor over a period of just two decades, an official investigation into major wave activity was launched by the European Commission.

The investigators used satellite information from the European Space Agency about the state of the oceans during three weeks spanning February and March 2001. They proved that during that short snapshot of time, there were more than ten giant waves around the globe measuring over 23 m.

'Two large ships sink every week on average, but the cause is never studied to the same detail as an air crash. It simply gets put down to "bad weather"', explained senior scientist Wolfgang

> Satellite information proved that over three weeks, there were more than ten giant waves around the globe measuring over 23 m.

Rosenthal, of GKSS Forschungszentrum in Germany, one of the major partners of the probe. 'Having proved they [rogue waves] existed in higher numbers than anyone expected, the next step is to analyse if they can be forecasted.'

Of course, it is not only ships that are at risk. In twelve years, no fewer than 466 giant waves were recorded to have unleashed their power over the North Sea's Goma oilfield.

With broad acceptance of rogue waves in the scientific community, it now seems likely that at least one enduring ship mystery has been solved. But one dramatic episode has gained a place in history for the bizarre circumstances surrounding the disappearance of a ship.

In 1909, the SS *Waratah* vanished in broad daylight after setting sail from Durban, taking with her 211 passengers and crew.

Subsequent generations have been fascinated by this sudden disappearance, not least since several passengers displayed a strong sense of foreboding about the ship's fate.

In 1910, the Board of Trade carried out an inquiry into the disaster in London, where company director Claude Sawyer, a first class passenger travelling on the *Waratah*, related his lucky escape. Together with fears about the ship's listing, he suffered from troubling dreams. 'I saw a man with a long sword in a peculiar dress. He was holding the sword in his right hand and it was covered with blood. I saw this vision three times.

'The second time it came I thought "I will know it again" and the third time I looked at it so intently that I could almost design it, sword and all, even now.

'Next day I mentioned the dream to a gentleman and he said: "It's a warning." Then I began to think why I should be warned and I was anxious to leave the ship.' Sawyer took heed of his dreams and decided to remain in Durban, while his fellow passengers boarded the ship again.

Rogue waves of up to 30 m can rear up out of relatively calm seas, dwarfing even large ships.

On the night the 3-year-old *Waratah* disappeared, Sawyer was once again subject to a vision. 'That night I had another dream. I saw the *Waratah* in big waves, one went over her bows and pressed her down. She rolled over on her starboard side and disappeared.'

He was not the only passenger to have qualms. But he was luckier than one girl, known as Evelyn, who confided to a friend that on three consecutive nights before embarking she had dreamt the *Waratah* would sink. After the disaster, this friend wrote to a British newspaper saying that the last time she saw 15-year-old Evelyn she had been 'frantically clutching the handrail as she was led weeping up the gangway'.

Another passenger, Nicholas Sharp, declared the life-saving apparatus on board was inadequate. The ship's chief officer had advised him to secure passage on another vessel as 'this one will be a coffin for somebody'.

...the last time she saw 15-year-old Evelyn she had been 'frantically clutching the handrail as she was led weeping up the gangway.'

The *Waratah* was sighted on the morning of 27 July by another steamship. Only when she failed to turn up in Cape Town was the alarm raised. Despite a widespread search, no wreckage or bodies were found.

It was known that bad weather swept across the ship's route on 28 July. That same day a mounted rifleman on shore reported a ship foundering at the mouth of the Xora River. Nearly a month later crew from a steamer called the *Tottenham* may have spotted wreckage and corpses in the water, but the captain refused to deviate from his course. The Board of Trade inquiry did not conclude that either of these sightings positively related to the missing vessel. A lifebelt belonging to the ill-starred ship finally washed up on the shores of New Zealand in 1912, a poignant symbol of the fate of those on board.

Speculation about the *Waratah* caught the attention of Sir Arthur Conan Doyle, author and spiritualist, who decided to hold a seance to determine what had happened to the doomed ship. Spirits of the passengers told him the *Waratah* had been hit by a giant wave, which sent it immediately to the ocean floor.

Ninety years after the *Waratah* vanished, marine historian Emlyn Brown thought that he had located its wreckage using sonar and filmed it with closed-circuit television cameras during a deep-water dive. He had been financed by Adrian White, whose grandfather, a ship's steward, perished in the tragedy. The ship in fact turned out to be the *Nailsea Meadow*, a cargo ship carrying British Honey tanks torpedoed in the Second World War by a German U-Boat.

The *Waratah* may well be one of the untold thousands of ships to be claimed by rogue waves, yet its loss remains remarkable for the psychic sub-text now firmly attached to the story. For those embarking on subsequent voyages, it is spine-chilling to think that the incredible sight of a rogue wave was the last thing those unfortunate passengers ever witnessed.

KRAKEN

Sailors have long believed that gruesome beasts with a taste for blood lurk beneath the waves, occasionally surfacing to attack a passing ship and its unfortunate crew. On land, people have been swift to dismiss their tales as ludicrous exaggeration. But the latest scientific evidence says that they were right to be fearful of mighty creatures from the deep.

The Kraken was said to have flailing arms or tentacles that could reach as high as the top of a ship's mast.

The monster most feared by sailors down the centuries was known as the Kraken. Its flailing arms reached as high as the lookout nests in the masts of sailing ships, it had eyes the size of footballs and it was commonly depicted with the dimensions of a small island. Probably seen over 2,000 years ago in classical times, the Kraken has been variously described as a squid, an octopus, a whale, a crab and a lobster.

Persuasive records of the Kraken exist in the *Speculum Regale*, or *King's Mirror*, a Scandinavian text in the form of a conversation between a father and son dating from 1250. 'I can say

It is believed that giant squid can reach up to 18 m in length and that their daily diet typically consists of 50 kilos of fish.

nothing definite as to its length...for on those occasions when men have seen it, it has appeared more like an island than a fish. Nor have I heard that one has ever been caught or found dead. It seems likely that there are but two in all the ocean and that these beget no offspring, for I believe it is always the same ones that appear.'

When Erik Pontoppidan made records of the natural world in Norway in the eighteenth century, he also referred to the Kraken. And in 1802, an illustration of the monster by Pierre Denys de Montfort was circulated, who based his drawing on the recollections of sailors from a French vessel apparently attacked by the Kraken off the shores of Angola in Africa.

Speculation about a hitherto unidentified underwater beast was fuelled when a partly decayed body was discovered on a Florida beach in 1896. The body was 5.5 m long and some 3 m wide. Tentacles were in the order of 11 m in length. Local naturalist De Witt Webb was sure it was an octopus, although other experts believed it could have been the remains of a whale.

But an octopus, even one of gigantic proportions, tends to be a shy creature and would be unlikely to attack ships. His cephalopod cousin the squid, with ten rather than eight tentacles, is far more aggressive and seems a more convincing candidate for Kraken. Two particular types of squid are in the frame but, until a short time ago, evidence for both was in short supply. Until recently, mystery cloaked the activities of the giant squid (*Architeutis dux*), thanks to its secretive nature. The best indicator scientists had of its existence was the presence of a few tentacles in the stomach of predator whales. In 2001 a body was discovered off the coast of Spain, spurring scientists on to make fresh calculations about its lifestyle. It is believed that giant squid can reach up to 18 m in length and that their daily diet typically consists of 50 kilos of fish.

2003 proved a pivotal year for squid-watchers. In January of that year, a French yacht taking part in the round-the-world race for the Jules Verne Trophy became enveloped in the arms of a giant squid. Yachtsman Olivier de Kersauson realized the creature was clamped to his boat's hull when he caught sight of a tentacle through a porthole.

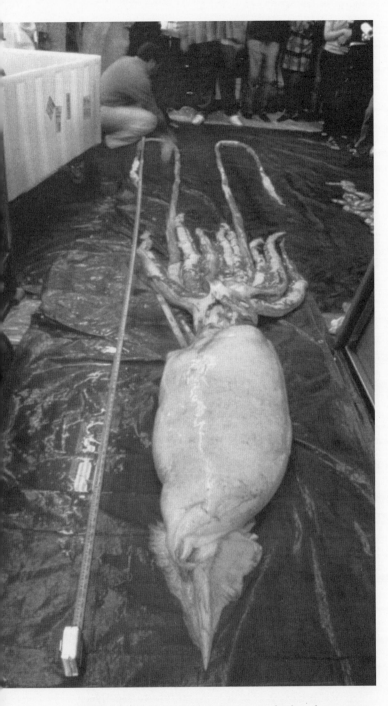

A giant squid has an extremely long, strong beak, and can exert a huge amount of strength using the flaps of muscle at the end of its tentacles.

'It was thicker than my leg and it was really pulling the boat hard,' said de Kersauson, who was close to the Portuguese island of Madeira when the incident happened. The squid, measuring an estimated 8.5 m in length, was jamming the rudder of the boat, effectively putting the vessel out of action. Giant squid can exert an amazing amount of strength by using the visible flaps of muscle at the top of their tentacles. The suckers that help them to cling onto boats and other surfaces are the size of dinner plates. Fortunately for de Kersauson and his crew, the squid released its grip when the vessel stopped. 'We didn't have anything to scare off this beast, so I don't know what we would have done if it hadn't let go,' de Kersauson said. 'We weren't going to attack it with our penknives. I've never seen anything like it in forty years of sailing.'

De Kersauson was one step ahead of marine scientists, who have never yet seen a giant squid alive. But, more significantly still, in April that year a colossal squid (*Mesonychoteuthis hamiltoni*) was retrieved almost intact from the Ross Sea in the Antarctic. Although it was dead, it gave scientists their first opportunity to study the species, first officially identified in 1925.

Its overall length could not be calculated due to tentacle damage, but its mantle (body) measured 2.3 m, already exceeding the maximum body length of the giant squid. Startlingly, scientists believed it was not yet fully grown. One feature that set it apart from other squid were swivelling hooks on the clubs at the end of its barbed tentacles. It also has the largest beak of all known squid.

Both the giant and colossal squid stay well away from mankind at depths of between 60 m and 300 m in cold waters. Evidence of their sinister strength has been found on the washed up bodies of mighty sperm whales that appear to have sustained deep cuts following squid attacks. A famous battle between these two ocean-going titans featured in Herman Melville's *Moby Dick*, and it seems that this is the stuff not just of fiction, but of reality.

Wedging itself on to the bow of the Kuranda, the weight of the enormous jellyfish began to push the vessel down.

Scientists now believe that the colossal squid is not only the biggest invertebrate known to mankind but also one of the most aggressive predators on earth. Unexpectedly, their assertions have given credence to the stories of sailors from a bygone age.

Just as stories of enormous squid were once treated with disdain, so tales of giant jellyfish are also cautiously received. Jellyfish have been around for 650 million years, and are believed to pre-date even the dinosaurs. They comprise 95 per cent water and have no heart, blood or brain. And they are even rarer and harder to come by than the elusive squid. Yet there is conclusive evidence that at least one large, rogue jellyfish haunts the oceans.

In 1973, a ship called the *Kuranda*, travelling between Australia and the Fiji Islands, literally hooked up with a gigantic jellyfish. It is assumed that the jellyfish mistook the ship for prey before it latched on to the craft. One unfortunate seaman who came into contact with the jellyfish's stinging cells (nematocysts) experienced severely burned skin and later died from his injuries. The captain of the *Kuranda*, Langley Smith, said the tentacles of the lethal stinger measured some 60 m long.

Wedging itself on to the bow of the *Kuranda*, the weight of the enormous jellyfish began to push the vessel down. A swiftly-issued SOS brought another ship, the *Hercules*, to the extraordinary scene, whose crew managed to dislodge the jellyfish by using a high pressure hose. Later, when the slime from the jellyfish was analysed, it turned out to be from a species called Arctic Lion's Mane. The largest known Arctic Lion's Mane was washed up on a beach in Massachusetts in 1865, measuring 2.3 m across with tentacles of 37 m long.

In 1969, two divers reported seeing a jellyfish measuring upwards of 46 m. However, swimming at great depths in the remotest corners of the world's oceans have helped the jellyfish retain its largely obscure existence.

Safe on land, we tend to forget that two-thirds of the surface of the earth is taken up by the oceans, vast and mysterious watery territories that plummet to depths of several kilometres. Much of this ocean world remains unexplored by humans, and we have much to learn about the life forms that exist there. What does seem clear is that the stories of seafarers, so often dismissed over the centuries, in fact provide a glimpse of sea monsters that are all too real...

SOUNDS OF THE DEEP

The earth's oceans are huge, unexplored underwater kingdoms that have held mankind in their thrall for thousands of years. Today, these inaccessible areas remain as mysterious as the infinite expanses of space, although scientific advances have recently attempted to push back the boundaries of sub-aquatic understanding in order to cast some light on the black depths that cover our planet. This has produced several surprising results.

Scientists have established that one of the most effective methods of obtaining information about the underwater world is through the use of hydrophones. The origins of these underwater microphones can be traced back to the 1960s when they were utilized widely by the US Navy for the purpose of detecting the presence of Soviet submarines during the Cold War. Today, they have been found to be ideal for tracing, tracking and identifying the many sounds travelling through the water.

The hydrophones, which are in essence a kind of listening station, are positioned hundreds of metres below the ocean surface. At this depth, factors such as pressure and temperature trap the sound waves within a layer known as the depth sound channel and, as a consequence, the waves travel for many thousands of kilometres without suffering distortion.

When the sound waves come into contact with hydrophones they produce a spectrogram, a visual representation of sound. This can be analysed and compared to other, known, spectrogram patterns. Many ocean noises – such as those made by boats, submarines, whales and earth tremors, for example – occur frequently and are easily identifiable in this way, but there remains a large number of eerie echoes that evade explanation.

While some sub-aquatic sounds last for just a few minutes, others continue for years at a time, baffling researchers.

Most of these inexplicable noises occur at a low frequency and, therefore, have to be speeded up in order to be rendered audible to the human ear. While some sounds last for just a few minutes, others continue for years at a time, baffling researchers. Although underground volcanoes, icebergs and even enormous, undiscovered animals residing within the ocean depths have all been suggested as possible reasons for these peculiar sounds, the truth is still unknown.

One particularly mysterious noise picked up by hydrophone has been nicknamed 'Bloop'. While scientists suspect that this strange sound may

The bottom of an iceberg that has fallen away or 'calved' from the edge of a glacier.

emanate from an animal, since the spectrogram pattern showed the rapid variation in frequency characteristic of that produced by deep-sea creatures, there is one surprising factor in this case – the sheer volume of the noise.

The fact that the Bloop signal has been detected simultaneously by sensors located more than 4,800 km apart indicates that the noise produced is louder than that caused by any known animal. It has been suggested, therefore, that a giant squid like the fabled Kraken (see page 39), or some other type of undiscovered monster, could be roaming the depths of our oceans.

'Slowdown' is the name given to another signal that, again, raises more questions than it answers. The sound has been detected in the Pacific and Atlantic oceans several times a year since 1997, and continues to baffle experts all over the world. One leading scientist, Christopher Fox, observed that the noise, which he likened to that of an aircraft, was coming from a southerly direction and so may have originated in the Antarctic. In order to rule out any obvious, man-made explanation, he consulted the US Navy. His suspicions that the sound could have been caused by top-secret military equipment were, however, unfounded.

Another theory which is currently being studied is that the noise could be caused by the shifting of Antarctic ice at the South Pole. The spectrogram pattern produced by Slowdown is similar to that created in cases where friction is a factor, and might have arisen in this instance from the moving and shifting of huge masses of ice over land.

Many further tests will be necessary before the true origin of sounds such as Bloop and Slowdown can be confirmed. Whether they are indeed caused by the movements of mysterious alien creatures in the underwater depths, or whether there are other – purely geological – explanations, only time will tell.

LAKE MONSTERS

Gazing across a glassy Scottish loch framed by rugged scenery, it is impossible to believe that such a tranquil scene could be shattered by the antics of a massive, possibly prehistoric monster lurking in the depths of the lake. Yet this is precisely what has happened on numerous occasions, if hundreds of people who claim to have seen a serpent-like creature are to be believed.

This monster-mania is not solely centred on Loch Ness, where the region's most famous extraordinary inhabitant apparently resides. Curious beasts have been spotted in various lochs in Scotland and in other deep lakes around the world, and the testimony from witnesses about them has been as persuasive as accounts about Nessie, the Loch Ness monster.

One venue for several famous sightings has been Loch Morar, where the monster is known as

A photograph of 'Champ' in the waters of Lake Champlain in the northeast of the United States of America.

'Morag'. Fishermen Duncan McDonnell and William Simpson were afloat on 16 August 1969, when they had a close-quarters experience with this being of gigantic proportions.

It was 9 pm and the fishermens' boat was travelling at a speed of about 7 knots when a splash in the loch nearby caught the men's attention. Natural curiosity soon turned to terror as the thing churning the water made a beeline straight for them. As McDonnell recounted: 'I looked up and saw about 20 yards [18 m] behind us this creature coming directly after us in our wake. It only took a matter of seconds to catch up with us. It grazed the side of the boat, I am quite certain this was unintentional. When it struck, the boat seemed to come to a halt or at least slow down. I grabbed the oar and was attempting to fend it off, my one fear being that if it got under the boat it might capsize it.'

'I looked up and saw this creature coming directly after us in our wake. It only took a matter of seconds to catch up with us...'

Later, Simpson wrote of the terrible experience: 'We watched it catch us up then bump into the side of the boat, the impact sent a kettle of water I was heating onto the floor. I ran into the cabin to turn the gas off as the water had put the flame out. Then I came out of the cabin to see my mate trying to fend the beast off with an oar, to me he was wasting his time. Then when I seen the oar break I grabbed my rifle and quickly putting a bullet in it fired in the direction of the beast.'

The shot was enough to see off the marauder, although neither of the men believed the bullet had wounded it. They estimated that the creature measured about 9 m in length and had a snake-like head extending some 0.5 m above the water. Its skin was rough and brown.

With a depth of 305 m, Loch Morar is deeper than Loch Ness and its waters run clearer. If this were the home of a beast it would remain a private one, as there are no roads running around the loch. One rumour is that Morag is the ghost of a long-extinct dinosaur.

Meanwhile, in Loch Ness, a creature has often been seen and sometimes even photographed. The first recorded witness to Nessie's exploits was St Columba, who allegedly saved a man from its attack. Sightings have escalated since 1933, when John McKay reported seeing 'an enormous animal rolling and plunging on the surface'. There have been photographs in abundance, most famously one taken in 1934, which made international headlines. However, most of the photos, including that one, have since been branded as fakes. Other sightings are usually assumed to be uprooted trees drifting in the wind.

In 2003 a BBC 'Nessie hunt' decided to test the waters using scientific expertise. The team sent 600 sonar beams into the loch without finding evidence of a deep-water creature. This result has fuelled the sceptics' cause, which assumes that Nessie has more to do with a buoyant tourist trade than any underwater phenomenon. There is insufficient food in the loch to support an animal of Nessie's dimensions and the sceptics claim that the sightings are more likely to be of giant eels, catfish or sturgeons. However, they do not explain how the loch would provide enough food for these fish. (One sturgeon was found to be 3.75 m long, weighed 400 kilos and achieved an age of eighty years.)

The latest attempt to debunk the Nessie story insists that the creatures spotted by witnesses were in fact elephants. During the 1930s, a travelling circus owned by Bertram Mills frequently fetched up on the banks of the loch and its elephants took a dip. The saga was stepped up by the sharp-witted impresario Mills,

who offered a vast reward for the capture of the Loch Ness monster, having realized his elephants were the root cause of a rash of sightings.

Yet still there are regular reports that Nessie has surfaced from people who are neither tourist trade operators nor circus proprietors, who appear to have no vested interest in proving her existence.

Although Nessie is the most well known, there are monsters reported in other freshwater lakes in different parts of the globe. The creature that allegedly resides in Lake Champlain, lying

The coelacanth fish was thought to have become extinct at around the same time as the dinosaurs, until it was discovered alive and well in 1938.

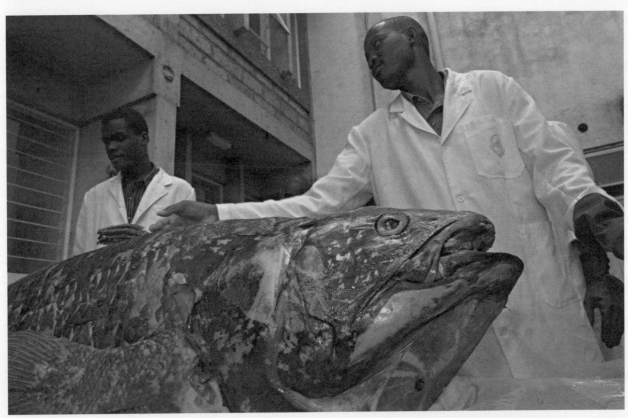

between Vermont and New York in North America, has become fondly known as 'Champ'. A French explorer by the name of Samuel de Champlain recorded the first sighting of the creature in 1609, and since then, reports have numbered in the hundreds. Native Americans in the region firmly believed in its existence and in 1873, circus owner PT Barnum offered a $50,000 reward for its hide.

In 1977, a photograph purportedly of 'Champ' stoked up the rumours and, as yet, the validity of the picture has not been entirely refuted. In 1979, sonar experiments on the lake apparently picked up evidence of a 5 m-long moving object beneath the surface but even this failed to convince sceptics of a monster-type existence.

The notion that something lives in the lake is so much ingrained into Canadian culture that it is against British Columbian law to harm it.

Meanwhile Canada, with its expansive wild terrain and deep lakes, has at least a trio of monsters to its name. In Lake Pohenegamook, Quebec, the reported resident is Ponik, a 12 m-long beast with a horse's head, humps and two flippers. Over in British Columbia, in Lake Okanagan, a creature called Ogopogo has been sighted on several occasions since 1850. The notion that something lives in the lake is so much ingrained into Canadian culture that, should the monster surface, it would be against British Columbian law to harm it. In Newfoundland, the Crescent Lake is reputedly the home of Cressie, a snake-like creature with a fishy head. Alleged appearances by all three in recent times have made headlines around the world.

The hunt continues for Selma, resident in Lake Seljordsvatnet in Norway. Also reportedly possessing a horse's head, Selma is said to be black, have flippers and measure somewhere between 3–12 m in length. Locals have reported sightings of their elusive neighbour since 1750.

So can these really be supernatural beings or creatures isolated from a bygone age? The jury is still out on the exact identification of the creatures that reside in the lochs and lakes. Yet we do know that some things have survived in the deep for centuries, unknown to mankind. The most prominent example is the coelacanth, the so-called 'fossil fish' thought to pre-date the dinosaurs by millions of years, that was assumed to have become extinct at around the same time. Then, in 1938, it was discovered alive and well and living in South African waters. Because of the extreme sensitivity of its eyes, the coelacanth is rarely caught by fishermen during the daytime or on nights with a full moon. If the coelacanth remained hidden from man for many millions of years, then it is more than likely that other species elude us too.

Indeed, for all our technological advances, there are plenty of things about life in the murky depths of the world's vast inland waters that remain a mystery. It is tempting to believe that Morag, Nessie and the rest of the world's lake monsters are among them.

NANDI BEARS

Of all Africa's unexplained animals, the Nandi bear is said to be the most ferocious and is consequently the most feared. It is renowned all over this huge continent, where it strikes terror into the hearts of both native people and Westerners alike. The nature of its existence is a mystery – is it really a bear, or could it be some other kind of animal? And how has it managed to avoid categorization by scientists?

There would certainly appear to be a strange, unidentified killer animal prowling around the villages on the east coast of Africa. Numerous eyewitness reports from both indigenous and Western inhabitants describe the beast as resembling a large hyena, being about the same size as a lion and having a dark, possibly reddish-brown, coat. It is said to be a nocturnal creature, and there are numerous reports of vicious attacks on humans.

Several accounts of this animal have been publicized in the Kenyan press, and one article, in particular, thrust it into the limelight. The report described the experiences of two of Kenya's most famous citizens, who were outside one moonlit night when they spotted what they believed, at first, to be a lioness. This initial identification was quickly proved to be inaccurate, however. As the animal became more visible, it could be seen to have a snout and a back which sloped down to its hind quarters, just like that of a bear. It also had the thick, dark fur and shuffling gait commonly associated with members of the bear family.

Inhabitants describe the beast as resembling a large hyena, being about the same size as a lion and having a dark, possibly reddish-brown, coat.

Although it is known, from the writings of Pliny and others, that bears did once roam this continent, according to official animal demographic statistics, there are no native, wild bears living in Africa today. Moreover, there is no evidence of the creature that might provide further, vital information. Although natives claim to have killed several of the beasts by setting fire to them and Westerners report having taken shots at the creature, the fact remains that no-one has yet been able to make a positive identification.

It is known that one type of bear did once roam the continent, but this species is thought to have become extinct during the Palaeolithic period. With so many factors – such as the animal's shape, behaviour, appearance and ability to stand on its hind legs – suggesting that this creature

A modern-day grizzly bear in the United States.

might be a type of bear, it has been asked whether some of this supposedly extinct species could have managed to survive, and evade detection by scientists.

Although this so-called Atlas bear matches the descriptions of the modern-day Nandi bear, the identification raises a number of problems.

Not least of these issues is the fact that fossil records of the Atlas bear have been found solely in northern Africa, whereas the Nandi bear is only located in the east of the country. It is unlikely that the Nandi bear is a different species of bear altogether for, apart from the fact that the Atlas bear is the only type known to have inhabited Africa, not one single fossil record of the Nandi has been discovered on this continent.

Perhaps, then, this mysterious beast is not a bear at all? Many people believe instead that it is some sort of huge, bloodthirsty hyena, which could either be a previously undiscovered species, or else a remnant from prehistoric times.

In support of this argument is the fact that archaeologists have found evidence of the existence on the continent of a short-faced hyena, similar in size to a lion which lived until the Palaeolithic era.

Others suggest that the creature could be a chalicothere, a slope-backed animal related to the horse, but having claws instead of hooves. Like the hyena, this species is also believed to have become extinct in the Palaeolithic era. Although this description matches that of the Nandi bear, there is one crucial factor which makes the proposition less likely: the chalicothere, in common with all horses, was a herbivore, whereas the Nandi bear is known to be a vicious killer.

The Nandi tribe, from which the beast derives its most commonly used name, describe the bear as a primate, resembling a large baboon. Baboons are omnivores, known to make savage attacks on animals such as smaller monkeys and sheep, and are also able to stand on two feet. Differences in behaviour between the baboon and the mysterious animal – such as the fact that the baboon hunts in packs and is not nocturnal – have been noted, but can possibly be ascribed to the fact that the two creatures could have a slightly different genetic make-up.

On the evidence provided by the fossils of giant baboons and the description of the Nandi tribe, researchers are seriously considering the possibility that the Nandi bear could be some sort of hitherto unknown species of baboon. Alternatively, it might be a survivor from prehistoric times.

Until more thorough research is carried out, however, or a specimen has been caught, scientists and cryptozoologists are unable to verify exactly what kind of animal this is. Only once this is known can they start to solve the riddle of its origin.

ORANG-PENDEK

Tales of mysterious ape-like creatures are not uncommon. Indeed, the possible existence of animals such as the yeti or Bigfoot has gripped the imagination of mankind for many years, and is an endless source of debate and intrigue. One creature that has been the subject of marked interest in recent years is the orang-pendek or 'little man'.

Accounts of this animal come from a range of sources, most notably from the local people of Sumatra, who have accepted it as a part of the diverse habitat in which they live. It is, they say, a shy creature that only kills small animals for

Two monkeys which were taken captive and presented to Prince William of Orange in about 1800. The creature on the left was described as a 'Man Ape'.

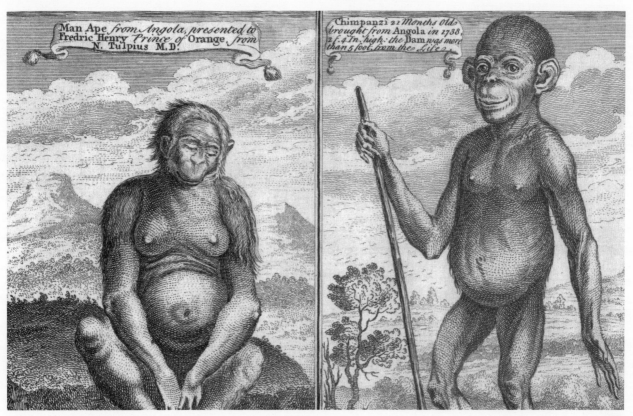

food and has never attacked a human. It is therefore not regarded as a threat and is generally left alone by the natives.

The orang-pendek is described as short in stature, walking on its hind legs at a height of just 0.7 m–1.5 m. Its pinkish-brown skin is covered with a coat of short, dark body hair and it has long, flowing hair around its face. Its arms, unlike those of most normal apes, are considerably shorter than its legs, and it appears more human than ape-like.

Many footprints have been discovered over the years, and these have been used as proof of the animal's existence. Although these prints are said to resemble those made by a child of around 7 years old, they are in fact much broader than a human's and some accounts actually describe the feet as pointing backwards.

To add to the natives' accounts of the orang-pendek, a number of sightings of the creature by Western explorers have further corroborated the story. The first sighting of the orang-pendek by a Westerner occurred in 1910. The man described it as: 'a large creature, low on its feet, which ran like a man and was about to cross my path; it was very hairy and it was not an orang-utan; but its face was not like an ordinary man's'. This description was echoed by that of a Dutch hunter thirteen years later, who added that he felt unable to kill the beast because its appearance was so similar to that of a man.

More recently, in the late 1980s, interest in the animal was re-ignited by the findings of the English travel writer, Deborah Martyr. Although initially sceptical that such a creature did in fact exist, after sighting it on several occasions and studying its footprints, she went on to become one of its most reliable and trusted witnesses.

Following the emergence of poor-quality photographic evidence of the creature a decade later, it was decided that conclusive evidence of the orang-pendek was needed; as the shadowy and blurred images that had been captured on film were deemed to be inadequate proof of its existence. Accordingly, a number of expeditions have set out lately to the Sumatran swamps to try to gather definite proof. The discovery of hair and faecal samples, casts of footprints and a clear and incontrovertible photo, for example, would not only prove once and for all that this creature exists, but would enable scientists to determine if it is an example of a species of ape previously unknown to zoologists.

'...it was very hairy and it was not an orang-utan; but its face was not like an ordinary man's'.

Scientists are, alternatively, debating whether the orang-pendek might be linked in some way to the discovery, in a limestone cave on the Indonesian island of Flores, of a new species of miniature human. Evidence has been uncovered to show that these tiny people, nicknamed 'hobbits' on account of their diminutive stature, lived and hunted on the island 18,000 years ago. Perhaps this creature is not an ape at all, but, rather, an example of a sub-species of human being? It seems that further evidence will be needed before a definitive answer to the mystery of the orang-pendek is provided.

THE JERSEY DEVIL

Could a corner of North America really be haunted by a devilish beast from a species unknown to mankind? It certainly seems unlikely yet, in the early years of the twentieth century, a cluster of appearances by a grotesque winged creature paralysed villages across the state of New Jersey.

A string of sightings of this mysterious beast, which came to be known as the Jersey Devil, led to panic amongst local people. Schools were closed and factories barricaded. Small town streets were deserted as residents retreated behind closed doors for fear of meeting the monster.

Policemen, postmasters, trappers and vicars were among those who reported sightings of the devil in and around New Jersey during January 1909. Although the descriptions sometimes differed in detail, the beast was unquestionably one and the same. After spotting it outside his Gloucester house on 19 January, Nelson Evans gave the following detailed description:

'It was about 3½ ft [1 m] high, with a head like a collie dog and a face like a horse. It had a long neck, wings about 2 ft [60 cm] long, and its back legs were like those of a crane, and it had horse's hooves. It walked on its back legs and held up two short front legs with paws on them. It didn't use the front legs at all while we were watching. My wife and I were scared, I tell you, but I managed to open the window and say, "Shoo", and it turned around, barked at me, and flew away.'

During the month-long episode, witnesses of the Jersey Devil numbered in the hundreds. Could they all have been subject to some manner of mass hallucination? The creature has frequently been described as being similar to a traditional horned Satan, and perhaps the news of an extraordinary beast at large infected the fertile imaginations of local people and led them to believe the devil was roaming in their midst. Yet the communities where sightings occurred were scattered far and wide, so it was highly unlikely that the panic and rumours rife in one village should spread to the next.

If it did exist, the Jersey Devil made its home in the Jersey Pine Barrens, some 5,180 km² of forested wilderness once inhabited by gangs of thieves. The area had a fearsome reputation for being dangerous and lawless, so the devil might well feel at home there.

Over time, various explanations have been proffered for the Devil's existence in the state of New Jersey. One of these holds that a local woman, frustrated at falling pregnant again, cried out that the devil should take her next child away. Although it was born normally, her baby then sprouted wings and flew away up the chimney. Another version of the story maintains that when a local woman fell in love with a British soldier during the American Revolutionary War, people cursed her, swearing that her offspring would be a devil.

Other explanations are that the Jersey Devil is the product of a local liaison between a witch and Satan, or that a devil was installed in the region to punish a community after they mistreated a minister.

Mysteriously, the people involved in the mythology often have the surname Leeds or live at Leeds Point. For this reason, the beast is sometimes alternatively known as the Leeds devil.

Sometimes the appearance of the Jersey Devil is taken as a sign that things are about to take a turn for the worse, although there is no immediate evidence to back up this theory.

Sightings have been an occasional feature of the region for several hundred years. Among the most notable witnesses are Commodore Stephen Decatur (1779–1820), who allegedly shot at the beast although failed to harm it, and Joseph Bonaparte (1768–1844), one-time King of Spain

Is this the image of the devilish creature that has haunted New Jersey for centuries?

and brother of the French emperor Napoleon Bonaparte, when he was living in America.

But the number of accounts that came pouring forth during one week in January 1909 was unprecedented. The Jersey Devil was seen in flight and on the ground. The fire department of West Collingwood allegedly trained its hoses on the beast, but it escaped uninjured. Its bizarre tracks were to be found everywhere – even on rooftops – in the snow that blanketed the district. Two trappers who tried to follow a trail discovered the owner of the prints leapt over fences 1.5 m high – and also squeezed through 20 cm gaps. Many people, although they did not see it in the flesh, heard its barks and piercing screams. It left behind a trail of farm animal corpses and even attacked pet dogs.

With good reason, the small communities scattered around the Pine Barrens were riveted by the stories and limp with fear. No one could explain the oddities surrounding the Jersey Devil. Some hoaxers took advantage of the fevered atmosphere to play tricks on the public, including planting tracks with a stuffed bear's paw. Two men, Jacob Hope and Norman Jefferies, even claimed they had captured it. They covered a kangaroo with green paint and feathers, placed deer antlers on its head and charged gullible punters a fee for a peek. However, even when the pranksters had been discovered, there was still plenty of evidence that defied explanation.

Clearly it has not been a kangaroo causing a stir in New Jersey, but the precise identity of the flying fiend remains unknown. Some people think it is a prehistoric relic that has lived – and may still be living – hidden in a subterranean cavern. The evidence for this theory is based on the proportions of the footprints, recorded in 1909 and at other times, that are similar to those of a pterodactyl.

Others are convinced that a large bird, such as a crane, is to blame, and another alternative is that the creature is of supernatural origin. Since 1909 sightings have diminished in number, although they do still occur. Some locals believe the advent of street lighting, wide roads and fast cars is keeping the creature at bay.

> Many people, although they did not see it in the flesh, heard its barks and piercing screams. It left behind a trail of farm animal corpses and even attacked pet dogs.

In 1957 the Department of Conservation was believed to have discovered the corpse of an unknown beast, with prominent hind legs and feathers. Could this have been the remains of the Jersey Devil? If so, could it be that the beast has finally been laid to rest, or will he continue to haunt the residents of New Jersey? At the moment there is little to indicate exactly what struck terror into the hearts of witnesses almost a century ago. It is hard to believe that their collective imagination was the only thing fuelling the whole episode. Yet until another body is discovered and undergoes analysis, imagination is all that underpins the story of the Jersey Devil.

THE AFRICAN DINOSAUR

From an urban or Western perspective it seems inconceivable that there is a corner of the planet that remains obscure. Yet the part of the African continent most closely associated with dinosaur sightings is so remote and dense with undergrowth that it is impossible to explore it thoroughly and record all the species that live there.

In 1932, a British scientist roaming in the region heard some unidentifiable sounds and recorded gigantic tracks.

Lake Tele is in the People's Republic of Congo, a country recently torn by conflict and all too often rife with disease. It is fed by numerous tributaries, and it lies at the heart of some 142,450 km^2 of swampland, only an estimated 80 per cent of which has been explored. Even in the twenty-first century, the number of visitors to the shores of the lake is startlingly few. If dinosaurs had survived largely unseen anywhere on earth, then it would be here.

The evidence for the existence of a dinosaur is mostly anecdotal. However, these are stories that have persisted for centuries and are particularly potent among the indigenous population.

As long ago as 1776, before the existence of dinosaurs was even known about, the French missionary Abbé Proyart wrote a description of the clawed tracks he saw embedded in African mud. Their dimensions were 90 cm in width with about 2 m between steps.

In 1913, a German explorer revealed the name given to the mysterious creature by locals, 'mok'ele-mbeme'. It was, he claimed, 'of a brownish-grey colour with a smooth skin, approximately the size of an elephant, at least that of a hippopotamus. It is said to have a long and very flexible neck and only one tooth but a very long one, some described it as a horn. A few spoke about a long muscular tail like that of an alligator'.

In 1932, a British scientist roaming in the region heard some unidentifiable sounds and recorded gigantic tracks.

The waters were muddied in the years following the Second World War by a hoax and by claims that creatures of similar dimensions were residing in the Congo River, the swamps of Gabon and also Lake Bangweulu in Zambia.

Nevertheless, a series of expeditions to the Congo from the UK, America and Japan was dispatched between 1972 and 1992 – with largely disappointing results. Most had difficulty breaching the shores of Lake Tele or even of the Congo river. Those that did often claimed that they heard noises that they presumed belonged to mok'ele-mbeme. Two men saw the monster but in both cases film taken of the momentous event failed to come out.

In 1981 Herman Regusters took a number of pictures of a swamp beast but the film was apparently damaged by the extreme climatic conditions of the jungle. Two years later Congolese zoologist Dr Marcellin Agnagna was so awestruck when the creature reared up in

front of him that he neglected to take the lens cap off his movie camera. The resulting footage was useless.

A Congolese zoologist was so awestruck when the creature reared up in front of him that he neglected to take the lens cap off his camera.

In 1992 the most convincing film was shot as a Japanese documentary crew flew over Lake Tele, not on the trail of the elusive monster, but in search of panoramic views of the region. As the plane sped over the lake the cameraman noticed a disturbance in the water. He struggled to maintain a focus on the object, which was creating a noticeable wake. By the time the plane banked around and returned the thing had vanished, although ripples in the surface of the water were still visible.

The film is indistinct. It could be the first genuine footage of mok'ele-mbeme or it might be an elephant on the move. The blurred shape in the frame mostly resembles two people travelling in a motorized canoe, although it is said that no people travel across this part of the lake. One inexplicably strange aspect of the film is that whatever is in the water ends up entirely submerged – unlikely for either an elephant or a canoe.

Africa was once home to hundreds of thousands of dinosaurs. Could one have survived the passage of time, hidden deep in the jungles of the Congo?

But the most irresistible evidence to date has come from people living in the vicinity. The swamp inhabitants are various pygmy tribes, all of whom appear to have some knowledge of mok'ele-mbeme. Shown pictures of gorillas, hippopotamuses and elephants they have quickly registered recognition and put a name to them all. When shown a picture of a sauropod – the dinosaur that best fits the description of what lives in the lake – a consensus has also swiftly been reached. It is mok'ele-mbeme.

One hunter, Nicolas Mondongo, was a teenager when he encountered the monster. He said it had a head and neck some 2 m long, crowned by a frill like that of a cockerel. Its four legs were stout and its tail was greater in length than its neck.

Another persuasive tale was recorded among the people of the river villages who remembered when a monster was attacked and killed by fishermen. The corpse was cooked and eaten by selected tribespeople. All those who tasted the flesh died soon afterwards, although no one as yet knows why. The event apparently occurred in the later 1950s and there is still the hope that explorers will discover the bones discarded after the fatal feast.

From the villagers of the swamp, expedition members have discovered that mok'ele-mbeme is vegetarian but nonetheless ferocious, using its tail to lash out at anyone who gets too close. Tribespeople are also convinced there is enmity between mok'ele-mbeme and hippopotamuses as they do not cohabit the same stretches of water.

In November 2000, Adam Davies undertook one of the most recent expeditions to this inhospitable region and the following year he reported his findings in the *Fortean Times*, a journal that specializes in cryptozoology.

Although Davies did not see or hear mok'ele-mbeme himself, he picked up two vital pieces of information. The first was a description from a village elder who claimed to have seen it many times.

'It has feet like an elephant and a neck like a giraffe. It does not live on the lake but in the forest. It travels across the lake for food'.

The second fact that he gathered was from Dr Agnagna, who told him not to concentrate his search on Lake Tele but on other lakes close by that were even more remote.

At the end of this examination, the facts are maddeningly few. Something has been seen in the vicinity of Lake Tele – and at other locations – that has led a significant number of people to believe that dinosaurs still exist in the heart of Africa. A series of expeditions has brought various pieces of evidence to light, but these are mostly anecdotal and a definitive photograph has not yet been produced. Rather than an unknown beast, there is a possibility that the sightings were of unexpected activity by elephants – although local people well acquainted with wildlife might be expected to distinguish between elephants and other creatures. Testimony from local tribes might be coloured by superstition or imagination.

The density of the jungle works both for and against sceptics. While hostile terrain makes the dinosaur idea difficult to prove, it likewise means the notion is perhaps feasible, as this is uncharted territory and no one can say with certainty what does, or does not, reside there.

CHUPACABRAS

In the 1990s the world was gripped by a crytpozoological mystery that has yet to be solved. Across the Americas, attacks in the dead of night left farm animals dead, their bodies drained of blood. But just who or what was responsible for the vampiric assaults, no one could say.

At first the attacks occurred solely in Puerto Rico, a Caribbean island lying some 1,600 km off the Florida coast. Then the focus switched to Mexico, where a cluster of similar events made the news headlines. Before long there were reports of farm animals with single puncture wounds in their lifeless necks or chests in countries as diverse as Brazil, the Dominican Republic, Argentina, Bolivia, Chile, Columbia, El Salvador, Panama, Peru and the United States. Conspicuously, the flesh of the dead animal was left intact.

A suspect came to the fore, dubbed El Chupacabras which, translated from Spanish, means 'goat-sucker'. There were numerous

Could the attacks on farm animals have been carried out by starving vampire bats, desperate for food?

The gargoyles that adorn historic buildings such as Notre Dame in Paris bear a marked resemblance to descriptions of chupacabras.

sightings of it, and these appear to fall into three different categories.

The first is an upright lizard standing some 1.25–1.75 m, with scaly green-grey skin and sharp spines on its back. The horrific picture is completed with a forked tongue and fangs. Alternatively, the chupacabras has been described as a wallaby or kangaroo-style creature with a dog's face covered by coarse fur. The last of the trio of descriptions is a hairless dog with a pronounced spinal ridge.

All of the above have in common red eyes, three-toed tracks and a distinctive screeching or hissing sound. Sometimes witnesses detected a sulphurous odour in the vicinity of a chupacabras. More tantalizing still are the reports that the goat-suckers have been seen at the same time that UFOs were spotted cruising in an area.

The first chupacabras attack is generally recognized as being in Orocovis in Puerto Rico in 1995 when eight sheep were found dead. Allegedly, their bodies were entirely drained of blood. In August the same year at least 150 barnyard animals were slaughtered in the same ghoulish manner. Three months later came another spate of deaths and the first sightings of the creature deemed responsible.

A hairy, crimson-eyed beast came through the window of an urban home to rip a child's teddy bear to pieces. In its wake there was a slime puddle and a piece of rancid meat. Another witness claimed the chupacabras disappeared before his eyes, while a third decided it was a member of the monkey family.

Unsurprisingly, the population of Puerto Rico was terrified by events. Mobs several hundred strong roamed the countryside at night on the trail of the monster but failed to capture it.

In the early months of 1996 there was a lull in the killings, coinciding with some unseasonably cold weather. Observers came to the conclusion that the goat-sucker had hibernated to escape the chill. In March he was back, though, having killed thirty cocks and hens belonging to farmer Arturo Rodriguez. Shortly afterwards a strange creature walking on two legs, with red eyes, pointy ears, fangs and claws was spotted by a boy called Ovidio Mendez. The creature made no threatening moves towards young Ovidio before it finally bolted. Police were called to the scene, but they failed to find any further clues about the

A hairy, crimson-eyed beast came through the window of an urban home to rip a child's teddy bear to pieces. In its wake there was a slime puddle and a piece of rancid meat.

beast's identity. Scientists on the island stuck to their theory that dogs or perhaps even rhesus monkeys were to blame.

By 1996, when chupacabras activity was focused on the United States, the response from the population was similarly fearful. In Florida, a police department spokesman commented: 'People here are hysterical'. Meanwhile in San Salvador, attacks of the same nature were firmly blamed on vampire bats. The bats were starving, the government minister elaborated, for vampire bats are parasitic and rarely, if ever, kill their prey. By the end of 1996, one Mexican newspaper reported that there had been forty-six domestic attacks involving more than 300 animals and four people.

Since then, chupacabras killings have diminished, but are certainly still in evidence. Farming folk in affected areas remain cautious or even terrified. Different national authorities are united in their dismissal of events as being the work of wild animals or the product of fertile imaginations, fatally combined with sensationalism in the press.

Were chupacabras around before the 1990s? There are sporadic reports of bizarre animal slayings in the Americas before this date, which some observers now believe fit the modus operandi of the beast. Cattle deaths in one area of the United States in the 1970s were thought to have been the work of a rogue condor, but perhaps the truth was more sinister.

Speculation that chupacabras existed years ago is mainly based on their apparent facial likeness to the gargoyles that adorn old European buildings. If we accept that this string of farm animal killings is more than a bizarre coincidence that can be blamed on various starving predators, then what is the explanation? The hypotheses are fascinating, even if some are barely credible.

Biblical scholars pointed to the fact that demonic creatures of this type were forecast as a precursor to the apocalypse in the Book of Revelation. Elsewhere, a clairvoyant monk claimed the chupacabras were representative of a race of vampires that could only be countered with a laser beam or silver bullet. Another group decided these were creatures from space almost certainly infected with deadly diseases, whose intention was to cripple the human race. Failing that, they could be alien pets given some freedom on the planet after a long space voyage, with the mother ship hovering nearby.

Thinking along similar though not identical lines, there were those who felt the chupacabras were the horrible results of a genetic experiment that had gone badly awry. Humans or aliens could have carried out such experiments, and then let loose the hideous spawn of their research. This would explain why the governments of afflicted countries were slow with a response at times of crisis, unwilling to admit to clandestine or unethical experimentation.

There is, of course, the suggestion that chupacabras is a supernatural beast. The paranormal argument is given credence by the few examples of animals attacked by the beast and killed within cages that have remained intact. As in the case of the child whose teddy was ripped to pieces, there are often traces of slime among the animal corpses. There is no firm evidence yet as to what this substance might be.

The mysterious chupacabras looms large for those faced with the consequences of its actions, but there is no consensus about what it actually is. For now its activities provoke more questions than answers. The prospect of this cryptozoo-conundrum being resolved in the near future appears remote.

SKINWALKERS

The state of Utah is home to numerous supernatural occurrences and strange beings. Of these, the so-called 'skinwalker', or 'Wendigo', is perhaps the most terrifying and the question of its existence continues to mystify and bewilder the inhabitants of this part of the USA.

According to native American legend, the skinwalkers are a band of shape-shifting Navajo witches that roam the countryside terrorizing humans and animals alike. They can take on the form of any animal at any given moment, acquiring the inherent strengths and attributes of that particular creature while at the same time retaining their innate human cunning.

This ability to maintain human intelligence

Many believe that skinwalkers are linked to a region called 'Skinwalker Ridge' which, according to extra-terrestrial enthusiasts, is close to a region of intense UFO activity.

while gaining the sensory or speed advantages of a specific animal renders the skinwalker a truly awe-inspiring and formidable foe. In addition to the possession of everyday human knowledge, these witches are blessed with those powers that lie outside the realms of common wisdom. So a witch in the guise of a coyote will have amazing agility, strength and speed, combined with the dark powers of mind control and a knowledge of curses and other occult crafts.

Native tradition relates that the skinwalkers have no choice about their metamorphoses, and that each change causes them much pain and torment. Perhaps it is for this reason that they show such ferocity towards the creatures around them, jealous of their ability to maintain a fixed identity and so remain exempt from the perpetual torment of mutability.

As a result of the witches' constantly changing identity, very little is known about their origins or habits. Many believe that they are linked to a region called 'Skinwalker Ridge' which, according to extraterrestrial enthusiasts, is close to a region of intense UFO activity and which native Americans studiously avoid. Could this region be a portal to another dimension from which the shape-shifters originate? Some people think so.

What is known about these eerie beings has been gleaned from the many reports in existence. Sightings by Navajos tell of the creature's glowing yellow eyes and ability to strike terror into even the bravest observer. Encounters are not restricted to the Navajos, however, as the events of 1983 show. The isolated stretch of Route 163 that runs through the heart of the Monument Valley Navajo Tribal Park, although stunningly beautiful, is renowned for being the site of strange, otherworldly activities and local people warn outsiders that they should never venture into the region at night.

On this particular occasion, four members of a family were returning home from Wyoming, where they had been visiting friends. The most direct route was along Route 163, and having driven along this road without incident on the outward journey, they thought nothing of taking this course again on the way home.

The isolated stretch of Route 163...is renowned for being the site of strange, otherworldly activities and local people warn outsiders that they should never venture into the region at night.

The family reported that, on this pitch-black, moonless summer's evening, they had been driving for several hours without seeing another human being. They were making steady progress when the father, who was driving, mentioned that they were no longer alone. Looking behind them, the whole family saw headlights some distance behind the car.

They continued on their journey, keeping the distant lights in their sights and afterwards said that they felt slightly comforted in the knowledge that there would be help at hand should their vehicle break down.

Suddenly, however, the lights from the other car disappeared. Disquieted by this fact, the daughter, Frances, asked her parents whether they should go back to see if the occupants of the vehicle required any assistance.

Her father was anxious not to prolong their journey, however, and instead insisted that they should press on and reach their destination. Frances afterwards said that it was at this time that the atmosphere in and around the car changed ominously. Her sixth sense was proved to be justified a few minutes later. As they slowed to round a sharp bend, the father saw something ahead on the road. Crying out in surprise, he struggled to maintain control of the car and it almost veered off the road.

The rest of the family, alarmed by the evident panic in his voice, pushed down the locks and held fast onto the door handles, even though at this point they had no idea what had caused him to yell out and swerve. Everything became all too clear when he slammed on the brakes to prevent the vehicle from careering over the edge of a steep drop.

Although dressed in a man's clothing, the monstrous being could not be described, by any stretch of the imagination, as a normal human.

Leaping towards their vehicle was a creature unlike any the family had ever seen before. Although dressed in a man's clothing, the monstrous being could not be described, by any stretch of the imagination, as a normal human.

Describing the course of events later to a Navajo friend, Frances recalled that the beast was black and very hairy, with long arms which clung onto the side of the car, and an anguished face that stared in at them for a few seconds before they sped away along the road.

Having reached the relative civilization of the nearest town, the family felt able to discuss the terrifying sight that they had recently witnessed. Shaken by what had happened, they were keen to see some evidence that their imaginations had not been responsible for the strange events, and so made a thorough inspection of the car. Incredibly, there was not one single mark or print to be seen in the thick dust that had inevitably accumulated on the vehicle during its long journey. Neither was there any sign in the town of the vehicle that had been following them until the time of its sudden disappearance.

Although reports of encounters with the skinwalkers in one form or another are not uncommon among the Navajo, what is notable about this occurrence is that this family was not of native American origin.

Among the many questions to be raised by these bizarre happenings are the following: why were these particular people chosen by the strange supernatural beings? And what exactly did they want from them?

These curious shape-shifting witches have aroused great debate in this part of the USA and all over the world. Other beings that are said to possess a similar mutability are the werewolves of European renown, which also have the same ability to inspire awe and terror in the unlucky observer.

The provenance and purpose of these malevolent beings remains a matter of intense controversy and, until more evidence comes to light, the mystery will continue.

THE VENEZUELAN APE MAN

It is among the most notorious images in the annals of natural history. Seated on a gasoline crate, and propped up grotesquely by a stick, the dead ape had been photographed in a mountainous forest district of Venezuela. The problem for early twentieth-century zoologists was that no such animal was believed to exist in the continent of the Americas.

The photograph was taken around 1920 by François de Loys, a Swiss geologist on a three-year expedition to explore rivers and swamps southwest of Lake Maracaibo. Their aim was to identify lucrative oil reserves, but it was a mission that extracted a heavy price from de Loys and his men. Of the original twenty-strong party only four survived; the others were all victims of disease or attacks by hostile local tribes.

During the last year of the survey, the beleaguered group was camped beside the Tarra River when two red-haired creatures around 1.5 m tall emerged from the forest in an excitable state. De Loys thought at first they were bears, but as they moved closer he realized they were apes, probably male and female. The animals screamed, waved their arms, broke off branches (seemingly to use as weapons), defecated into their hands and threw their faeces at the camp.

The notorious photograph taken by de Loys shows the dead ape sitting on a crate, propped up by a stick.

This type of behaviour is a common aggressive response among spider monkeys and some apes and it suggested an attack was imminent. De Loys did what any self-respecting European explorer would do under the circumstances and shot them, to defend himself and his party. The female was killed and the injured male ran off.

Gathering around the carcass, everyone in the party agreed that the species was extremely interesting and unusual. Unfortunately, given the circumstances, the chances of getting the body back to Europe in a recognizable state were non-existent. De Loys decided to take a photograph as documentary evidence, and the picture was taken from a distance of about 3 m away.

What happened next is not clear. Some reports suggest the flesh was cooked and eaten by de Loys' men; others that the remains were partly preserved and later lost in a battle with Motilones tribe. Either way, when de Loys finally returned home, his only evidence was the photo.

Curiously, it was nine years before this emerged. Even then, it was not de Loys who presented it to the scientific establishment but one of his close friends, George Montandon, a Swiss anthropologist, who apparently chanced on the picture while inspecting some of de Loys' ageing files. Montandon published it in the *Illustrated London News*, naming the creature *Ameranthropides Loysi*, in honour of its intrepid discoverer.

Soon after this, the Academy of Science in Paris met to discuss the implications of the find. The cornerstone of primate evolution theory was that apes and humans emerged only in the Old World, in Africa. If, after all, they were present in the Americas, then long-established rules would have to be rewritten. It would be a leap in the dark and, unsurprisingly, the Academy did not take it.

The scientists concluded that the animal was a sapajou, a fairly common New World monkey.

The only evidence to the contrary, they argued, was its size and lack of a tail. Assessment of size was dependent on de Loys' word and the tail could have been either cut off or tucked out of shot.

The ape theory was further undermined when sceptics waded into the debate. Sir Arthur Keith implied that the animal was a spider monkey, while others went further, accusing de Loys of blatantly fabricating a crude hoax. Throughout the twentieth century the same questions were asked: Why did de Loys not photograph a man beside the ape to provide size context? Why such an odd pose? Why wait nine years before allowing a friend to reveal such a major discovery?

As late as 1996, cryptozoologist Loren Coleman, writing in the *Anomalist Magazine*, argued that George Montandon had been working to a secret racist agenda. This theory held that different races were descended from different apes and consequently some were superior to others. Until the Venezuelan apeman appeared, Montandon had struggled to explain which ape was the ancestor of Native Americans.

In fact, the hoax argument is itself hardly watertight. For one thing why would de Loys, a serious geologist, wish to risk the wrath of the scientific establishment by pulling a silly stunt in an area outside his expertise? Secondly, in an expedition dogged by disease and violent deaths, he surely had more urgent priorities – such as getting home alive. And as for the nine-year delay, isn't it possible that de Loys did not fully appreciate the significance of what he had seen?

Supporters point out that an analysis of the gasoline crate seat revealed it was 50 cm high, putting the de Loys creature at 1.55 m, almost exactly the height he claimed in his report. If so this would certainly rule out a spider monkey, which has an average height of between 38–68 cm. Other researchers say that while there are some likenesses to a spider monkey – the round ridges surrounding the eyes, the long hair and long fingers and toes – there are also several contradictory features. These include the shape of the face (oval rather than triangular) and the lack of a prognathism (a protruding lower jaw).

If Montandon had been alone in reporting a mysterious ape-like animal in the Americas, his claim would be easier to dismiss. But in fact there are many accounts. A chronicle written in 1533 by the conquistador Pedro de Cieza refers to a Spaniard finding one dead in the woods. In the eighteenth century Edward Bancroft, doctor, naturalist and British spy, recounted Native American legends of a 1.5 m-tall creature which walked upright and was covered in hair.

Nineteenth-century science writer Philip Gosse, in his *Essay on the Natural History of Guyana*, suggests the existence of 'a large anthropoid ape not yet recognized by zoologists', and in 1876 explorer Charles Barrington Brown wrote of a beast dubbed 'Didi' by Guyanese natives – 'a powerful wild man whose body is covered in hair and who lives in the forest.' More recently, in 1987, an American mycologist called Gary Samuels was working in Guyana, when, hearing footsteps, he looked up to see a 1.5 m-tall, bipedal, ape-like animal which bellowed at him before running away.

It is easy to dismiss the de Loys photograph as a hoax, perhaps because we are uncomfortable with the idea that such a significant species could exist without our knowledge. Yet natural history is littered with similar examples – the okapi, the Komodo dragon and the coelacanth (see Lake Monsters on page 45) were all twentieth century finds – and there remain surprisingly large swathes of the planet that have not been properly explored. De Loys may be a charlatan…but the jury is still out.

KONGAMATO

Although dinosaurs are known to have been extinct for thousands of years, a strange tale emanating from African natives in Zambia might, in fact, suggest otherwise. Over the centuries there have been numerous reports of ferocious flying reptiles that bear an uncanny resemblance to a supposedly extinct species of dinosaur called the pterosaur.

These claims have inspired such curiosity that, in 1932, the traveller Frank H. Welland ventured into the Jiundu swamps in the Mwinilunga district of western Zambia to investigate further.

The natives gave him detailed accounts of monstrous, reddish birds, with a wingspan of 1–2 m, long beaks full of teeth and leathery skin in place of feathers. They called these creatures 'kongamato', which translates as 'overwhelmer of boats', due to the fact that the huge birds would often overturn small vessels, attacking and sometimes killing the occupants. So terrified were the locals of the kongamato that it was thought that just one look at it would result in certain death. Welland wrote an account of the natives' descriptions in his book, *In Witchbound Africa*, which received great publicity for it also revealed that, when Welland showed the Zambians drawings of the prehistoric pterosaur, they unanimously and unhesitatingly agreed that these sketches identified precisely the creature they knew as the kongamato.

Many people were sceptical of these claims, and argued instead that the Zambian people had obtained the description of the pterosaur from those natives who had worked on excavations in Tanzania where the fossilized bones of pterosaurs had been discovered some years earlier.

There are several problems with this theory, however. First, was it possible for descriptions of the dinosaur bones to have travelled from Tanzania to Zambia, a distance of 900 km? Second, even if the Zambians had heard about the skeletal structure of the pterosaur, how would they have known about the creature's leathery skin and lack of feathers? Finally, if the sightings were nothing more than the product of fervent imaginings, why did they not come directly from the excavation site in Tanzania, rather than from as far away as Zambia?

Sightings of the mysterious creature continued, one story being told to the English newspaper correspondent, Mr G. Price, by a civil servant living in Africa. The expatriate recounted how he had met a native who had suffered an almost fatal wound to the chest while exploring the much-feared swampland. The man claimed that he had been attacked by a huge long-beaked bird.

Such stories were not limited to the inhabitants of the Zambian swamps, however. One account came from the famous zoologist and writer Ivan

The natives gave him detailed accounts of monstrous, reddish birds, with a wingspan of 1–2 m, long beaks full of teeth and leathery skin in place of feathers.

Sanderson who, in 1933, was leading an expedition to the Assumbo Mountains in the Cameroons on behalf of the British Museum. He described how, while out hunting one day, he had shot a fruit bat over the fast-flowing river. Wading out into the water to retrieve the fallen animal, Sanderson lost his balance and fell. Having regained his footing, he heard a warning yell from one of his colleagues and to his horror saw a monstrous black creature bearing down upon him from the sky at great speed.

Sanderson ducked into the river to escape the huge bird and then made for the riverbank. At this point, the creature renewed its attack, diving down on him again and both he and his companion threw themselves on the ground, conscious only of the beating of the creature's wings. Fortunately, the animal then flew off into the night, leaving the two men to return to the safety of their camp. Here, they related their story to the natives, asking them if they knew what their attacker might have been. The locals fled in terror without answering the question.

Sanderson reflected on what he had seen – fortunately, due to his zoological expertise, he was able to give a precise description of the animal. He described it as having been about the size of an eagle, with a semicircle of sharp white teeth in its lower jaw. This report matched not only those of other sightings, but also corresponded with what is known of the pterosaur. Sanderson also remarked that the beast, like the pterosaur, resembled a bat. However, he discounted the possibility that it was only a fruit bat on the basis that these creatures are not known to attack humans.

Some years later, in 1942, similar stories from other areas in Africa, such as Mount Kilimanjaro and Mount Kenya, were related to the author, Captain C. Pitman. They described the existence of a large bat-like bird, which produced tracks suggesting that it had a large tail that dragged along the ground behind the creature.

In his book *A Game Warden Takes Stock*, Captain Pitman went on to describe how the animals were alleged to feed on rotting human flesh if corpses were not buried to a sufficient depth. Further accounts of the birds were contained in another publication, *Old Fourlegs*, in which fossil expert Dr J. L. B. Smith described 'flying dragons' in the region of Mount Kilimanjaro.

An artist's impression of a pterodactyl, a type of pterosaur known to have existed in prehistoric times.

Today the sightings continue in remote areas of Africa. In 1998, a Kenyan exchange student, Steve Romando-Menya, declared that the existence of the kongamato is common knowledge among the bush dwellers in his country. Moreover, all witnesses, when asked to draw what they have seen, are repeatedly reported to draw a pterosaur.

What are these mysterious creatures? Sceptics claim that it is impossible for the prehistoric pterosaur to be in existence today, and yet the number of confirmed reports from reliable sources would seem to indicate otherwise. The controversy and debate continue to this day.

Mysterious Monuments

The power of many ancient monuments is undeniable. Primitive populations pushed themselves to the limit to achieve such feats as Stonehenge and the Nazca lines, yet in many cases it is impossible to say what purpose they serve. Why were they built just there? Why were such rare and hard-to-come-by materials used? Investigating the power of these ancient wonders, we are struck not by how much we have learned, but by the amount we have yet to find out.

THE NAZCA LINES

Across a 434 km² stretch of Peru's Nazca desert, archaeologists have identified 13,000 lines and pictures etched into the sun-baked surface. That these images were produced by an ancient civilization is beyond doubt. But their purpose is far harder to explain.

The designs were first noticed in the 1920s, as manned flights began to venture into South America. Pilots reported seeing straight lines which ran for miles, traversing mountains and occasionally ending on cliff edges. Geometric shapes included triangles, rectangles, spirals, wavy lines and concentric circles. Animal geoglyphs included birds, whales, a dog and lizard. Some images were drawn on a truly vast scale: a 305 m pelican, a 285 m bird with a curiously zig-zag shaped neck and a monkey complete with 100 m spiral tail.

There were also more surreal pictures – specifically an 'astronaut' figure and a bizarre creature with two colossal hands, one of which had only four digits. Was this, as some have claimed, an attempt to record contact between prehistoric humans and alien beings?

Before considering this and other interpretations of Nazca, it is worth setting out areas of agreement among experts. Firstly, it is obvious that the lines were made by removing the desert's top layer of iron-oxide-coated stones to reveal lighter-coloured soil underneath. Secondly, it is accepted that this must have been a colossal effort, perhaps lasting a thousand years, and that because of the scale of the work the artists could never have seen the full fruits of their labours from the ground. The lines are so unobtrusive that during the last century the pan-American highway was built straight through them without anyone noticing. Thirdly, it seems likely

> The lines are so unobtrusive that during the last century the pan-American highway was built straight through them without anyone noticing.

that the patterns were made by ancient Nazca Indians sometime between 400BC–AD600. This estimate is based on radiocarbon analysis of Nazca fire and ceramic debris, although it is not conclusive, since the lines themselves cannot be radiocarbon-dated.

It is possible that an even older civilization did some of the hard work, perhaps evolving from the Paracas culture which blossomed in southern Peru between 1100–200BC. The Paracas people are thought to have constructed the giant El

Candelabro geoglyph. Also known as the Tres Cruces or the Trident, this form stretches to more than 120 m wide. It is situated on a slope overlooking the Bay of Paracas, together with some fifty figures – humans, birds, cats and monkeys – near the Peruvian city of Palpa.

The first academic to make a proper study of Nazca was Paul Kosok, an American who stumbled across the site in the late 1930s while researching prehistoric irrigation systems. He suspected that the lines were linked to astronomical alignments, a theory reinforced when in the late afternoon of the southern hemisphere's winter solstice (22 June) he and his wife witnessed the sun set precisely at the end of one line. Kosok enlisted the help of a German astronomer, Maria Reiche, and together they developed the idea that some Nazca shapes were used as a calendar to help farmers calculate crop planting times. The animals, they believed, represented major constellations.

Another American scientist, Gerald Hawkins, used a specialist computer program to calculate the number of significant solar alignments produced by the Nazca lines. He decided that alignments would have to point consistently to a specific celestial event, such as the rising or setting of stars, sun and moon. Neither was it enough merely for some lines to fulfil the criteria. If the astronomical link were to be proved, then it had to account for all the lines.

Hawkins instructed his computer to show how many were aligned on extreme positions of the sun or moon. The answer was thirty-nine out of 136, barely better than would be expected by chance. Worse, only a few of these thirty-nine

An aerial view of the Nazca lines criss-crossing the Peruvian desert. Could these really be some kind of communication for extraterrestrial visitors?

alignments could be linked to significant solar or lunar positions. Hawkins tried a similar experiment with the stars, inputting a catalogue of their positions dating back to 10,001BC. Again, the alignments were statistically insignificant.

In 1968, as Hawkins published his results, the Swiss writer Erich von Daniken inflamed the Nazca debate by claiming that the lines marked out a giant alien spaceport. His book *Chariots of the Gods* essentially argued that it was impossible for ancient people, incapable of flight, to have

One of the more bizarre geoglyphs has few recognizable features other than two huge hands, one of which has only four digits.

produced the drawings themselves and that they must have been taught by visiting aliens.

Critics accused von Daniken of making the facts fit his theory. His cause was not helped by a television investigation into pottery fragments which, he claimed, dated from biblical times and depicted flying saucers. Unfortunately, von Daniken's fragments proved to be of more recent vintage, after television journalists found and interviewed the potter who made them.

As if to rub salt into his wounds, a flamboyant American publisher and adventurer called Jim Woodman set out to prove that Nazca people could, in any case, have known how to fly. Using cloth and rope based on samples found in Indian graves, and reeds cut from Lake Titicaca on the Bolivian border, he constructed a 2,260 m³ hot-air balloon, powered by heat from a bonfire on the ground. Together with the British balloonist

Julian Nott, Woodman ascended to a height of 90 m, neatly illustrating that Nazca designers could well have had the technology to fly and monitor progress of their work. This theory may sound far-fetched, but archaeologists have already shown that at least 500 years earlier, Paracas doctors were performing brain surgery through trephination – the removal of skull sections with a cylindrical saw (see Trepanning on page 293).

Yet even if the ancient inhabitants of South America had the means to make the lines, this still does not explain what they were for. Few archaeological sites have spawned quite so many theories, and in recent years Nazca has been cast as a giant map of subterranean water sources, a focus for earth energies, a cathedral plan, an athletes' racetrack and even a giant loom on which vast teams of weavers produced cloths or nets. Even harder to grasp is the idea that the Nazca lines are located on a global 'Code Matrix' in which the world's significant ancient sites correlate precisely to the Great Pyramid at Giza. Evidence for this is reportedly found in the geometry of Nazca's layout.

The most likely explanation is that the lines were linked to religious or magical ceremonies. Nazca was an agricultural society skilled in planting, irrigation, harvesting, storage and distribution, but it was also vulnerable to natural disasters and disease. Could the lines have been communal sites for appeasing or worshipping specific gods? Perhaps they served as a gentle reminder of the needs of the Nazca people, and a prompt for regular help from on high. The truth is that, even discounting the role of alien architects, the purpose of the lines remains elusive.

STONEHENGE

The towering, mysterious circle of rocks that rises out of Salisbury Plain has inspired awe in millions of people over the ages. But the reason for its existence baffles archaeologists to this day. Various theories suggest a ritual site, an astronomical observatory, or a focus for some mystical form of 'earth energy'.

In piecing together the complex Stonehenge jigsaw, we can at least be confident of some basic facts. Using radiocarbon measurements, scientists have dated the earliest work on Salisbury Plain to around 3,100BC. At this time the site was far more primitive, comprising a circular 97.5 m diameter ditch, a single entrance and a central wooden 'temple' or sanctuary. Around the edge of the ditch were fifty-six holes, each containing cremated human remains. On the summer and winter solstices the whole structure aligned with rising and setting points of the moon.

By 2,500BC, the wooden sanctuary had been replaced with two circles of the famous bluestones that had been transported 390 km from the Preseli mountains of south-west Wales. An entrance avenue of parallel ditches which aligned to the midsummer sunrise was added,

The mammoth bluestones used to construct Stonehenge were transported almost 400 km from the Preseli mountains of south-west Wales to Salisbury Plain.

together with outlying single megaliths such as the Heel Stone, Slaughter Stone and Station Stones. However, the bluestones were pulled down within a century and recycled for a new design.

The new Stonehenge had a very different emphasis. At its centre was the Altar Stone (now fallen), a large sandstone shipped from the Cleddau Estuary in Pembrokeshire. Over the next 500 years, some of the re-used bluestones were raised around it in a horseshoe shape. Beyond these were placed five massive sarsen trilithons (two uprights bearing a horizontal), a ring of

The ancient architects of Stonehenge possessed a level of mathematical and engineering sophistication that defies explanation.

bluestone pillars and an outer ring of sarsen uprights linked by lintels. The bus-sized sarsen blocks are by far Stonehenge's largest, typically weighing 30 tons and at least one as much as 50 tons. Most are thought to have been transported from the chalklands of Marlborough Downs, some 32 km west.

According to some estimates these three building phases must together have required more than thirty million hours of labour. For Stone Age people to allocate this amount of time – even over two millennia – seems extraordinary. It suggests a level of co-operation far above what we might expect; a society in which Stonehenge labourers would have had to be fed, watered and

sheltered in order to build a seemingly useless monument. How did they do it? More importantly, why did they do it?

The how is comparatively easy to fathom. Many of north-west Europe's Neolithic monument builders used large quantities of stone transported from a great distance. The architects of Newgrange in the Irish Midlands, which predates the Stonehenge megaliths by at least 500 years, brought quartz and granodiorite from sites 48 km away. It seems likely that Stonehenge's bluestones were brought to Salisbury Plain by a combination of raft-borne river, sea and overland transport. Once the raw materials arrived, the construction of the circle itself would have required a phenomenal amount of manpower, relying on a levering system of wood and rope.

Manpower aside, the thorny question of quite why it was necessary to lug the bluestones 390 km is far from clear. A study led by Geoff Wainwright and Timothy Darvill in 2004 suggests that the dolerite crags of the Preseli mountains would have held particular appeal. The stone is naturally fractured into 'ready-made' pillars, so they just needed to be levered off for removal. The stones themselves – strong, durable, and speckled with white feldspar – may have been invested with a symbolic, mythical power.

Which brings us back to the key question, what was Stonehenge for? It may well have had different functions at different times. But the prevailing archaeological view is that Stonehenge was a ritual and burial site, linked to astronomical observations. It was almost certainly not used to predict the agricultural crop cycle. In England the summer solstice occurs long after the start of the growing season and the winter solstice misses the harvest by a good three months.

In 2005, tests on some Neolithic pig bones showed that large numbers were slaughtered in the months of December or January. This lends weight to the idea that a winter solstice festival was held at Stonehenge. It also seems to have been an important burial site. Around the standing stones are a large number of burial mounds, and in 2002 an archer's grave was discovered that contained more than 100 precious items such as gold earrings, copper knives and pottery. Tests have shown that the deceased – dubbed the 'King of Stonehenge' – was born in the Alps around 2,300BC. This is the richest known burial of the age anywhere in Europe, and the implication is that the 'King' was a settler who played a key role in constructing the monument.

The link between Stonehenge and the ancient Druid religion has taken a battering in recent years. Experts believe this connection was always tenuous (based as it was on the observations of Julius Caesar) and it is now clear that the heyday of the Druids came a thousand years after work on Stonehenge ended. However, we cannot be certain how early the Druid traditions came into existence, so a link cannot be ruled out.

The idea that Stonehenge was used as a celestial calendar is simple to prove. If you stand in the centre of the circle at 5 am on a clear Midsummer's Day you can see the sun rise precisely in line with the Heel Stone, 37 m beyond the ring. This is the most obvious and impressive of the circle's mysterious alignments. During the 1950s and 1960s a further twenty-three alignments were recorded by Oxford University engineer

Alexander Thom and the astronomer Gerald Hawkins. Hawkins speculated that Stonehenge was used to predict eclipses, although critics now say his methodology was flawed and that he overestimated the number of alignments.

What is clear is that the ancient architects of Stonehenge possessed a level of mathematical and engineering sophistication that defies explanation, knowledge that appears to have pre-dated both the Egyptian and Mesopotamian cultures. How can we explain that 2,000 years before Euclid's Pythagorean 'breakthrough', and more than 3,000 years before Arya Bhata 'discovered' the value of Pi, Neolithic Britons were using these concepts to construct Stonehenge?

Putting aside questions of science, another theory behind the existence of Stonehenge is that it focused some intangible 'earth energy', a natural force field that could be tapped by those in the know. Hard evidence for this theory is lacking, although footage of UFOs in the skies above the circle in October 1977 has never been properly explained. All we can say for certain is that Stonehenge seems to be in a significant place: it stands on a known 35 km ley line (see page 86), which also bisects three earthworks and three tumuli (burial grounds).

Maybe the greatest barrier to solving the mystery of Stonehenge lies in our own prejudices. Today we live a hectic urban lifestyle that isolates us from the subtle rhythms of nature observed by Neolithic societies. Perhaps we are concentrating too much on scientific knowledge, and our problem in unravelling the mystery of the mammoth stones is that we have started in the wrong place.

BAALBECK

Temples have stood at Baalbeck, in Lebanon, for thousands of years, enduring the rule of numerous civilizations and the worship of many changing gods. They have been altered, but never destroyed, because of their incredible beauty and grandeur. In fact, it is the sheer scale of the temples that has provoked such intrigue and wonder, with archaeologists the world over mystified as to how such impressive structures could have been built so long ago.

Baalbeck was originally a Phoenician settlement which became successively Greek, Roman, Byzantine and then Arab, through conquest. The Greeks occupied the town in 331BC, renaming it Heliopolis (city of the sun). Located on principal trading routes, the city flourished and became a large religious centre.

Wherever structures have survived this long, they have usually been built from stone with the express intention of permanence, and Baalbeck is no exception. In fact, this structure contains the largest cut blocks of stone in the world. Some of these are so large, and quarried from so far away, that experts are mystified not only as to how they were transported to the site, but also how the temple was ever built.

The reason for the inconceivable vastness of the stones was Phoenician tradition, which dictated that the podium for the temple must consist of no more than three layers of stone. When a large extension to the temple site was suggested, the ancient architects realized that they were going to have to work on a scale not previously imagined.

Undeterred by the daunting scale of their task, they commissioned the carving of what were in effect colossal building bricks, hewn from solid

The remains of the Temple of Jupiter (foreground) and Bacchus (background) at Baalbeck.

rock. Several of these are to be found on the western side of the podium, in the area named the 'Trilithon', after the three largest blocks. These stones are around 20 m long, 4.5 m high and 3.6 m deep, and each is estimated to weigh around 800 tonnes. By way of comparison, these stones are four or five times larger than those at Stonehenge (see page 75), and approximately three hundred times heavier than those used to build the Egyptian pyramids.

Amazingly, the largest of the stones was even heavier than this. At more than 1,000 tonnes, the size and weight of 'the stone of the pregnant woman' would test the greatest cranes in existence in the world today. However, this stone still remains in its quarry, as building work ceased before it ever came to be used.

Aside from the fact that the huge blocks of stone were transported more than a kilometre from their quarry and then raised more than 7 m into their final positions, there is yet another mystery attached to them. The craftsmanship shown in the construction is of such a high standard, with the stones arranged in such a precise fashion, without the use of mortar, that it is impossible to wedge even the slightest object between them.

The scale of Baalbeck has fired people's imaginations to such an extent that each successive culture to occupy the site has linked the Trilithon with some kind of popular myth, be it giants, biblical figures or even the intervention of extraterrestrials.

Whatever the explanation for the construction of this vast monument, it looks likely that Baalbeck will continue to draw countless visitors in the future. Like thousands before them, these people will marvel at the beauty of this remarkable ancient monument, that suggests so much about the possibilities of human achievement.

YONAGUNI

In 1985, a discovery was made in Japan that still baffles the scientific community today. A Japanese dive tour operator, Kihachiro Aratake, strayed from his regular area into the waters off Yonaguni Island, near Okinawa. About 30 m beneath the surface, he found a strange formation which, on further examination, appeared to be a man-made pyramid.

Ever since this date, the Yonaguni finding has been a source of immense controversy. Experts are unable to agree upon whether it is actually a man-made structure at all, or simply a remarkable natural formation. If it can be confirmed to be man-made, it will undoubtedly revolutionize the way in which the history of our own species is viewed.

Scientists agree that this area of coastline became submerged by the rising oceans at least 10,000 years ago. Following the end of the last Ice Age, there was a huge global thaw that altered the world immeasurably and, over time, sea levels are believed to have risen by up to 30 m. This means that any civilization in place at that time would have been destroyed, engulfed by the rising waters, with all traces of it remaining hidden to this day.

A Japanese dive tour operator strayed from his regular area into the waters off Yonaguni Island, near Okinawa. About 30 m beneath the surface, he found a man-made pyramid.

Furthermore, it is known that human civilizations have thrived on coastlines for thousands of years, because the sea is not only an excellent source of food, but also facilitates important activities such as trading and transport. Yonaguni would, therefore, have been a likely location for a settlement to arise. Such a civilization would, however, have pre-dated all known cultures by thousands of years, since the oldest known city is believed to be Sumeria in Mesopotamia, which dates back to around 5,000 years ago. To double the accepted timescale of human development is to take a drastic leap. This, however, is not impossible, especially if there is real evidence to support it, as Yonaguni might prove to be.

Perplexing scientists still further is the fact that similarities have been noted between the architecture that appears to exist at Yonaguni and that which can be found above the sea on the coast of Peru.

Yet even the oldest of these Peruvian structures, built by the Moche people, are at the most 2,000 years old, leaving an inexplicable gap of many millennia.

Further controversy has arisen over the actual appearance of the Yonaguni structure. Underwater photographs of the site appear to show the presence of ramps, terraces and steps. While American geologists argue that these are nothing more than natural formations, Japanese scientists have claimed that tool markings can be found along the structure, suggesting that it might have been tampered with.

One person, however, has seemingly taken both sides of the argument, asserting that the site is both natural and man-made. Dr Robert M. Schoch, a geologist who made frequent dives to the site, actually suggested that the majority of the structure was indeed a natural formation, but one that had been chosen and modified by humans, in a process known as 'terra-forming'. The discovery of what appeared to be a small staircase on the site was prime evidence of such modification.

The discovery of structures beneath the sea always generates intrigue and excitement, with people proclaiming that the lost city of Atlantis (see page 272) has been uncovered. However, the location of Yonaguni means that it is unlikely to have been Atlantis. Rather, it would seem to have closer parallels to the lost continents of

Mu or Lemuria, as both were said to exist in the region of Asia, spanning the Pacific and Indian oceans respectively.

Although the comparatively modern science of tectonics has largely discredited the notion that there were ever 'lost continents', many believe that they did, in fact, exist. Lemuria and Mu are supposed to have been destroyed by immense natural disasters that engulfed the continents. It is not impossible that ancient myths telling of the demise of whole civilizations have become altered and enhanced over time to encompass the destruction of entire continents. In this respect it could actually be possible that the end of the Yonaguni culture could have been mythologized or exaggerated into a story such as that surrounding Lemuria.

In drawing these parallels between Yonaguni and the mythical continents, the experts involved are hoping to advance the theory that there is a great lost culture of the Pacific. Tantalizing glimpses of such a culture are offered by the mysterious stone heads of Easter Island or the oral traditions of the Polynesian islands. Apparent similarities between Yonaguni and stone constructions on Hawaii and Tonga suggest a cultural bridge from prehistoric Japan to the coast of South America.

This theory also attempts to explain the similarities between many different cultures of the world, a large number of which shared a belief in astronomy and adopted the pyramid as a favoured type of construction. Some theorists, such as Graham Hancock, believe that this serves as evidence of an ancient seafaring culture that spread its wisdom around the globe. It is certain,

A scuba diver embarking upon an exploration of the underwater world.

however, that further proof will be required before the sceptical world of archaeology accepts such a drastic reinterpretation of man's early history.

Perhaps, if the site around the pyramid is explored further, this evidence might be found after all. Or, if not, it is possible that proof could be located at other formations that have been discovered on the seabed close to the Japanese islands of Kerama and Chatan, and in the Straits of Taiwan. Now that technology is able to reveal more and more about global changes as a result of the Ice Age, it seems likely that further discoveries of this kind will be made in shallow coastal shelves around the world.

This offers us the exciting prospect of possible answers as to the nature of the origins of human civilization, but as always, each discovery is likely to raise further questions. Why, for example, has the pyramid been so evident in disparate cultures at different times of mankind's history? The answer to this question looks set to remain one of the greatest mysteries of the ancient world.

NEWGRANGE

The megalithic tombs of Newgrange, in Ireland, are more than 5,000 years old, so they pre-date the pyramids of Egypt, and even the arrival of the Celts in Ireland. As is often the case with such ancient monuments, very little remains today to give a clue as to the greater purpose behind their construction and this fine Stone Age necropolis is a source of speculation all over the world.

Located near the banks of the river Boyne, to the east of Slane, the Newgrange tombs are known in the native tongue as Bru Na Boinne. According to pagan lore, Newgrange was the dwelling of Aengus, the powerful god of love. The site is also associated with the mystical race of the goddess Danu, also known as the Tuatha De Dannan. According to local superstition, these nature-loving pagans have left something of their spirit in the landscape and it is thought that Cuchulain, the legendary hero of the Celtic warriors, was conceived at Newgrange.

The Newgrange tomb is said to be the burial place of the high kings of Tara. Their ashes would have been contained in large bowls in each of the three recesses of the burial chamber.

The builders of these tombs demonstrated considerable devotion to their construction. First, they made use of materials that were not readily available – the quartz must have been quarried and transported from the Wicklow Mountains, a considerable distance from Newgrange. Second, the builders were involved in a huge project – it has been estimated that the construction of the monument would have taken a workforce of 300 men more than twenty years to complete.

In common with the people of other ancient cultures, the lives of the Newgrange community would have been closely regulated by the natural rhythms and cycles of the earth, with the summer and winter solstices assuming great importance. At Newgrange, at the winter solstice, the dawn sun shines through a 'roof-box', down a short, straight passage and into the heart of the burial chamber, illuminating intricate carvings that are believed to represent the sun and the moon.

Intriguingly, similar effects can be found at Stonehenge, in the pyramids of the Maya and the Aztec, and in King Khufu's pyramid in Egypt, where a curious shaft of light enters the tomb at the time of the solstice.

Did these cultures have a common spiritual identity, or is there something innate in human nature that relates to the movement of the stars and the cycles of the planet? These ancient farming communities possessed knowledge far ahead of their time. It is impossible not to marvel at the skill that enabled them to make the precise calculations necessary in order to align the passages of the tombs with the light of the stars or the sun.

THE ARTHUR STONE

The legend of King Arthur is one we are all familiar with, but we are not so sure of the historical facts concerning his life. On 4 July 1998, an archaeologist working at Tintagel Castle in Cornwall unearthed an inscribed chunk of slate. It bore the name Arthnou – an early version of Arthur – re-opening a furious academic controversy about where the 'Once and Future King' of the Britons resided.

> 'It is remarkable that a stone has been discovered with the name "Arthnou" inscribed on it at Tintagel, a place with which the mythical King Arthur has long been associated.'

The discovery of what became known as 'The Arthur Stone' caused a sensation in archaeological circles. The chief archaeologist of English Heritage, the government-backed body which manages the castle site in North Cornwall, declared it 'the find of a lifetime'. Dr Geoffrey Wainwright added: 'It is remarkable that a stone has been discovered with the name "Arthnou" inscribed on it at Tintagel, a place with which the mythical King Arthur has long been associated.'

What so excited Dark Age historians was that the stone emerged from a proven 'sealed context', meaning it had lain undisturbed since at least the seventh century AD. Measuring 20 cm x 35 cm, and 1 cm in depth, it was originally a plaque of some kind, and bore the Latin words: *Pater coli avi ficit artognov* – 'Arthnou, father of a descendant of Coll, has had (this) made/ built/ constructed'.

Quite what he had constructed remains unclear, because the slate had been broken and recycled as a seventh-century drain cover. However 'Arthnou' was clearly once a leader of means and stature. In Britain of the Dark Ages, literacy was the preserve of monks and the educated nobility.

Previous excavations at Tintagel had produced fragments of wine and oil pots imported from the Mediterranean, suggesting that the castle was a high-status, secular site, possibly the royal court of a chieftain of Dumnonia (the ancient kingdom of southwest Britain). The slate's significance was that it proved people here were reading and writing Latin, and living a Romanized way of life, 200 years after the Romans left in AD410, which is exactly the period when King Arthur was supposed to have been in power.

In unravelling the mystery of the Arthur Stone, it is important to separate the legendary story of the King from the historical version (such as it is). Few other areas of ancient British history produce quite so much disagreement among scholars and given that there are at least nine competing claims for 'ownership' of Arthur – Brittany, Cornwall, Cumbria, Scotland, Somerset, three areas of Wales, Wiltshire, Warwickshire and Yorkshire – it is hard to see a consensus emerging.

What is clear is that Arthurian legend has been much reproduced and embellished over the years. Fantasies such as Malory's fifteenth-century tome *Le Morte D'Arthur*, Tennyson's *Idylls of the King* and T. H. White's *The Once and Future King* have all contributed to Arthur's legendary status. In these books we learn how Arthur founds his court on the principle of 'might for right', valiantly defending his kingdom against the invading Saxons. He thrives under the counsel of the wizard Merlin but is eventually betrayed by the adultery of his best friend, Sir Lancelot, with his Queen, Guinevere, and dies a hero's death in the 'last battle' against evil forces led by his nephew Mordred. Despite this, according to the old stories, he lies buried in a secret tomb and will return to aid his people in their hour of need.

The Arthur legend is loosely based on the writings of the twelfth-century canon Geoffrey of Monmouth, whose *History of the Kings of Britain* was widely read in Europe. Geoffrey's declared aim was to promote patriotism by extolling the glories of the early Britons, but unfortunately the distinction between fact and myth is lost in his work. When Geoffrey wrote of Arthur's birthplace as Tintagel, he was mistranslating an earlier text which used the term 'din-dagol', an old Welsh word meaning 'double-banked

hillfort'. He also wrongly believed the Cornovii tribe, supposed ancestors of the King, were based in Cornwall, although they actually controlled what is now the West Midlands. In fact some historians argue that Cornwall has the weakest claim of all to an Arthurian link.

However, just because the written history of sixth and seventh-century Britain is unreliable, this does not mean that traditional folk tales and oral records should be discounted. An oral system worked pretty well for the Vikings, who relied on it for centuries in matters of law and governance. In Iceland there was even an elected Lawspeaker whose job was to hold the law in his memory and recite a third of it each year, for three years, at the

The ruins of Tintagel dominate the dramatic Cornish coastline.
Could this have been the home of the legendary Arthur?

main annual assembly. The problem of course is that oral history is easier to manipulate.

The story of Arthur's quest for the Holy Grail (see page 218) is a case in point. Portraying the king as a defender of Christianity against pagan Britain was nothing more than skilful spin-doctoring by missionary monks keen to claim converts. Just as they built churches on sacred pagan sites, so they adapted traditional stories to suit their religious agenda. Arthur, if he ever existed, was almost certainly a pagan.

And yet the legend of the Holy Grail may be an oral allegory for actual events. It draws heavily on the concept of a freezing wasteland where no crops grow, where famine is rife and plague stalks the countryside. Climatologists now believe that the Arthurian period may have seen just such a scenario, perhaps caused by a mass of debris from comets in the atmosphere which partially blocked light from the sun. Contemporary records from elsewhere in Europe bear this out – the Mediterranean writer Zachariah for instance talks of 'fire from heaven' – and an analysis of oak tree rings suggests growth was severely curtailed between AD539 and AD541.

So was there ever a 'real' Arthur figure? Many Dark Age historians now believe that a militarily successful and charismatic leader did emerge in Britain after the fall of the Roman Empire and that his name lived on in folk memory well before any meaningful written accounts. The ninth-century historian Nennius tells us that Arthur was a former Roman general, but offers little by way of explanation. To confuse matters further, it is likely that the name 'Arthnou' (which originally meant 'known as a bear, known to be a bear') was common among the ancient Britons.

Could Arthur's court have at been Tintagel? There are certainly plenty of legends linking the King to Cornwall, among them a stone slab at Slaughterbridge, near Camelford, which is said to mark his grave. Other stories claim his magical sword Excalibur lies at the bottom of either Dozmary Pool on Bodmin Moor, or Loe Pool near Helston, where it was thrown by St Bedivere as Arthur lay dying. The waterfall at St Nectan's Kieve, near Tintagel, is supposedly the place where Arthur baptized his knights before they embarked on their search for the Grail.

English Heritage has been careful to play down any clear, evidential link between the Arthur

It is likely that the name 'Arthnou' (which originally meant 'known as a bear, known to be a bear') was common among the ancient Britons.

Stone and either the historical or the legendary king. However as Dr Wainwright puts it: 'Tintagel has presented us with evidence of a court of the Arthurian period with buildings, high-status finds and the name of a person, Arthnou. Arthnou was here, that is his name on a piece of stone.'

Shrouded in mystery and yet somehow familiar, the Arthur stone is an exciting and unique archaeological find where, as Dr Wainwright put it, 'myth meets history.'

LEY LINES

In 1921, a mill owner called Alfred Watkins discovered a strange feature of the British landscape – the alignment of ancient sites and natural features across many miles. He called these connections 'ley lines' after the Saxon word ley, meaning 'clearing'. Today the debate over their purpose still rages.

Most open-minded archaeologists accept that ley lines exist. True, it is possible to quibble over detail – a burial mound is bisected at one edge rather than the centre for instance – yet given the effects of agriculture and land management over several thousand years such imprecisions must be expected. The real issue lies not in proving the leys are there, but in interpreting them.

Watkins built up knowledge of his subject over

many years travelling the rolling hills of his native Herefordshire. During visits to mills and farms he would note familiar landmarks, photograph them and plot their locations on a map. Combined with his expertise in local history, folklore and place names he soon had an unrivalled insight into the county's geography. When he eventually realized what he had discovered, he likened the feeling to 'a flood of ancestral memory'.

In his first short book, *Early British Trackways*, Watkins describes how the flash of insight occurred one summer's day: 'I had no theory when, out of what appeared to be a tangle, I got hold of the one right end of this string of facts and found to my amazement that it unwound in an orderly fashion and complete logical sequence,' he wrote.

'A visit to Blackwardine led me to note on the map a straight line starting from Croft Ambury, lying on parts of Croft Lane past the Broad, over hill points, through Blackwardine, over Risbury Camp, and through the high ground at Stretton Grandison, where I surmise a Roman station. I followed up the clue of sighting from hilltop, unhampered by other theories, found it yielding

An ancient trackway typical of the ley lines discovered by Alfred Watkins. The network of trails extends across the whole of the British landscape.

astounding results in all districts, the straight lines to my amazement passing over and over again through the same class of objects…'

In his main book on the subject, *The Old Straight Track* – published in 1925 and still the definitive work on leys – Watkins explains his theory in depth. He believed he had uncovered an ancient system of trackways, initially laid out as far back as the Stone Age. These would then have been adopted by subsequent cultures and preserved, some of them right up to the present day. The tracks were marked by obvious reference points to assist travellers, and they might bisect man-made landmarks such as castles, churches, burial mounds, standing stones and stone circles, as well as natural features like hilltops, 'notches' on a ridge, ponds and even prominent groups of trees.

There were some obvious flaws in Watkins' argument, not least that many castles and churches were constructed long after the Neolithic period when he believed leys were created. However it is generally accepted by historians that these structures were often built on significant sites. It follows that certain ley markers are original and others evolved from their predecessors. As for trees, while it is true that a few British species date back thousands of years, it is also quite possible for their descendants to occupy the same spot. Very often, clumps of trees are found atop the sites of their forebears.

As mentioned earlier, some sceptics accuse ley hunters of being too 'flexible' in their enthusiasm to plot lines through map landmarks. They argue that a ley is either straight or not, and that a few metres out is not good enough. Watkins himself was more relaxed about these measurements, noting that 'ancient methods of alignment …tended to pass through the edges of circles, not taking their centres as is now the case.'

But how would the ancient inhabitants of Britain have planned straight tracks, without modern methods of measurement and navigation? Watkins believed the 'straight-sighted track' would have been planned using fire beacons at strategic points and a team of men with staves.

How would the ancient inhabitants of Britain have planned straight tracks, without modern methods of measurement and navigation?

(He even suspected that these surveyors were the inspiration for the chalk figure of the Long Man of Wilmington in Sussex.) Once the ley was plotted, scrub and woodland along the line would be cleared and additional markers added.

Place names formed a key component of Watkins' theory. He pinpointed fields called ley or lea as possible sites. Place names containing references to the colours red and white suggested pottery or salt trade routes respectively. It followed that a place name referring to the colour gold was linked to the transport of precious metals, but Watkins later discovered that the answer was more mystical: a 'gold ley' was aligned to the midsummer sunrise.

Black was harder to explain, until Watkins realized that in Anglo-Saxon times the word meant something quite different. Black could mean shining, white or pale – perhaps a reference either to the signal fires or reflective ponds. Watkins decoded many ley names, tracing their symbolism back into the mists of the past.

But however mysterious and captivating this might be, a key question remained. What was the motivation for constructing leys? To our

The Long Man of Wilmington in Sussex. Could this be a depiction of one of the ancient surveyors who plotted the ley lines?

knowledge, there were almost no straight roads and paths in the ancient British landscape, apart from the Roman legacy. Are we expected to believe that a tradition of straight track-building simply died out, and that ley lines are all that remain? Isn't it just as likely that landmarks form purely chance alignments and that ley followers are all wishful thinkers? Over the years, leading mathematicians have attempted to illustrate this, with varying degrees of success.

Watkins answered his critics with a crude, though intriguing, experiment using a map of the Andover district. He noted the positioning of fifty-one churches on the map and counted the number of alignments between them. He found that there were thirty-eight alignments of three churches, eight alignments of four churches and one of five churches. He then marked fifty-one random crosses on an identically-sized piece of plain paper. This produced thirty-four three-cross alignments, one of four crosses and none of five crosses. Watkins concluded that the number of four-church alignments in Andover was more than would be expected, providing 'exceedingly strong evidence of deliberate alignment'.

If this sounds unscientific, remember that dozens of known leys bisect considerably more than four landmarks. For example, at Glastonbury there are at least seven landmarks aligned over 34 km, at Stonehenge there are eight over 35.5 km, and one ley line bisecting Cambridge has ten landmarks aligned across just 22 km. Nor are 'old straight tracks' unique to the British Isles. In the western Cordillera of the Andes one track stretches for 32 km across a hilly landscape at a height of 3,960 m.

The question of what leys were for remains a tantalizing mystery. It could be they were simply a Neolithic version of motorways, allowing travellers to take the straightest, clearest, safest route irrespective of whether this meant climbing a hill or traversing a river. In the busy, urbanized world of today, we generally prefer to take the easiest path between two points, avoiding hills

Watkins concluded that the number of four-church alignments in Andover was 'exceedingly strong evidence of deliberate alignment'.

and obstacles even if it is longer as the crow flies. But it does not follow that Stone Age humans would have done the same. Given their active, outdoor lifestyle, striding up a hill or two would hardly have counted as strenuous.

Leys may have had other practical or religious purposes – perhaps they were used for astronomical alignment (see Stonehenge on page 75). Inevitably they have taken their place in New Age thinking, and some pagans believe they were intended to channel an undefined 'earth energy' between sacred sites. Others claim they are linked to UFOs, perhaps functioning as ground markers for alien visitors coming in to land.

Our landscape is criss-crossed with these mysterious lines, but the truth is, we still do not know why they are there. More than eighty years after Watkins' breakthrough discovery, their presence in the British countryside remains as enigmatic as ever.

The Enigmas of Space

Events that occur in the furthest reaches of space rarely register on our planet, and even our own moon remains shrouded in mystery. Yet occasionally, signs of life in the boundless universe do impinge on us here on earth, keeping us guessing about what is really out there. Reports of alien abductions and UFO sightings have become increasingly frequent, suggesting that perhaps we are not the only life form to have broadened our horizons beyond our own planet. But at the moment we possess just pinpricks of knowledge that shimmer enticingly like distant stars in a night sky.

BLACK HOLES

Scientists have been trying to unravel the mystery behind the phenomenon known as the black hole for well over one hundred years. No-one has been able to offer any real proof that black holes exist; nonetheless, the existence of this dark force of the universe is largely accepted in theory, based on the work of some of mankind's most brilliant minds.

The mysterious black hole is formed when a 'white dwarf' star collapses in on itself completely.

It was in 1844 that the German astronomer Friedrich Wilhelm Bassel first postulated the existence of the black hole, based upon his observations of the 'dog star' Sirius. Sirius is the brightest star in the galaxy and Bassel was observing it through one of the most advanced telescopes of the day. He noted that, rather than moving in a straight line, as he would have expected, this star seemed to be subject to very slight undulations.

Bassel concluded correctly that this must be the result of some invisible force of gravity acting upon the star. Through the studies that he initiated, great discoveries have been made about the life stages of a star. For instance, it is now known that a star passes through four such stages in all, and at least 90 per cent of all known stars are thought to end up as black holes.

In the initial phase of a star's life, it is primarily comprised of the elements hydrogen and helium. Fusion takes place between the two elements, causing great energy to be released, and the entire nuclear process sees the build-up of immense gravitational forces at the centre of the star itself. A good example of a star at this stage of its life cycle is our own sun – the energy emitted by the sun is felt by us on earth as radiation in the forms of heat and light.

As time passes and the fusion continues, the core of the star will grow continually denser, due to the fact that helium is a denser material than hydrogen, with a greater atomic mass. At the same time, the exterior layers of the star will expand and the star will grow in size. At this stage the colour of the light emitted will also change and the star will become classified as a 'red giant'. At the core of the star, immensely powerful reactions will still be taking place.

In the next part of the star's life, the outer layers of the red giant will gradually disperse until all that remains is the super-dense core. At this point, when it begins to emit a different wavelength of light, it is known as a 'white dwarf'. It was when Sirius was in this phase of its history that it was spotted by Bassel back in the mid-nineteenth century. Although, by today's standards, he was restricted in what he could see through his telescope, he noted that Sirius consisted of a pair of twin stars, and that the super-dense mass of one seemed to be affecting the other. It was only with the advent of more advanced technology that it was possible to see the light being emitted by the star in its 'white dwarf' stage, and so begin to understand more fully what was happening.

Eventually, the star reaches its fourth and final life stage, represented by the concept of the mysterious black hole. This is formed when a 'white dwarf' star collapses in on itself and its matter becomes super-dense. The star is now millions of times smaller in size than when it started out, in contrast with its gravitational pull, which will be many millions of times greater.

Anything that comes into the gravitational range of the black hole will be drawn into it, whether this be planets, other stars, or even light. In fact, it is only because black holes draw light into them that scientists have been given any clue as to their existence. Although, without light, the black hole itself cannot be captured on film, what have been filmed are scenes showing matter being drawn into these pockets in space.

By using this method, astrologers are attempting to pinpoint the location of existing black holes within our universe.

Scientists have studied black holes and tried to suggest ways in which the enormous power of these peculiar facets of our universe could be harnessed in the future. Some maintain that they could hold the key to time travel, or to crossing large distances in space. Whether this is possible

is not known, but what is guaranteed is that if any human being on a future space mission were to stray anywhere near a black hole, it would spell certain death.

Others, such as the famous physicist Stephen Hawking, have postulated that black holes could actually provide humanity with a power source for the future, through the extraordinary energy they produce. It is unlikely that such a proposal would ever be met with anything other than resistance, however, as it would take only the smallest black hole to completely devour the entire earth and, indeed, the whole solar system, meaning that there could be no margin for error whatsoever.

It would seem, according to the principles laid out in the theory of the 'big bang', that this is the eventual fate of the universe anyway. At present, the cosmos is still expanding as a direct result of the original 'big bang', but it is believed that the balancing force of this expansion will be its eventual contraction. Stars will collapse into black holes and the mass of these black holes will accumulate to incorporate whole galaxies, until the universe returns to the same state in which it started.

Whether scientists will ever succeed in making use of the awesome energy contained within the black hole is unknown – at the moment, certainly, it seems far too great a risk to contemplate. Perhaps one day black holes will come to represent something other than an inconceivable power of destruction, but until that time they will be viewed with awe, wonder and respect.

This is the sort of astronomical effect that may be caused by a black hole.

WORMHOLES AND WARP DRIVES

Mankind has been fascinated by the notion of space travel for many years. The universe is a huge place, however, and we have to ask ourselves just how far it is possible for us to journey. Einstein's famous theory of relativity ($e = mc^2$) deems it impossible for a human being to travel faster than the speed of light and yet, if this is true, the vast expanses of space will remain forever inaccessible. Despite this, mankind still dreams of interstellar travel and many people believe that one day the human race will walk upon, and even colonize, alien planets. If this dream is to become a reality, one wonders how it will ever be possible.

To date, the farthest distance that human beings have explored lies just beyond the reach of our own solar system, a truly colossal distance of more than 6.5 billion miles. This journey was completed by two space probes, Pioneer 10 and Voyager 1. Launched in the 1970s, these probes have outlived their planned lifespans and explored further than was ever expected.

However, even at the remarkable speeds at which these probes can travel, it would still take them many tens of thousands of years to arrive within reach of our nearest stellar neighbour. Our closest lone star is approximately 26 trillion miles or four and a half light-years away and those stars that have been linked to surrounding planets are many, many times further away than even this. By the time a probe reached its ultimate destination, humankind might no longer exist.

Current methods of space travel use a system of direct propulsion, involving igniting fuel and blasting a jet of it behind the craft to provide forward thrust. If this method were used for the purposes of interstellar travel, the amount of fuel required would be beyond the realms of the possible. It is clear that if mankind is ever to journey to other star systems, a radical new approach to space travel will be necessary.

A computerized illustration of Voyager 1, which has travelled more than six billion miles during the thirty years that it has been orbiting in space.

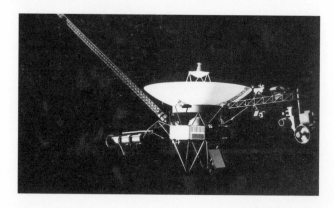

In pursuit of this, scientists have studied systems of nuclear fission as well as ion drives, but these have proved unfeasible. What has greatly interested researchers, however, in their search for entirely new possibilities in space travel is the use of warp drives and wormholes. While these cannot actually break the laws of physics, it is thought that they may be employed to bend, or ingeniously bypass, such constrictions.

Research into black holes has proved that space-time can be warped, and it is believed that, intriguingly, the fabric of space-time could be warped for the purposes of space travel.

The theory is that, by forcing the space-time behind a spaceship to expand, while simultaneously causing it to contract in front of the ship, the law of light speed could be conveniently side-stepped. Bizarrely, this would enable the spaceship to travel faster than the speed of light, without actually travelling through space at such a speed. In order to cause this warping effect, immense quantities of energy would need to be controlled very carefully.

An alternative method of space travel involves the creation of a wormhole – which is a hole in the very fabric of space-time itself. In layman's terms, a wormhole amounts to the idea of folding space, bringing close together two places that are normally very far apart. For example, if there are two points on a map, A and B, the distance between them can be shortened immeasurably by folding the map so that A and B are touching each other, and are essentially in the same place. Physicists believe that it might be possible to do this with the concept of space-time.

The problem with this remarkably simple sounding theory centres around the enormous amounts of energy that would be required to turn such an idea into reality. The only forces that are capable of distorting space-time are immense quantities of mass and density, which produce huge gravitational power. To harness these we would need to learn how to manipulate the power of black holes and neutron stars. Even if we succeeded in mastering this technique, we would still need to learn how to control and navigate the space that we were using.

Research into black holes has proved that space-time can be warped, and it is believed that the fabric of space-time could be warped for the purposes of space travel.

Although it is true that we have a great way to go before these ideas might become real possibilities, we have only to look at history for inspiration. For hundreds of years, suggestions that man might one day be able to fly were greeted with ridicule, as were notions of journeying to the moon or splitting the atom – however, these are all achievements that we now take for granted.

Unless we are prepared to allow the mysteries of the universe to remain unsolved forever, we must confront the incredible complexity of these matters with the same spirit that has led mankind to previous scientific victories.

ANGEL HAIR

Angel hair is a rare and perplexing phenomenon that has so far defied explanation. It is a delight to behold, made up of silken threads that rain down on to the earth and look startling against a cloudless blue sky. But reach out to touch it and it will almost certainly vanish before your eyes.

In September 1741, one corner of Hampshire, England, became remarkable for a blizzard of gossamer that continued for hours. Residents from three small towns – Bradley, Selbourne and Alresford – saw the widespread downpour. One witness related what he had seen in a letter written four years after the astonishing event:

'As the morning advanced the sun became bright and warm, and the day turned out one of those most lovely ones which no season but the autumn produces; cloudless, calm, serene, and worthy of the South of France itself.

'About nine [in the morning] a very unusual appearance began to demand our attention, a shower of cobwebs falling from very elevated regions, and continuing, without any interruption, till the close of the day. These webs were not single filmy threads, floating in the air in all directions, but perfect flakes or rags; some near an inch broad [2.5 cm], and five or six long [13–15 cm], which fell with a degree of velocity which showed they were considerably heavier than the atmosphere.

'On every side as the observer turned his eyes might he behold a continual succession of fresh flakes falling into his sight, and twinkling like

A very unusual appearance began to demand our attention – a shower of cobwebs falling from very elevated regions, and continuing, without any interruption, till the close of the day.

stars as they turned their sides towards the sun…Neither before nor after was any such fall observed; but on this day the flakes hung in the trees and hedges so thick, that a diligent person sent out might have gathered baskets full.'

This account is one of the most familiar stories of an angel hair shower, but by no means was it an isolated incident. Since then, there have been reports of this strange occurrence from all over the world, although the greatest number are from North America, Australia, New Zealand and western Europe.

In 1914, soon after the first winter rains arrived in South Australia, there were accounts of angel hair falling in pieces between 15 cm and

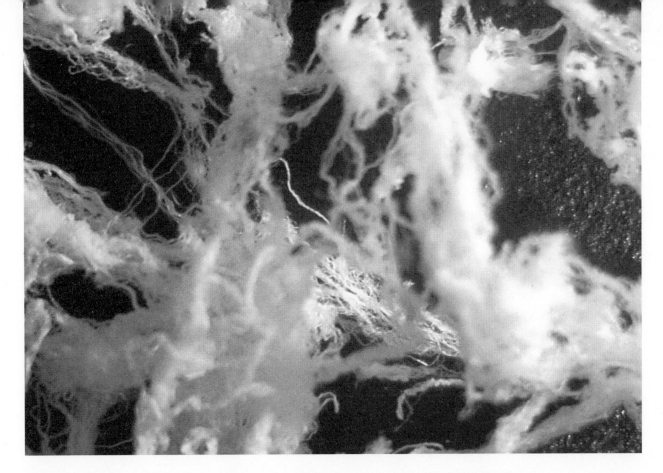

Angel hair is described as being similar in substance to a spider's web, made of gossamer-like intertwined fibres.

23 cm long, and then swiftly dissolving on the ground. Three weeks later another shower, lasting for an hour, was reported.

According to a 1950 edition of the *Philadelphia Inquirer*, two police officers in South Philadelphia in the United States were on evening patrol when they saw what they thought must be a parachute falling to earth. When the 1.8 m-long object finally landed, the officers saw it glow in purple and crystalline colours. As one of the men reached down to touch the substance, 'the mass on which he laid his hands dissolved, leaving nothing but a slight, odourless, sticky residue.' Within 25 minutes it had all disappeared.

Two years later, a school headmaster in Oloron-Sainte-Marie in south-west France saw objects in the sky that he could not identify. In the wake of these objects came trails of an unknown substance, which was described as gelatinous at first, but that quickly turned into vapour.

Global reports about angel hair have continued with surprising frequency, sometimes detailing that it arrives in balls rather than flakes. Indeed, descriptions vary from fluorescent filaments, through to flecks and strands and even to jelly and goo. One conclusion is that the substance has come from spiders or perhaps another silk-spinning insect. Spiders do sometimes migrate by flying in wind currents, but there is a marked absence of spiders in the material described as 'angel hair' and no link has yet been proven.

The mystical qualities of this substance are enhanced by the fact that some – although not all – accounts of angel hair are associated with the sighting of an unidentified flying object (UFO).

So far, there has been little orchestrated research into the qualities of angel hair. This is primarily due to a lack of reliable data, as it tends to disappear after coming into contact with human flesh. However, one woman is trying to change this. Analytical scientist Phyllis Budinger, from Ohio, has used the restricted number of angel hair samples available to draw

some conclusions about its chemical content.

She investigated four samples, drawn from across North America. Incredibly, the first dated from 1977 and had been stored in two airtight glass jars for more than twenty years before being analysed. It fell in Los Gatos, California, and the samples lay forgotten until 1998.

In 1999, a bemused driver who had driven for some 24 km through a fall of angel hair near Sacramento, California, collected the second sample. Some strands were just a few centimetres long, while others measured up to 17 m long.

At Oloron in south-west France, a headteacher saw UFOs trailing strands of angel hair. Could this mysterious substance be extraterrestrial exhaust?

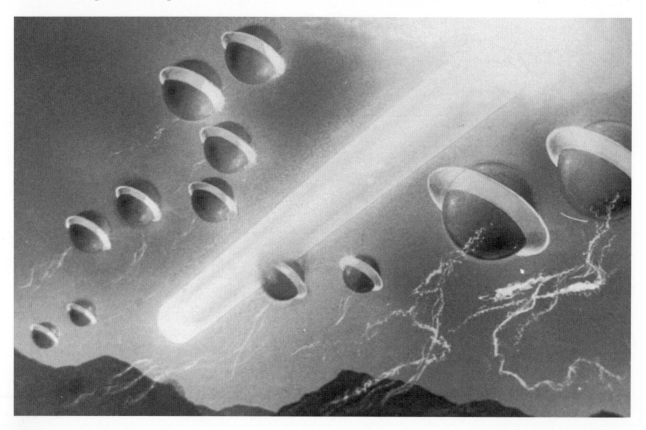

The third sample came from Burlington, West Virginia, in 2000, and was discovered after the householder heard a mysterious droning noise lingering outside her home the previous night. It was only in this case that the substance was described as transforming into a slimy goo. Inexplicably, both the householder and her dog fell ill after finding the angel hair, although it is not known if the events were linked.

Shenandoah in Iowa was the location of the fourth angel hair sample. The fall occurred in 1981 and lasted for nearly six hours. This case was notable for being concurrent with the sighting of a UFO.

Budinger was able to scrutinize the Los Gatos samples through an extremely powerful microscope and saw bundles of fibres rather than single strands. They were even thinner than spiders' silk, and the droplets often seen with arachnid webs were not apparent. However, while it is true that spiders' silk is frequently characterized by the presence of droplets, this may not always be the case. Only further research into the nature of spiders' webs will clarify this.

Budinger was able to determine that all four specimens had similar molecular structure. She defined this as 'a polymer containing protein-amide type linkages'. A polymer is formed from repeated units of smaller molecules, while amides are ammonia-based compounds.

Budinger's findings indicate that angel hair originates from a biological source. But to date, she has been unable to identify this source. There are similarities between angel hair and spider or caterpillar silk, but they do not seem to be identical.

Angel hair is not only difficult to collect, but it is also highly sensitive. It is subject to contamination from car exhaust fumes, or even from the human hand, which might skew the chemical results of analysis.

The two most compelling samples of angel hair are those collected at Burlington and Shenandoah, where there is a strong suspicion of UFO activity. Indeed, a different analysis of information about angel hair falls in Australia discovered that in eleven cases there were no reports of UFO sighting, while in eight there were. It is this extraterrestrial aspect of angel hair that both baffles and intrigues investigators today.

Some – although not all – accounts of angel hair are associated with sightings of a UFO.

Budinger is in no doubt as to what is now needed to resolve the mystery of angel hair. 'Clearly a broader database is required. Most important is the need for angel hair from events coinciding with witnessed UFO activity. More samples are needed from a variety of locations and from falls at different times of the year. Unfortunately, a predominance of data is from falls in the United States and in the month of October…Proper sampling is needed. It should be done as soon as possible after the event…Proper analytical testing is required.'

Until such a thorough scientific approach is adopted, the unusual sight of a fall of angel hair can be valued as one of today's enduring mysteries.

GREYS

A spindly body with a bulbous, hairless head and large, dark almond eyes. Sound familiar? Probably, since this is the uniform description given of alien life forms spotted here on earth. These beings are known as 'greys', after the colour of their smooth, rubbery skins. In recent years, reports of alien sightings have been relatively frequent, and it is striking how similar most descriptions are.

Greys are described as having spindly bodies, with bulbous, bald heads, and large almond-shaped eyes.

Sceptics do not believe the image of the grey to be the real likeness of alien life forms, but rather that which appeared in an ABC sci-fi show made in the early 1960s called *The Outer Limits*. They believe this image has somehow seeped into international consciousness as the definitive portrayal of extraterrestrial life, when previously the image was predominantly of 'little green men'. Yet surely this cannot explain why, even under hypnosis, literally scores of people have come up with the same descriptions? The life forms they speak of communicate telepathically, have wasted muscles and closely resemble foetuses.

There has been plenty of speculation about what part of space these extraterrestrials might come from. Among the most frequently cited places is Zeta Reticuli, a binary star, visible in the skies of the southern hemisphere, thirty-nine light years away from earth.

Why would aliens want to visit earth? Perhaps they are on a quest to save their dying race, or maybe they want to clone human beings for an unknown purpose. It is doubtful that they would come here to wonder at our technology, since their own appears to be far superior. Nor does it seem to be their aim to share their knowledge with us, because the recall of abductees is often hazy.

Reports of UFOs began surfacing after the Second World War, when the world was gripped in the paranoia of the Cold War and the fear of the atomic bomb. Rocket technology had advanced during the war years to a point where fast, long-distance flight appeared to be a distinct possibility for the first time. Americans were fearful of a communist invasion and they were sure that, in the event, both nuclear and psychological weapons would be dispatched by the USSR. It was in this climate of fear that pilot Kenneth Arnold saw what he described as 'flying saucers' soaring in formation above the Cascade Mountains in Washington State in June 1947. Arnold's testimony marked the beginning of a flood of UFO sightings in America and around the world.

On 7 July 1947, these stories reached their climax, with the revelation of the now notorious Roswell incident. The wreckage of an odd-looking craft and its equally unusual humanoid crew was apparently discovered on the Foster ranch, near Corona, New Mexico. The following day a press officer for the nearby Roswell Army Air Fields announced that an alien vessel had crash-landed there. But a high-ranking military officer was swift to refute the claim, saying that an experimental balloon had gone down near Roswell. As he explained it, the bodies at the scene were in fact crash dummies. However, many people did not accept the official explanation, and they remained convinced that the US government had evidence of aliens in its grasp.

The debate was fuelled in 1995 when a film allegedly showing an alien autopsy following the Roswell incident was unveiled. But there was immediate doubt about the film's authenticity, not least because the creatures which featured in it did not match descriptions given of them at the time.

Since then, theories about what really happened at Roswell have abounded, the latest being that emaciated Japanese prisoners of war were being used as test pilots on an experimental flight. This would certainly explain why the military were keen to have the whole incident hastily covered up.

Many people remained convinced that the US government had evidence of aliens in its grasp.

The entire Roswell episode has been marked by inconsistencies, controversy, claim and counter-claim. It is known that at least two crucial official documents from the era have gone missing. But if some of the original descriptions of the Roswell Army Air Fields crew are to be believed, then this was the first known human contact with greys.

Since the Roswell incident, large numbers of stories involving contact with greys have circulated, some of which seem convincing, others less so.

In July 1952, Truman Bethurum was sleeping in his truck when he was woken by the voices of eight diminutive figures standing close by. Outside his cab, Truman was astonished to see a 90 m-wide spaceship, hovering soundlessly. The beings, he reported, had olive rather than grey skin. According to his account, they told him: 'Our homes are our castles in a faraway land'. Then they allegedly took him aboard the spaceship to meet its captain, Aura Rhanes, who told him they were from the planet Clarion, obscured from earth by the moon.

Ten years after this incident, a UFO that reportedly crashed south of Alamogordo, New Mexico, yielded the bodies of two greys. They have been described as being about 1 m tall with large heads, pink-grey skin, large eyes, small noses and mouths and holes for ears. It is said that the bodies were sent to a leading university hospital in America for analysis.

In 1973, student Masaaki Kudou was working as a security guard in a timber yard close to the sea on Hokkaido, Japan, when he apparently saw a spaceship taking off from the water. He claims he saw one humanoid figure, accompanied by another two that were smaller. Other spaceships joined the first before they sped off together, leaving Kudou astounded.

In 1989, mother Linda Cortile announced she was literally beamed up into a spaceship by aliens who were short and grey with round heads and apparently frail bodies. Curiously, the incident happened on Manhattan Island and reportedly had a host of witnesses. Alien appearances are more commonly associated with rural areas rather than metropolitan places like New York.

Cortile recalled that during the abduction she was given a medical examination, before abruptly being returned to bed in her twelfth-storey apartment. Scrutiny of Cortile's case continues even today.

The internet has enabled the exchange of stories like these to proliferate. There are also many on-line tales from people who claim to have seen spaceships in US air force hangars and

Linda Cortile announced she was literally beamed up into a spaceship by aliens who were short and grey with round heads and frail bodies.

spoken to aliens captured from these craft. However, most of these are experiences related by a third person, rather than by first-hand witnesses, and are therefore less reliable.

Sceptics sneer at the stories of contact with aliens, sometimes known as 'close encounters of the third kind'. And some of the stories are so exaggerated that they are hard to believe.

Yet just as the cynics dismiss all claims of alien contact, so ufologists feel able to scoff at many of the earthly explanations given for episodes of this nature. When detailed descriptions of an alien encounter are given by several witnesses, the explanations that those involved mistook a fast-moving mystery disc for Venus in the night sky or for high-flying weather balloons do seem simplistic. To dismiss all reports of extraterrestrial contact is closed-minded, given the size of the universe and possibility of advanced life forms existing far from earth. And the notion that alien sightings are the product of people's subconscious has yet to be proved to anyone's satisfaction.

ALIEN IMPLANTS

Accounts of extraterrestrials abducting humans for close quarters examination have been frequent for the last fifty years. And recently it has come to light that those who believe they have had close encounters may be marked out forever by an intravenous implant. For over a decade, implants have been reported in the hands, feet, nose and abdomen of abductees. Only x-ray technology can discern whether aliens have left their extraordinary calling card, as there are no obvious indications remaining on the skin. However, those afflicted are frequently dogged by illness, even before any suggestion of an implant is made.

So why would aliens implant humans in this way? It is a matter for conjecture, but there is one generally accepted opinion – that the implants might act as transmitters or beacons so that when the aliens return they can trace their human subjects. So far, though, hard evidence for implants is in short supply.

Indeed, there is no conclusive proof that humans have ever been inside spaceships. All the evidence is anecdotal, leading the sceptics to claim that the experiences reported by abductees are nothing more than lucid dreams. Yet how can we explain that the accounts of kidnappings by aliens number in their hundreds? Furthermore, the stories all bear a curious similarity. Stories of abduction usually begin with the

sighting of a UFO. The accounts that abductees give of dancing lights in the sky or cigar-shaped craft shooting overhead are sometimes verified by other people in the area.

Abductees then apparently walk, float or fly up into the spacecraft inside a beam of light. Inside, they find the craft brightly lit and clinically clean. They recount how the examination takes place in this surgical setting, with the human subject naked and quivering beneath the eyes of

Alone and helpless, the abductees are reportedly taken to a brightly lit, clinical room on board the spacecraft, where the aliens proceed to examine them.

Accounts of alien abduction usually start with the sighting of mysterious lights in the sky, or an encounter with a UFO.

apparently friendly and keen to give advice that will benefit mankind.

Returned to their homes or vehicles, the abductees typically discover they have only been missing for a few minutes, although it seems to them that hours have passed by. Immediately, the events inside the craft become a hazy memory, but then return in haunting and vivid dreams. After abduction experiences, people often sense that they are being observed, although they do not generally feel that the surveillance has sinister motives.

Hypnosis is one of the methods used to try and understand what has happened to abductees – or experiencers as they are sometimes called – during the time lapse inside the spacecraft. In the absence of film footage or other incontrovertible evidence, this information would otherwise remain hidden in their subconscious. In the 1980s, 270 cases of claimed abduction were analysed in detail using hypnosis. All accounts showed astonishingly close consistencies. However, the accuracy of using hypnosis for the purposes of recall is not proven, and it is believed that interviewers' beliefs on the subject may influence the outcome. The results are open to debate.

So what about the implants? Surely they must provide hard evidence of abductions. If experiencers submit to a second examination, the implanted particle or device can be analysed. However, results have proved disappointing. One item believed to be an alien implant was sneezed out, and turned out to be a ball bearing. Another was proved by chemical scrutiny to be a dental filling. There is no conclusive proof about the nature of implants, although recent

the aliens. It is presumably at this point that an implant is inserted. Afterwards, the human interlopers might be offered a tour of the craft. Attempts to remove a keepsake have always ended in failure, although the aliens are accounts allude to small, tear-shaped rocks of an unknown substance.

Perhaps more worryingly, there is an oft-repeated allegation that women are implanted with sperm and become pregnant, only to be robbed of the foetus before giving birth. If these accounts are to be believed, the aliens take a special interest in human reproductive organs.

In September 1961, Betty and Barney Hill were driving along the isolated Interstate Route 3 in New Hampshire when, as they relate, they encountered a spacecraft that looked like 'a big pancake'. Later, they were to reveal the details of their encounter while under hypnosis and their convincing stories became a kind of benchmark in terms of alien experience. They recounted how they ended up aboard the craft, where there were uniformed men with large eyes, flat noses and lipless mouths. Betty, a social worker, was given 'a pregnancy test' by some futuristic machinery through the navel. Meanwhile, mail sorter Barney endured the extraction of his semen.

Although Barney died years later, Betty has always maintained that she was taken by aliens. Yet her approach remains underpinned by common sense. Her experience, she insists, does not reflect any extraordinary personal talents. 'I'm about as psychic as a dead fish,' she jokes.

Likewise Elaine Darlington, a former Royal Air Force servicewoman living in Newquay, Cornwall, enjoyed an ordinary life before her alleged contact with aliens. She cites four different encounters with aliens, and it was during the last of these that she said an 'operation' took place.

'They zapped me with a light on the centre of my forehead. They seemed to be able to manipulate matter or body energy,' she said. 'The operation began – I think it was on my stomach. There was no pain but they had some problem with my blood…I came round in my own bedroom with no side effects, apart from one small blotch on my left rib cage. It vanished within 24 hours.'

There is an oft-repeated allegation that women are implanted with sperm and become pregnant, only to be robbed of the foetus before giving birth.

Because the mark on her body disappeared so quickly, evidence was once again in short supply. However, Elaine's home was hit by power cuts around the time of the visits and she herself suffered electric shocks. Curiously, her local electricity board could find no problems with supply.

On a final alien encounter on Newlyn Downs, Cornwall, Elaine's husband Ian was there to share her experience. Elaine had woken in the early hours, convinced she was to make an excursion to the Downs. On arrival, they recount how they both saw a bright light through the window of their vehicle and watched it shoot up at high speed to the sky.

The lack of hard evidence to prove alien abduction makes it all the harder for experiencers to convince sceptics, but they will not give up. 'My memories of being taken are real,' insists Elaine. 'It isn't like remembering dreams'.

THE 1969 MOON LANDINGS

On 20 July 1969 the world watched in amazement as film footage depicted US astronauts Neil Armstrong and Buzz Aldrin taking their historic steps upon the surface of the moon. As politicians and statesmen offered their congratulations to the USA, people all over the globe were inspired by this incredible feat.

Many experts who have studied the footage of the first moon landing have suggested that it was, in fact, faked.

It was called mankind's greatest achievement ever, and it was generally believed that it would usher in a new age – the space age – with moon bases, space colonies and expansion through our solar system. Why then, several decades later, has none of this come about? Why has mankind not set foot on the moon for over thirty years? Could the answer be that man never actually set foot on the moon in the first place?

Almost as soon as the Second World War ceased, the USA and the Soviet Union started competing to land a man on the moon. Both sides worked long and hard in their quest for victory, and seemed to have no qualms about utilizing the knowledge accumulated by Nazi scientists during the war to enable them to achieve their goal, as it was acknowledged that there was a great deal of political capital to be gained by the side that won.

The USSR enjoyed a series of advances, leading the way with the Sputnik programme and putting the first man, Yuri Gagarin, into space. For a considerable time, it seemed as if a Communist victory was inevitable, with the USA's space plan suffering a series of disastrous setbacks. Yet this was not to be, because it was the USA that, in the end, gloried in the moment of stepping onto the moon's surface and planting its flag – or did it?

What was previously accepted as indisputable fact is now more frequently being viewed as a mystery – or even a conspiracy. Many experts who have studied the footage of the first moon landing have suggested that it was, in fact, faked. But was it really possible to fake the moon landings and maintain the secret so successfully for so long? This would be a task almost as difficult as flying to the moon itself, and no one claiming to be involved in such a deception has ever come forward to expose it. Nevertheless, there are many sceptics who still present some very convincing evidence for their arguments.

To start with, there are those who are suspicious of all the secrecy surrounding the space project, who view the restricted access to the facts as concealment of the evidence and a sure sign of conspiracy. All that we have as proof is the widely released footage of the two astronauts performing their tasks on the moon surface, and it is this that has sparked most of the substantial allegations of deception. Many have claimed that there are enough errors and discrepancies in these images to illustrate the forgery convincingly.

The first, and most famous, of these concerns relates to the American flag. The footage depicts the astronauts planting the flag in the moon surface and the 'Stars and Stripes' flapping wildly while they endeavour to keep it upright. What is peculiar is that, even after the flag has been firmly positioned, it continues to move as if it were blowing in the wind, an unlikely scenario in the light of the absence of any atmosphere on the moon to cause such movement. Conspiracy theorists have argued that the motion of the flag was, in fact, caused by some kind of fan located within the photographic studio used to create the faked images. These claims have been countered by the suggestion that the moving flag may indicate that there is, after all, an atmosphere on the moon, although, on the basis of established science, this seems highly unlikely.

Perhaps more difficult to dismiss so simply is the controversy relating to the surface of the moon and the blast crater. The Apollo

The Apollo 11 Saturn V lifts off into space in 1969.

photographs clearly show that the lunar landscape is covered in a large amount of dust – this is obvious from the famous pictures of the astronauts' footprints and the later images of the tracks of the lunar rover. Samples of dust and rock were even put on display when the mission returned to earth.

When the moon lander came to rest on the surface of the moon, it controlled its descent with a powerful rocket thruster which acted as a brake to stop it from crashing into the lunar surface. It stands to reason, therefore, that the photographs would be expected to reveal a large amount of displaced dust around the landing module and at least a small crater beneath it.

However, what is curious is that, on examination of the pictures of the lunar landing site, it appears that the lander has touched down without disturbing the lunar surface at all. There are no visible scorch marks anywhere and the area around the module seems undisturbed. The lander looks shiny and clean, with no trace of any settlement on its surface and even the module's feet are clean, despite sitting on large amounts of lunar dust.

A third point of contention in the lunar photographs is that relating to the shadows visible. While, on the moon, there is only one light source – the sun – discrepancies in the shadows captured in these pictures suggest that more than one light source was, in fact, present.

For example, some of the shadows of rock and objects can be seen to converge or cross, which should never happen if all of the light originates from one source.

In another image, Armstrong's and Aldrin's shadows appear to be of different lengths, again suggesting that more than one light source is being used. In one telltale shot, both astronaut and moon lander are visible, with the sunlight illuminating them from one side.

The shot is particularly patriotic, for not only is the astronaut seen saluting the American flag, but he is also standing next to the lunar module that again displays the flag, as well as the words, 'United States'. The darkness of a lunar shadow should be pitch black, and yet the flag and words are highly visible on the dark side of the lander.

The conspiracy theorists argue that these irregularities with the lighting, and the movement of the flag, are evidence that the footage of the landings was not actually taken on the surface of the moon at all, but rather, in a studio somewhere here on earth. Further supporting this idea is the fact that in each of the photographs a peculiarly dark sky is visible, and yet, in the absence of any atmosphere on the moon, the stars should have been especially visible from its surface.

Although the moon landscape, the equipment involved and even the appearance of low gravity could all have been replicated by the film effects units of Hollywood, it would have been impossible to try to reproduce an accurate astrological representation of a starry sky.

It seems, therefore, that there may be evidence to suggest that man may not, after all, have landed on the moon. And yet, even if this evidence were correct, it seems an improbable suggestion that man has not ventured into space at all. Global communications rely upon satellites that orbit the earth at various altitudes and this would be impossible without space travel. Much of the work being done today in the fields of

The controversial picture with the US flag and the words 'United States' clearly visible on the lunar module.

astrophysics and astronomy is conducted from orbiting telescopes such as the Hubble, which exist outside the earth's atmosphere. Once again, the technology required to put these instruments into space was developed in the space race that culminated in the moon landings.

One cynical suggestion about the possible reasons for faking the moon landings is that they were actually a politically motivated ruse to divert public attention away from the Vietnam War. During the run-up to the moon landings, there was increasing opposition to the war, as well as a level of military failure. By landing on the moon, the USA demonstrated victory, in scientific terms at least and, interestingly, the missions to land on the moon ceased at around the same time as the war in Vietnam.

A completely alternative theory combines the ideas of conspiracy and deception. Based upon the belief that there are unusual artificial structures, and even cities, built on the moon and perhaps also on Mars, it has been suggested that the publicly disseminated footage of the moon landings was a cover for the amazing nature of what was, in fact, found there.

With the advances in technology that have taken place over the last few decades, there are few who doubt that mankind could now fly to the moon successfully. Whether, however, this was achieved back in 1969 is still doubted by some – in fact, it may require another trip to the moon to prove that the flag still stands. Until that time, it seems likely that the satellite will remain a bewitching enigma.

MOON CITIES

The two main theories put forward to explain the existence of mankind are, on the one hand, those that spring from religious notions of creation and, on the other, those that arise from scientific ideas, such as the process of evolution. A third theory is, however, gaining in popularity with many people all over the world, and they are awaiting further space exploration and technological advancement to prove them right. Their belief is that human life actually

originated on a planet other than earth, and has been in existence for much longer than is currently thought.

The discovery of the 'face on Mars' in 1976 (see Martian Cities on page 112) – an apparent geological construction resembling human facial features – was greeted with great enthusiasm and sparked extensive research into the possibility of extraterrestrial life within our own solar system. While many enthusiasts focused on examining the pictures of the Martian surface, others brought their attention to bear on other areas of our galaxy. Little did they expect such astounding discoveries.

Scientists such as Richard Hoagland, the American astronomer who pioneered this research, decided to examine the only other body of our solar system on which we possess any sort of detailed information, namely our moon. In his close inspection of photographs of the lunar surface, Hoagland discovered several peculiarities that seemed to have been overlooked by the scientific establishment.

Within the radius of the Ukert crater is the unmistakable image of an equilateral triangle.

Clearly visible in some of the moon photographs are structures that seem highly unlikely to have been formed by natural means. The first of these appeared in the Triesnecker and Ukert craters, which were created eons ago by meteor impacts. Within the radius of the Ukert crater is the unmistakable image of an equilateral triangle, one of the very foundations of geometry and almost impossible to explain as a natural phenomenon. Each side of the triangle is 26 km long, and it can be viewed from earth during a full moon with just a small telescope.

Impressed by this remarkable discovery, astronomers scoured the existing lunar footage for more evidence of such anomalies. To many people, the existence of this triangular shape alone was evidence of some form of intelligent

life and, if further proof could be found, then maybe a case could be made for looking for lunar inhabitants.

So, the examination of the lunar surface continued. All the areas of interest seemed to be located in that part of the moon known to astronomers as the 'Sinus Medii' (Latin for 'Central Bay'). If one were observing a full moon, this is the region around the centre of the visible disk. Within this area, in particular, investigators were drawn to a strange protuberance from the moon's surface, known as 'the shard'. This geological feature is remarkable because it projects from the surface of the moon to a distance of more than 1 km, in an otherwise sparse and flat landscape.

Perhaps the strangest of all formations to be detected on the lunar surface are those that appear in one of the photographs taken during the Apollo 10 mission. In frame number 4822, a structure can be discerned that appears to be floating just a few kilometres from the moon's surface – this configuration is known as 'the tower' as it appears to have a cube-shaped top to it. Some sceptics have argued that this must be part of the mission probe's photo array, as such an object would defy the laws of physics. Others, however, are more willing to consider less conventional theories, and believe that this structure is strong proof of a former lunar city.

It is the latter group of people who are particularly interested in some of the other National Aeronautics and Space Administration (NASA) photographs, which appear to show large chasms in the lunar surface being spanned by a number of bridges. While this is not geologically impossible in itself, the proximity of such bridges to what have been described as ruined lunar cities may suggest that they were constructed artificially for the purpose of transport, rather than having arisen from any natural cause.

In examining these pictures, some people also claimed that the remains of a colossal dome are visible. It appears to contain a kind of grid pattern, suggesting that at some time it might have contained a lunar city. Using a system of dating based on the number of fresh impact craters in the area, it is estimated that the area that might have contained such a city has been ruined for around half a billion years.

Many people believe that the true extent of the lunar discoveries, as well as the evidence compiled from the surface of Mars, has been covered up by the government. They argue that the photographic footage released to the public has in some way been doctored to conceal the truth. These views, however, have been given no credence by scientists or by NASA, who attribute the objects themselves to quirks of geology and photographic defects.

Whatever the arguments, it seems safe to say that, as technology improves, it will not be long before people are able to use their own telescopes to look in ever greater detail at planets and moons in our solar system.

It is likely that they will therefore soon be able to make their own judgements about these mysterious structures and their possible origins. It would certainly give mankind much to think about if any of these theories were proven to have their basis in fact after all.

An image of the moon that shows craters on the surface.

MARTIAN CITIES

In recent years there has been much excitement over the notion that there may, indeed, be life on a planet other than our own and, in particular, on Mars. Various governments have pledged to launch an exploratory mission to Mars with the aim of landing a man on the planet, and this may well take place in the future. However, the majority of people who hope to find some evidence of present or past life on Mars expect this to be of the microscopic microbial variety, perhaps existing in a small amount of water beneath the planet's surface.

The expectation of the discovery of life on Mars received an unexpected boost in 1976, when mankind's first Martian probe reached the red planet. Named the Viking Orbiter 1, the probe's mission was to scan and map the surface of the planet, as this information was considered vital to scientists in their efforts to understand the mysteries of our nearest planetary neighbour. The maps would also help them to choose a suitable location for the planned future landing of a mission to the planet in order to gather samples of the Martian surface for analysis.

When the scientists and astronomers involved in the project were examining the data from the Viking probe, they made a wholly unexpected discovery. In the Cynodia region of the planet there appeared to be a large hill, more than a kilometre wide, which in its formation unmistakeably resembled a human face.

After extensive investigation, the National Aeronautics and Space Administration (NASA) declared that the image was a purely chance formation, and that it had no real scientific significance. As such, the image was released to the public.

Many believe that the Martian face is an artificial structure, created by some kind of intelligent life form.

To many, however, this explanation was unsatisfactory, and the image generated great enthusiasm for the concept of life on Mars. Proponents of this idea have stated their belief that the Martian face is an artificial structure, created by some kind of intelligent life form. To build such a formation, its creators would have required knowledge and understanding of the physiology of the human face, and therefore it seemed that they were either humans themselves, or else they had come into contact with mankind at some point.

Further underpinning this theory are claims that a number of other features in the photograph could also represent artificial structures. For

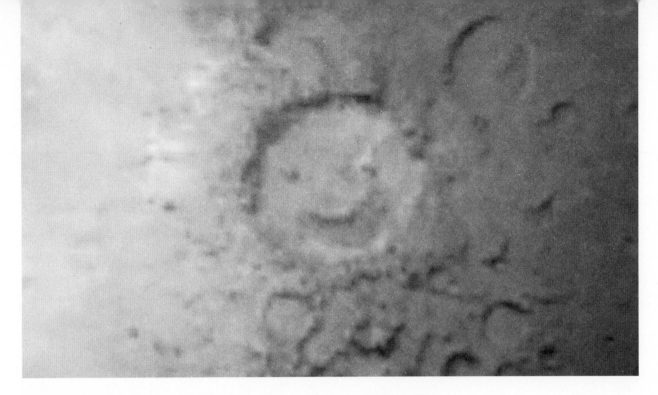

The Galle Crater, also called 'The Happy Face', photograped on the surface of Mars in 2003.

example, it has been suggested that several angular hills in the same Cynodia region were actually pyramids – if so, such a structure would provide an interesting link between our own world and the Martian environment. Unfortunately, the resolution of the photograph was too poor to be able to gain a conclusive answer either way.

Could it be possible that a civilization of humans, or at least one that was aware of humankind, had lived on Mars thousands of years ago? The debate continued, but the pictures had generated sufficient interest to warrant further investigation of the Cynodia region of the planet. During the late 1990s and early twenty-first century, the Mars Global Surveyor was charged with making a sophisticated map of the Martian surface, and in 1998 and 2001 the orbiting satellite took photographs of the disputed area.

At first it seemed that NASA's original verdict had been correct and the 'face on Mars' was simply a freak geological formation. Then, however, a fresh theory arose, which declared that the images revealed the existence of an entire city frozen beneath a Martian glacier near Mars' polar ice cap.

It seems that the information gleaned to date from the red planet is open to interpretation in a number of ways. Although there is a large base of established opinion ranged against the claims of life on Mars, many – such as American scientist Richard Hoagland – view the discoveries as evidence of a lost space culture that spanned our solar system, and perhaps even extended beyond it. Interestingly, even NASA agrees that it will take further investigations before the mystery is fully uncovered.

Ghostly Encounters

Chilling tales of brushes with the dead and frequent reports of ghost sightings suggest that after death, part of us will linger on here on earth. Haunting houses, churches, ships and even film studios, the dead seem here to stay. Some famous ghosts are said to haunt the area where they died in the hope of seeking justice. Others are said to serve as a warning. Many people who encounter spirits say that they are benevolent, and the ghosts are regarded with affection, but some spirits appear as negative and, occasionally, angry forces.

HAUNTED SHIPS

The creaking timbers of a swaying ghost ship looming through swirling mists, with red warning lights on its bow, is sufficient to strike fear into any stout heart. For the phantom crew of the vessel the threat is past, but for unfortunate observers, it lies just ahead.

So goes the tale of the *Flying Dutchman*, a ship that foundered on the tip of Africa after being lashed by a ferocious storm more than three centuries ago. The ship's captain, Hendrick Vanderdecken, refused either to seek shelter or to

> Before the phantom ship vanished, no fewer than thirteen men had witnessed it first-hand.

drop anchor despite the raging tempest. Following curses made either to God or the Devil, he was allegedly condemned to sail around the region forever with, quite literally, a skeleton crew. Moreover, anyone who sights the phantom vessel is also doomed.

Since the dawn of the sea faring age, sailors have been notoriously superstitious. They are quite likely to interpret cloud formations and naturally forming prismatic effects as ghost ships haunting the high seas. Curiously, though, there have been numerous reports about the *Flying Dutchman*, some from highly reliable sources.

On 11 July 1881, a lookout on the HMS *Bacchante* rounding the Cape of Good Hope was the first to see what he believed to be the *Flying Dutchman*. Before the phantom ship vanished, no fewer than thirteen men had witnessed it first-hand. In the ship's log, the midshipman recorded: 'During the middle watch the so-called *Flying Dutchman* crossed our bows. She first appeared as a strange red light, as if a ship all aglow, in the midst of which light her spars, masts and sails, seemingly those of a normal brig, some 200 yards [183 m] distant from us, stood out in strong relief as she came up. Our lookout man on the forecastle reported her close to our port bow, where also the officer of the watch from the bridge clearly saw her, as did our quarterdeck midshipman, who was sent forward at once to the forecastle to report back. But on reaching there, no vestige, nor any sign of the ship, was to be seen either near or away on the horizon.'

The writer went on to become George V of England – and he fared notably better than the lookout, who fell from the rigging and died later in the voyage.

Among other definitive sightings of the *Flying Dutchman* was one off South African shores in 1939. Bathers on Glencairn beach were united in their description of the sailing ship heading towards the sands, although few can have known details about merchant vessels of the seventeenth century. According to the *British South Africa Annual* of that year: 'Just as the excitement reached its climax, however, the mystery ship vanished into thin air as strangely as it had come.'

Once one of the most prestigious liners afloat, the *Queen Mary*, now has the reputation of being the most haunted. The spirits that frolic in the ship's first class swimming pool area are so prolific that a 'ghost cam' is trained on it at all times. Staff have seen child-sized wet footprints appear around the pool when no accompanying body is visible. Sounds of water-borne high jinks are heard from outside when the pool is empty. A medium invited aboard to investigate the sights and sounds believed one of the changing cubicles to be 'a portal to another realm'. If there are ghosts in the pool, they appear to belong to the years between the maiden voyage of the *Queen Mary* in 1936 and its war service, which began in 1940.

From the same era come accounts of the ghost of a white lady who, once spotted, disappears behind a pillar. However, some of the unearthly sounds that emanate from the ship are thought to be later in origin, stemming from the death of 17-year-old John Pedder, who perished trying to escape a fire onboard in 1966, just a year before the liner ended its service. Loud and frantic knocking sounds have been heard from behind door 13, and sometimes it feels hot to the touch. Could Pedder's ghost still be haunting the liner, condemned to relive his terrible last moments to the end of time? The *Queen Mary* is now a

The *Queen Mary* in dry dock. This vast and sumptuous liner is said to be the portal to another realm, teeming with ghostly passengers from a long-gone era.

permanent fixture in Long Beach, California, where she is a major tourist attraction, not least for the paranormal activity rumoured to take place aboard.

Another ghostly vessel spotted off the English coast is the *Lady Lovibond*. During her last voyage, she was bound from London to Portugal, carrying not only cargo but also Captain Simon Peel's bride and fifty of their wedding guests.

On deck, first mate John Rivers was contorted with jealousy. He had hoped to make Peel's bride his own wife, but his hopes had been dashed. By way of desperate revenge, he drove the three-masted barque in full sail on to the treacherous Goodwin Sands. All on board were killed as the ship's woodwork splintered and smashed down.

> By way of desperate revenge, he drove the three-masted barque in full sail onto the treacherous Goodwin Sands. All on board were killed as the ship's woodwork splintered...

The incident happened in February 1748, on an unlucky Friday 13th. However, that particular superstition is rooted in twentieth-century lore, so it would not have resonated with audiences of the time.

But this was not the last of the ill-fated *Lady Lovibond*. In 1798, exactly fifty years after the vessel foundered, Captain James Westlake of the *Edenbridge* reported seeing its apparition across his bow. The *Lady Lovibond* resurrected itself from that ship's graveyard again in 1848 and in 1898. On both occasions, it was seen in full sail by Kent fishermen. However, nothing was reported in either 1948 or 1998, despite the best efforts of

ghost hunters from across Britain. They might have been thwarted because an eighteenth-century calendar switch (when England adopted the Gregorian calendar) would have the ghost ship sailing some eleven days earlier than expected.

When it was launched in 1858, the SS *Great Eastern* was the largest ship ever built, with six masts in addition to paddle and screw propulsion. It should have been heading for a bright future.

But the ship was already associated with misfortune. Building the giant vessel had put one company out of business. On its eventual grand launch day it was so big it got stuck on the runway. Proud designer Isambard Kingdom Brunel died within four days of its first sea trials.

More significantly still, it suffered a series of mishaps at sea. Perhaps the worst of these was when a boiler overheated to such an extent that it launched a funnel of the ship into the air like a rocket, killing one crew member and injuring others. Furthermore, crew on the SS *Great Eastern* reported hearing hammering sounds loud enough to drown out any Atlantic gale.

In short, the SS *Great Eastern* was a commercial white elephant, which was eventually sold for a fraction of its building costs. It went on to lay 4,185 km of transatlantic telegraph cable before being sold for scrap. During the eighteen months it took to dismantle, it is said that a skeleton or even two were found within the double skinned hull. Although this may have been the case, skeleton stories like these are relatively commonplace in connection with haunted places. Still, there remains a chilling possibility that workmen became entombed during the building of the ship, and hammered to call for help.

Ghost ships are not only found on the open sea but also on lakes and even rivers. There are two similar stories from the great lakes of North America that have fascinated seafarers and public alike. The first dates back to September 1678 when the *Griffon* vanished from Lake Michigan. Although no trace of the vessel was ever found, several sailors in ensuing years reported seeing the ship sailing on the lake. Much later, in 1975, the *Edmund Fitzgerald* sank into the waters of Lake Superior, taking twenty-six crew members with her. Once again, sailors in the region have spotted the ship afloat and untouched by disaster. Mention should also be made of the SS *Iron Mountain*, which was not so much a ghost ship as a vanished vessel. In June 1872 it left Vicksburg, Mississippi, with its cotton and molasses cargo, towing a line of barges. Later that day, another steamship by the name of *Iroquois Chief* came across the barges floating freely down the river with the tow line apparently cut. Crew secured the barges and waited for the arrival of the SS *Iron Mountain*. It never came. Indeed, no one ever saw the ship, its crew or its cargo again. Nor was there a trace of wreckage along the river banks. The fate of the SS *Iron Mountain* remains unknown.

No one knows just how many ghost ships may be sailing the oceans and great lakes, lost in time and space. Whilst the sea swallows up some vessels and their crews without a trace, others seem condemned to return as haunting reminders of their watery fate.

In 1975, the *Edmund Fitzgerald* sank during a storm on Lake Superior, killing twenty-six crew members. But the ship has refused to sink into obscurity, and its ghost lingers on...

CREEPY CASTLES

Over the centuries, castles have borne witness to much human suffering, with numerous incidents of incarceration, illness, suicide and murder. Perhaps it is, therefore, not surprising that there should be such a high degree of spectral sightings within their walls.

For many hundreds of years, strange apparitions have been reported at the Tower of London, the oldest palace, prison and fortress of its kind in Europe. The Tower was built by William the Conqueror on ground which, one thousand years earlier, had been the site of a Roman fort, constructed by the Emperor Claudius. Today, this monument attracts a huge number of visitors, many of whom are lured there in the hope of seeing one of the many ghosts rumoured to stalk its grounds.

During its time as a prison, the Tower was home to many famous inmates, including Queen Anne Boleyn, Guy Fawkes, Thomas More, Princess Elizabeth, Lady Jane Grey and Walter Raleigh. Many of these unfortunate prisoners endured agonizing torture before being executed in the most barbaric way – often they were beheaded, or hung, drawn and quartered. Their heads would then be impaled on spikes on the perimeter walls to serve as a gruesome warning to the public.

There has been a long line of reports of hauntings at the Tower, the first of which were made in the mid-thirteenth century. Construction workers building the inner curtain wall claimed that the ghost of an irate Thomas Becket appeared before them and reduced the wall to rubble by striking it with his cross.

The ghost of the 70-year-old Countess of Salisbury also lingers at the site of the executions,

This prayer book belonged to Anne Boleyn and was used by her during her incarceration in the Tower of London.

where she met a truly grisly end. Henry VIII had ordered that she be beheaded, but at the last moment she tried to escape her death by running from the block. The executioner chased her, swinging his axe, and eventually hacked her to death. Some have spoken of seeing the execution re-enacted before their eyes, while others have observed the shadow of the fateful axe on the walls in the vicinity.

Of all the sad souls still said to be roaming the Tower, it is the figure of Anne Boleyn that seems to be the most persistent. This tragic figure was tried and executed for adultery and treason after miscarrying the potential heir to the throne. Her headless body, recognizable from the dress she was wearing on the day of her execution, is reported, even today, to drift from the Queen's House to the Chapel of St Peter Ad Vincula. Here, it leads a spectral procession of dignitaries down the aisle to the site of her final burial place under the altar.

The Salt Tower is the most feared and thus the most avoided area of the Tower of London. Yeoman Warders are reluctant to go near it at night after one of their members was inexplicably strangled. Dogs – who, in common with many animals seem to have a sixth sense regarding supernatural beings – refuse to go near it, further fuelling intrigue and superstition.

The presence of ghostly apparitions in the Tower was captured on camera as recently as 2003, when a photographer reported strange incidents while attempting to conduct a photo shoot. Bulbs kept blowing and flashes went off unexpectedly. Most eerily of all, when he came to develop the film, he discovered, among the many blank pictures, a photo containing a mysterious ball of light in the centre of the image.

Another famous British tourist attraction, Windsor Castle has been a home to royalty since the eleventh century and is still a royal residence today. Over the centuries it has seen innumerable births and deaths and has been connected with countless legends of witchcraft and treachery.

The footsteps and groans of King Henry VIII are allegedly heard by visitors to this day.

Of all the spectres rumoured to stalk the castle grounds, those of three kings, in particular, have made their presence felt within the castle walls. The footsteps and groans of King Henry VIII are allegedly heard by visitors to this day, while the ghost of King Charles I, beheaded in 1649 at Whitehall, is also said to roam the grounds, and has been sighted, complete with head, in the library and the canon's house. Sightings of 'mad' King George III, who was incarcerated in the castle before his death, have also been recorded.

Of similar renown in Scotland is Edinburgh Castle, a fortress magnificent in its austerity. Built on the site of a once-active volcano, this almost 1000-year-old construction has seen an unusual degree of violence and death, factors that could account for the large number of ghostly apparitions in the vicinity. The most famous of these are the figures of the headless drummer and piper who are said to patrol the castle's battlements, still playing their instruments.

A view of Edinburgh castle illuminated against the night sky.

In recent years, there have been tales of encounters with spirits arising from a fascinating discovery that was made in the city in the early 1990s. During renovation work, remains were uncovered of buildings buried beneath the existing city. It is known that during the Black Death in 1665 Edinburgh was blighted by a terrible plague that decimated the population. As the disease dwindled, surviving officials deemed it best to build over the top of the old, ravaged city, entombing the affected buildings and any remaining living sufferers under the new constructions. Since this forgotten world has come to light, many people have heard ghostly voices and seen beautiful flashing lights emanating from the subterranean city.

Another Scottish fortress, Glamis Castle, was famously recorded by Shakespeare in his tragedy *Macbeth*. The mysterious happenings at the castle are not restricted to the realms of the theatre, however – many dark deeds and hauntings have taken place within its ancient walls.

Legend tells of the misdeeds of the second Lord of Glamis, whose dalliance with the Devil is said to have left its legacy in the brutal acts of violence that ensued. 'Earl Beardie' or 'the Wicked Lord', as he was nicknamed, was apparently a violent gambler and drinker. One evening, unable to find a gambling partner, he is supposed to have announced that he would resort to playing with the Devil himself. Moments later there was a knock at the door, and a tall, bearded man dressed entirely in black asked the lord if he still required someone with whom to gamble. When the servants heard shouts and the sound of furniture being flung around the room, one of them crept to the keyhole to try to get a glimpse of what was going on, where he was caught by his master. When Lord Glamis returned to the room, the dark stranger had vanished, taking with him the soul of the gambling aristocrat. He died five years later, and his drunken, tortured spirit is said to still roam the castle, waiting to return to the room to play with the Devil.

The gambling aristocrat's drunken, tortured spirit is said to still roam the castle, waiting to return to the room to play with the Devil.

The castle is also home to the ghost of Janet Douglas, who was the wife of the sixth Lord of Glamis. Following his sudden death, she was accused of murder and witchcraft, even though there was no evidence to this effect. She was put on trial, during which she was found guilty of plotting the murder of the King of Scotland and summarily executed in Edinburgh in 1537. Her spirit is said to wander the halls of Glamis and she is frequently seen praying in the small chapel where she had vainly sought refuge almost 500 years ago.

Could it be that, in common with many other ghosts that inhabit some of Britain's oldest castles, she is seeking justice? Whatever the motives of these spectral beings, they are likely to continue to haunt some of our most ancient monuments, and remain an enduring source of fascination to mankind today.

HAUNTED CHURCHES

Vast numbers of the deceased are buried every day in churchyards all over the world, and so it is perhaps hardly surprising that many churches contain evidence of ghostly beings, not yet ready to rest. Every year there are hundreds of reports of spectral sightings in these holy houses, some of which have been captured on camera and evade all explanation.

One of the most famous photographs was taken in the picturesque village of Newby, Cumbria, in 1963. It was a quiet day, and the Reverend Kenneth Lord decided that it was an ideal opportunity to photograph the altar, having promised some days before to supply a picture to the village magazine.

He loaded his antique black and white camera, set up the shot and took the picture. Everything appeared normal until he developed the photograph, which clearly showed a tall, hooded, transparent figure to the right of the altar. The reverend gentleman was unable to explain the anomaly and vehemently denied having faked the apparition in any way at all.

Experts analysed the picture to see if any kind of forgery had taken place. However, even after the most rigorous testing, scientists remained baffled. Recent examination using modern technology has further deepened the mystery, as it has shown that not even the latest computer software could produce the same photographic image.

What is the answer to this mystery? Did Reverend Lord possess technological skills far in advance of those we have today? Or could this photograph be evidence of some kind of spirit world, invisible to the naked eye?

Everything appeared normal until he developed the photograph, which clearly showed a tall, hooded, transparent figure to the right of the altar.

A similarly perplexing picture was taken during the early days of photographic technology in 1891, on the site of Combermere Abbey, Shropshire. The abbey had a turbulent history – having originally been a twelfth century Cistercian monastery, all that remained following King Henry VIII's dissolution of the monasteries in the sixteenth century was the Abbots House and Hall. In the early nineteenth century, this highly desirable residence, set in 22,000 acres of rolling countryside, was presented to Sir Stapleton Cotton – along with the title Viscount Combermere – as a reward for his many services to his country.

This illustrious cavalry officer had had a dazzling career, having being made Governor of Barbados in 1817. While holding this post, he ordered an investigation into the famous mystery of the moving coffins. Despite his best efforts, he was ultimately never able to establish how a number of coffins in a sealed vault could repeatedly move around within the crypt.

The Viscount was to come to an unfortunate end seventy-four years later when he was knocked down and killed by a runaway horse-drawn carriage in his home village. On the morning of the funeral, a cold day in December, a Miss Sybil Corbet decided to bid the Viscount's residence a sad farewell and photographed the hall as a memento. This once vibrant place seemed eerily quiet when she took the picture and she reported feeling vaguely uneasy. When the photograph was developed, it proved that her sixth sense had been right, for she seemed to have captured on film more than just the spirit of the place.

It is said that if the picture is studied closely, the translucent outline of a head and chest can clearly be seen in the armchair, with an arm resting along the side. This apparition is said to resemble the deceased Viscount Combermere who perhaps, like the photographer, had decided to say one last goodbye to the hall.

Such ghostly apparitions are not confined to the UK, however. Across the Atlantic, in the USA, many strange sightings have been reported, of which perhaps the most famous have occurred at the burial ground of the Westminster Presbyterian Church in Baltimore.

In 1786, members of the church committee decided to build a war cemetery on the site of a former peach orchard, located just outside the city boundary. Word soon spread about the tranquility and beauty of the site, and soon all the most affluent citizens were building elaborate tombs there to house their deceased. Among these illustrious denizens were twenty-four generals, four congressmen, and, most notably, Edgar Allan Poe and his family.

Children were apparently seen digging up graves and running round the cemetery with skulls on top of broom handles.

During the first half of the nineteenth century, Baltimore experienced an increase in population and underwent radical change. Many new buildings were required, and the countryside surrounding Westminster church was soon built over. By 1850, such was the requirement for land that city officials declared that all burial grounds not directly attached to a church had to be relocated to outside the city. In order to avoid obeying this decree, the Westminster committee decided to attach the site to the church by building supporting arches in the vault and erecting walls around the existing pathways of the cemetery. Relatives were allowed easy access to the graves of their loved ones in the catacombs beneath the building.

As time passed, however, the city expanded and Presbyterian worshippers moved elsewhere. Eventually, the cemetery fell into disrepair, and suffered damage at the hands of vandals,

vagabonds and body snatchers. Children, adopting it as a playground, were apparently seen digging up graves and running round the cemetery with skulls on top of broom handles. Could so many sightings and supernatural experiences have been reported at this old cemetery because of the high level of disrespect shown to those buried there?

Of all the spirits to appear at the graveyard, the most frequent visitor is the ghost of Lucia Watson Taylor, who was interred in 1816 at the tender age of 16. There are numerous corroborating eyewitness reports that describe the benign apparition of this girl kneeling in prayer by her own grave.

The shadowy, mysterious figure of a man dressed from head to toe in black has also been spotted in the cemetery for a number of years. Apparently, he is always wearing exactly the same clothing – his head and face are covered by a fedora and scarf, and he holds a stick. Interestingly, he appears annually on 19 January, the birthday of Edgar Allan Poe. Could this be the ghost of the deceased author?

Such is the level of hauntings at this churchyard that it is frequently visited by psychics and ghost hunters. While all speak of the presence of otherworldly spirits, this would appear to be backed up by investigations using Electronic Voice Phenomenon (EVP). This technology has captured tape recordings of strange murmurs – could these be evidence of communication from 'the other side'?

The tomb of Edgar Allan Poe at the burial ground of Westminster Presbyterian Church in Baltimore.

HEXED HOUSES

Over the years, haunted houses have inspired generations of writers, artists and film-makers and captured the imagination of people of all ages, in every part of the world. By examining the history of these supernatural residences, we can gain a fascinating insight into the identity of their otherworldly inhabitants.

Temple Newsam House in Leeds, West Yorkshire, is an imposing Tudor-Jacobean house set in 1,200 acres of lush, rolling parkland. Dwellings on this site were listed in the Domesday Book of 1086, and in the twelfth century the house became the property of the Templar Knights. In the fifteenth century, it passed to the family of Thomas, Lord Darcy, a friend of Cardinal Wolsey, who became the first of a number of people to build parts of the house that still stand today. Following Darcy's brutal beheading for his involvement in the Pilgrimage of Grace revolt, the house was seized by Henry VIII and given to his niece, the Countess of Lennox.

It was in these spectacular historical surroundings that Henry, Lord Darnley, after whom the most famous room in the existing house was named, was born. Darnley grew up surrounded by political intrigue, eventually culminating in his fateful and turbulent marriage to Mary Queen of Scots, which ended with his mysterious murder.

Following this, the house was requisitioned by Queen Elizabeth I and since then has passed through many royal hands, undergoing several transformations along the way. It has remained a centre of political strife, and Darnley's murder has not been the only one carried out within its walls. Perhaps it is not surprising, then, that 'the Hampton Court of the North' seems to be home to more than just the living.

> The disturbing spectre of a small boy is said to appear from inside a cupboard and cross the room, screaming in pain and anguish.

Numerous spirits have been seen in various parts of the house over the ages, most notably in the Darnley Room, located in the south-west corner of the early Tudor part of the building. Frequent sightings are made of the spirit of a Knight Templar, still on guard after 900 years, and the disturbing spectre of a small boy who is said to appear from inside a cupboard and cross the room, screaming in pain and anguish.

Another ghost to haunt this property on a regular basis is the 'Blue Lady', the spirit of Mary Ingram, whose portrait hangs in the Green

Damask Room, and who lived in the property during the seventeenth century. One night, while returning home in her carriage, the unfortunate woman was attacked and robbed by highwaymen. Although not physically harmed, the incident seems to have damaged her psychologically, for from that point on she became obsessed with concealing her possessions. She roams the house to this day, dressed in a long blue dress and lacy shawl, hunting for her long-lost treasures.

Another former royal residence to see more than its fair share of scandal and intrigue is Cumnor House in Oxfordshire. During the sixteenth century it was home to Lord Robert Dudley and his wife Amy Robsart. Dudley was a close friend of Queen Elizabeth I and barely left the side of the young monarch during the early years of her reign.

Rumour was rife about an impending royal marriage, seemingly hindered only by the fact that Dudley was already married. In the pursuit of power and royal favour, Dudley abandoned Amy, who was only too aware that she remained the only obstacle to her husband becoming king.

Fearing for her life, she retreated inside Cumnor with just a few trusted servants for company. She became paranoid about her safety, taking great care over what she ate for fear of poisoning and not even venturing out into the beautiful grounds that she loved so dearly.

Despite these extreme precautions, however, Amy could not cheat her destiny. One day, when her staff had left her alone in order to attend the annual fair, she met with tragedy, and when her servants returned from their day out they found her broken body lying at the bottom of the stairs.

A commemorative effigy of Lord Darnley.

Slander and calumny ensued, with Queen Elizabeth and Lord Dudley as the prime suspects. The scandal forced the queen to abandon her plans to marry Dudley, as this would have seemed to confirm the rumours. Instead, she made him the Earl of Leicester, and they remained close friends until his death in 1564.

The truth of the mystery surrounding Amy Robsart's death has never been established. Perhaps it is for this reason that there were so many sightings of her restless soul drifting around the stairs where she met her unfortunate end. Eventually, in 1810, the owners decided to demolish the staircase. This had little effect since her sad spirit simply transferred its lonely wanderings to the gardens and parkland surrounding the house. Despite further attempts at exorcism by clergymen, locals to this day claim they see Amy in the vicinity.

Another haunted English residence is Raynham Hall in Norfolk. This ancestral home of the Marquess of Townsend is inhabited by a restless spirit called 'The Brown Lady', whose presence has, over the last 170 years, been felt, seen and even captured on film.

When the smoke cleared, the three were astonished to find no sign of the expected body.

This famous ghost is thought to be the spirit of Dorothy Walpole, sister of Sir Robert Walpole, the first prime minister to live at 10 Downing Street. Dorothy, like Amy Robsart before her, suffered at the hands of a cruel husband, who took custody of her children when she started to show symptoms of mental health problems. The unfortunate woman was then incarcerated in a first-floor bedroom and, again like Amy Robsart, died mysteriously after falling headlong down a flight of stairs.

Sightings of this unfortunate soul are well documented, and often involve those who were formerly sceptical of such supernatural activity. One of the most famous cases was recorded in 1835 by Frederick Marryat, a Royal Navy officer and politician's son, who, at the time, was staying at the house in the very room that had served as Dorothy's prison during her final days. Despite rejecting the allegations about the presence of the ghost, Marryat took the precaution of keeping a loaded gun about his person while in the building. The first two nights of his visit passed without incident, but on the third night an event, witnessed by two other people, was to shake his cynicism to its very foundations.

As the three friends were returning to their rooms one evening, they were surprised to observe a woman entering Marryat's room. The officer challenged the intruder who, in spite of being confronted by a gun, ignored his imperious command, whereupon Marryat opened fire. When the smoke cleared, the three were astonished to find no sign of the expected body. The only evidence that the shot had been fired was a bullet hole in the wall.

Then, almost exactly a century later, this house became the site of one of the most famous photographs to be taken of any supernatural entity. While shooting the property for a feature in *Country Life* magazine, a photographer made an astonishing discovery – one of his pictures clearly showed the outline of a woman descending the main stairway where Dorothy had met her death. Despite rigorous scientific testing, sceptics have been unable to label the picture a forgery. In fact, on the contrary, it seems to prove the existence of the ghost of a tortured soul who continues to haunt her former abode in the endless search for justice.

Further evidence of ghostly activity can be found many thousands of miles away, on the other side of the world in Australia. The Monte Christo Homestead in Junee, New South Wales was built in 1884 by Christopher Crawley, a local farmer. Today, it is known as the most haunted house in Australia.

Crawley was an intelligent man, who showed immense foresight in building the Railway Hotel at the same time as he built his home. With the Great Southern Railway Line having arrived in the area in 1878, he was able to take advantage of the sudden explosion in the town's growth, and thus his future was assured.

Crawley lived with his wife and family at the Monte Christo Homestead for many happy years, during which time he made improvements to the already impressive structure. Tragedy, however, struck this once happy home in 1910, when Crawley died as a result of infection. His wife spent the remaining twenty-three years of her life in mourning, reportedly so devastated by her husband's death that she only left the house on two occasions following the funeral.

In 1948 the last member of the family left the house and it stood empty and desolate until it was bought and restored in the early 1960s. Since that time, its many occupants have borne witness to an extraordinary amount of supernatural activity. Some have seen the spirit of a small boy playing in the gardens, and others have observed a woman dressed in period costume pacing along the balcony. The most frequent sightings, however, are of the Crawleys themselves, in particular the long-suffering Mrs Crawley. She is reported to roam around her former home, barring some from entering the property, and has also been seen in the chapel, wearing her mourning dress and a large silver cross.

Of the many visitors to the house over the years, the vast majority claim to be aware of a mysterious presence there. People speak of feeling uneasy, or of being watched, and report an inexplicable drop in temperature in certain areas of the building. Its current inhabitants say that bizarre incidents, such as the banging shut of the doors of empty rooms or the sound of footsteps on the carpeted floor of an unoccupied room, are so frequent that they no longer find them strange.

The number and similarity of these accounts lend them real credibility. As a result, the house has recently been the subject of a paranormal investigation, and was filmed as part of a documentary. The publicization of this investigation and the residence's ensuing widespread reputation have made this old house famous throughout Australia.

The famous picture of the 'Brown Lady' descending the stairs where she met her death at Raynham Hall.

CELEBRITY GHOSTS

Hollywood may seem like a place of glamour and lighthearted living, but behind the bright façade lie dark secrets. Many of the stars lured to Hollywood by fame and fortune have died untimely and mysterious deaths, and continue to haunt the luxurious settings of their success.

Perhaps the most famous of these Hollywood haunters is celluloid sensation Marilyn Monroe. In life, she was a tormented soul whose poignant pursuit for personal happiness touched a generation. So perhaps it is hardly surprising that she has remained a restless figure after her tragic early death.

Monroe's career started at the Roosevelt Hotel on Hollywood Boulevard. It was here that she posed on a diving board for her first advertisement, for suntan lotion, brimming with aspiration. The starlet, blessed with stunning looks and a voluptuous figure, appeared to have the world at her feet. But later she became embroiled in studio politics and struggled through many doomed love affairs. She even developed a draining drug dependency. On 5 August 1962, she was found dead at her Brentwood home, aged just 36. She is believed to have died from a self-administered drugs overdose, although some people doubt this explanation, and conspiracy theorists have since claimed she was murdered.

Since her death, Monroe's reflection has been seen in a full-length mirror that once hung in her favourite poolside suite at the Roosevelt Hotel, where she started out years before. Could it be that her restless soul is seeking to recapture youth and happiness? The dark-framed mirror that has captured her ghostly image has been moved to the hotel basement.

And Marilyn is not the only A-list celebrity making unscheduled appearances at the 320-roomed Roosevelt. Montgomery Clift – her co-star in the 1961 film *The Misfits* – can be heard up in room 928 labouring over his lines for the 1953 movie *From Here to Eternity*.

After becoming a star, Clift, like Monroe, led a tortured existence. He became an alcoholic and a drug addict. He was also homosexual, a fact he felt compelled to hide from the public for fear of people's response. He was found dead in his New York home at the age of 45, apparently suffering from heart disease.

Staff at the Roosevelt have been alarmed after hearing loud noises while standing outside room 928. Sometimes the telephone is found off the hook. One member of staff claimed a ghostly hand brushed her skin. It seems Clift never really checked out.

The last spooky site in the hotel lies in the Blossom Ballroom where a sizeable 'cold spot' has

been noted by some visitors, management and staff. This was the setting for the first Academy Awards in 1929. Perhaps the phenomenon is the result of some bitter disappointment suffered by an early Hollywood hopeful.

Comedy actress Thelma Todd starred in more than forty films before her death in 1935, aged 29. She had appeared alongside the Marx Brothers and Laurel and Hardy, and she also ran a restaurant called *Thelma Todd's Sidewalk Café* (situated on today's Pacific Coast Highway).

Her body was discovered in a car, in a garage above the café, still wearing evening clothes and a mink stole. The cause of death was presumed to be suicide through carbon monoxide poisoning. Yet there has long been speculation that it was murder, by a jealous former husband, an angry lover or perhaps even the Mafia.

If there was indeed an undetected murder, this might explain why Todd's ghost would want to return to earth. She has been seen descending a staircase at her old café, now owned by the religiously inclined TV and film company Paulist Productions. Employees have also smelled fumes in the building.

Clifton Webb is another wandering soul, witnessed close to his burial place in the Hollywood Memorial Park Cemetery. His spirit also reportedly appears from time to time at his old home in Retford Drive, Beverley Hills. Webb was famous for his roles as 'Mr Belvedere' and for an enduring friendship with playwright Noel Coward. However, nothing in his life took precedence over his beloved mother Mabelle.

The ghost of the young Marilyn Monroe (1926–62) is said to haunt the Roosevelt Hotel on Hollywood Boulevard.

The pair lived together until her death aged 91. Frustrated by Webb's excessive grief, Coward remarked with characteristic humour: 'It must be tough to be orphaned at 71.'

Another ghost has been heard in the same graveyard, that of Virginia Rappe. This ill-fated starlet died after apparently being shut in a hotel bedroom with outsized comedian 'Fatty' Arbuckle during a debauched party. Later she was discovered weeping and in pain. She died later from peritonitis brought about by a ruptured kidney. The ensuing scandal engulfed Hollywood and Arbuckle's career was ruined by it, although he was eventually cleared of wrongdoing.

The cemetery is also the last resting place of Douglas Fairbanks and Rudolph Valentino. Although Valentino's spectre has not been seen in the cemetery itself, it is thought to haunt the costume department of the Paramount Studios on Marathon Avenue.

Not only do staff see Welles' corpulent, caped frame, but they smell the cigars he was fond of smoking and the brandy he loved to swig.

Not to be outdone, Universal Studios has its own celebrity ghost, since the actor Lon Chaney is alleged to be haunting sound stage 28. But this does not seem to be his favourite haunt, since he was most often seen on a bus stop bench at the intersection of Hollywood and Vine. The son of deaf-mutes, Chaney learned to communicate with facial expressions. During his career he acted mostly in horror films and was heavily made up, becoming known as 'the man of a thousand faces'. He died in 1930 of throat cancer, aged 47. It is not known which of the thousand faces the ghost at the bus stop used to wear. When the seat at the stop was removed the ghost moved on.

Another man who has struggled to leave Hollywood behind is former bullfighter and *War of the Worlds* broadcaster Orson Welles. Since his death in 1985 aged 70, he has been glimpsed at his favourite restaurant, Sweet Lady Jane's in Melrose Avenue. Not only do staff occasionally see his corpulent, caped frame, but they smell the cigars he was fond of smoking and the brandy he loved to swig.

Guy Gibson was a different brand of celebrity. He came to prominence during the Second World War, after leading the 1943 raid against two hydroelectric dams in industrial Germany, using specially-designed bouncing bombs. The risks were incredibly high, and only eleven of the nineteen bombers from the celebrated 617 Squadron that embarked on the Dambusters raid returned. But the ambitious raid achieved its aim and, after the exploit, Gibson was awarded the Victoria Cross for his indisputable valour. He became well known on both sides of the Atlantic, went on a lecture tour in America and wrote a book about the raid called *Enemy Coast Ahead*. Gibson finally returned to active duty a year after the raid and was killed in a mission over Germany in September 1944.

As the fiftieth anniversary of the start of the Second World War beckoned in 1989, visitors saw the ghost of Guy Gibson relaxing in his

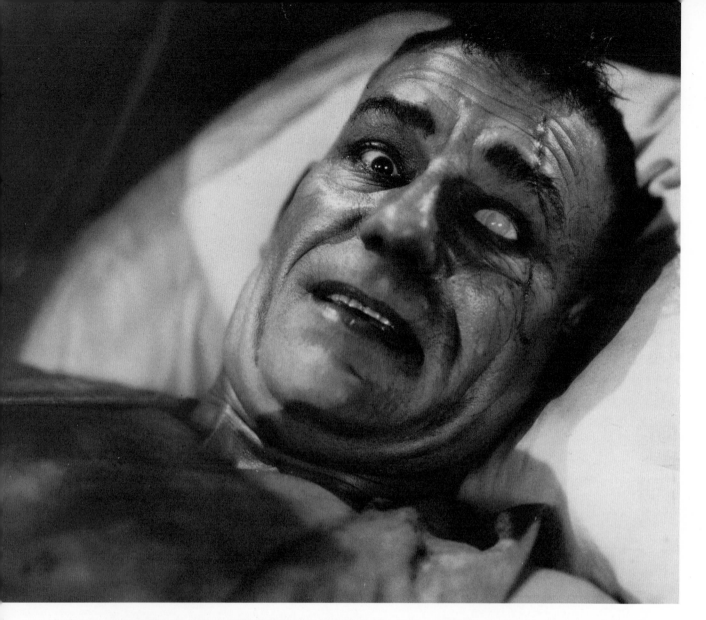

The actor Lon Chaney, 'the man of a thousand faces', in the 1926 film *The Road to Mandalay*. Chaney's ghost chose to divide his time between Universal Studios and a bus stop.

favourite armchair at the hotel that used to serve as an officers' mess for those in the Dambusters squadron. Guests also reported hearing a piano rendition of wartime songs in the hotel. The music continued to play, despite the fact that the bar containing the piano was firmly locked.

There is nothing to suggest that celebrities are more likely to return to earth in ghostly form than those with more mundane day jobs. But it is tempting to think that movie stars who once seemed larger than life, may have been bigger even than death.

TIMESLIPS

For the moment, time machines that transport people to the future and the past at the flick of a switch are strictly the stuff of science fiction. Yet there have been instances where people appear to stumble into a different era, and their memorable anecdotes offer serious food for thought.

In fact, time travel is probably not impossible, according to some of the greatest brains of the age. Albert Einstein left a window for it in his famous *Theory of Relativity*. However, although the theory is sound, we do not yet have the know-how to make time travel work.

What we do have is stories related by people who believe they have inadvertently seen a glimpse of another epoch. They can offer no explanation of how they got into this different dimension nor, by the same token, how they returned. The most compelling stories of time travel are those backed up by a number of witnesses.

In 1979, Len and Cynthia Gisby and their neighbours Geoff and Pauline Simpson, from north Lancashire, were driving through France on their way to Spain on a holiday. They decided to break their journey and stop for the night in the Rhône Valley near Montélimar, but the first hotel they tried was full. They were given directions to a second hotel that lay off the main road, down a bumpy track. Although the man at reception struggled to comprehend them, they finally secured two rooms for the night. They noticed the building was gas-lit, while the rooms had bedsteads with wooden bolsters and blankets rather than duvets. The windows had no glass in them and in the bathroom the soap was speared onto the wall by a metal spike.

Dinner was also a curious affair, with steak and beer. At breakfast they watched as gendarmes wearing cloaks and pillar-box hats arrived to speak with a woman in a long dress with button shoes. It seemed as if they had happened upon a theme hotel that paid particular attention to detail. And when it came to paying the bill, they discovered it was just a tiny sum. Each of them had been charged only a few pence for the hospitality.

Charmed by the rustic nature of the place, the four decided to pay a return visit on their way home. However, when they returned, the hotel seemed to have completely disappeared. Stranger still, all the photos they had taken of it previously came out blank.

The next bizarre timeslip had only one witness, and was therefore more open to doubt. But the man concerned was to become one of the stalwarts of the Royal Air Force during the Second World War, whose reputation was impeccable.

In 1934, Wing Commander Victor Goddard was flying a Hawker Hart biplane from Scotland

A squadron of British monoplane fighters, of the type that Goddard saw at the Drem airfield. During the Second World War, these were said to be the fastest warplanes in service in any of the world's air forces.

to Andover, in Hampshire. Turbulent weather enveloped the plane, and blinded by a deluge and dense cloud, Goddard went into a spin and only narrowly avoided crashing.

As soon as he had regained control of the rudimentary aircraft he suddenly found himself in radically different conditions. The clouds had parted and the sun was beating down. Below him, he recognized the Drem airfield he had visited the day previously, abandoned after the First World War and now derelict.

Yet the airfield was a hive of activity. Three biplanes were there, just like his own but painted yellow, and there was a fourth plane of a type he had never seen before. Goddard saw ground crew dressed in blue overalls, although as far as he knew all RAF uniforms were brown. The men failed to notice Goddard's plane above them, and when the Drem airfield was out of sight he found himself once more in the teeth of a storm.

Goddard put the strange incident to the back of his mind, although he never forgot it. And in 1939, as Britain geared up for war, he was astonished to see biplanes being painted yellow and mechanics' uniforms switching from brown to blue. Monoplanes like the fourth plane he had seen at Drem were finally being flown by the Royal Air Force. And after the outbreak of the Second World War, the airfield was put into use again.

Goddard, who had joined the Royal Navy in 1910 and switched to the Royal Air Force in 1918, held numerous senior posts during the Second World War and afterwards. Following his retirement in 1951 he was knighted. When he finally wrote about the eerie experience in 1966, he concluded that he must have flown into the future, and seen the airfield as it was to be during the Second World War. Goddard maintained an interest in the supernatural until his death in 1987.

Other timeslip witnesses have stayed rooted in

the present and seen people from another age passing through.

One such incident involved two men, only ever identified as L.C. and Charlie, who were driving on Highway 167 between Abbeville and Lafayette in Louisiana in 1969. The road ahead was empty, save for a vintage car bearing the distinctive plates '1940'. Behind the wheel was a woman dressed in old-fashioned clothes to match the car, and her only passenger was a child similarly attired. What caught the attention of the two men was not only the immaculate condition of the vehicle, but also the fearful expression haunting the driver's face. As they drew alongside the slow-moving car they asked through their open window if she needed help. She indicated that she did, so the men overtook her and pulled over onto the roadside. But when they looked back to see where she was, the vintage car had vanished.

As they battled their incredulity, another car pulled in. The driver insisted he had seen the old car ahead and watched as the modern vehicle overtook it. Then the old car had simply disappeared before his eyes. Together they searched the area, but found no clues. It is tempting to believe that the car had somehow time slipped into the year 1969, and then seamlessly returned to its own era.

Sometimes we all suspect time of playing tricks on us, when the hours race by like minutes, or drag by like days. But cases of time slippage are difficult to prove in isolation, without witnesses. In some cases, though, there are witnesses, and Eula White was one of them. Born in 1912, she grew up in rural Alabama. One day she went to a local farmhouse owned by the Hawkins family to sell peas and beans from the front porch. Mr Hawkins, who had gone into town on horseback for provisions, came into view with a white sack of flour over the saddle and a brown grocery bag in the crook of his left arm. As he came up the driveway, one of the boys playing nearby ran to open the farm gate for him. Then, right before the eyes of everybody there, Mr Hawkins simply disappeared. Astonishment soon gave way to fear, and Eula and her colleagues let out piercing screams. Eventually they calmed down and closed the farm gate again.

Then, right before the eyes of everybody there, Mr Hawkins simply disappeared.

Alarm rose in their throats once more when, some time later, they saw Mr Hawkins with flour sack and groceries riding into view for a second time. But this time he rode up to the gate, showed no signs of vanishing, and demanded that someone open up for him. Eula's feelings were of overwhelming relief, tempered by anxiety about the initial incident. It was an experience she would never forget.

Investigation into the possibilities of time travel did not end with the death of Einstein. Indeed, some of the most able brains of the age have wrestled with the notion, knowing that success would bring fame of a magnitude hitherto unknown for a scientist. But even today, the procedure still eludes them, and time remains a tangle no one has tamed.

CORNISH SPECTRES

Cornwall is an area of the British Isles that is steeped in folklore and mystery. Sinister tales of the deeds of smugglers and sailors, and eerie stories of ghostly beings abound throughout its wild, remote terrain.

Hotels and inns in the region have their fair share of spectral stories, one of the most famous of these being Jamaica Inn, near Bodmin. This hotel was immortalized in Daphne du Maurier's novel of the same name.

To this day, much to the discomfort of the visiting public, a murdered sailor is known to make regular appearances in the bar, seemingly intent on finishing his drink.

The Wellington Hotel in Lanreath is believed to be inhabited by not one, but numerous ghosts.

Many have seen the spirit of an eighteenth century coachman casually strolling past the hotel reception desk before disappearing through the wall. The fact that those who have witnessed the apparition are all in agreement about the exact details seems to imply that there might be some truth to this story.

Another ghost to inhabit the inn is thought to be that of a young girl who flung herself from the ramparts of the hotel's tower while overcome by love's despair.

Yet another seems to attract animals, which eagerly follow an unseen being, the only trace of whom is a shadow moving along the floor.

Another such benevolent spirit is to be found at the site of the ancient manor house at Duporth. Reports stretch back to a century ago when the original house was still standing. Its occupants spoke of a nun, affectionately called 'Flo', who was to be heard striking matches and unlocking cabinets on a regular basis. Although the manor house has long since been demolished to make way for a holiday village, it would seem that Flo is still in attendance. There are many reports of strange happenings – the roundabout in the playground is said to move of its own volition on a windless day, kettles housed in

An old mail coach of the type which used to thunder around the narrow lanes of Cornwall.

locked and empty rooms suddenly come to life and start to boil and sewing machines spring into action of their own accord. Staff at the holiday site say that if they ask Flo to stop her eerie behaviour the devices fall silent.

Blackaways Cove in north Cornwall is a more sinister site of otherworldly occurrences. This isolated inlet is situated perilously close to treacherous rocks, and has witnessed many shipwrecks over the centuries. Perhaps it is the ghosts of drowned sailors that are responsible for shrouding the region in superstition?

Alternatively, the eerie presence at the cove could be due to a particular drama that unfolded on land above the cove itself.

According to local legend, a father and his two sons once lived on a farm estate on the cliffs. When this man died, he left everything to his eldest son, while the youngest was cut off without a penny. This young man was driven to such a pitch of jealousy that, losing control, he set fire to the farm, totally destroying the property. Ironically, having burned the farmstead to the ground, he then discovered that his elder brother had died the day before, leaving everything to him. Distraught, the man lived out the rest of his days in guilty anguish and remorse. Perhaps the eerie presence at the cove can be attributed to the tortured wanderings of this jealous soul?

The narrow lanes that connect the pretty villages dotted around the coast and countryside also have their fair share of ghostly traffic. A particularly mysterious example of this occurred on the road between Mevagissey and Truro, much to the horror of a motorist, Cliff Hocking.

The terrifying sighting occurred one wet November afternoon while Hocking was driving to hospital in Truro to visit his wife. Upon rounding a bend in the twisting road, he was astonished to discover that he was heading straight towards an old stagecoach, bearing down on him at full speed. He gave a vivid, detailed description of the incident, stating that the coachman wore a wide-lapelled greatcoat, and was standing next to a guard dressed in a red coat and black hat and blowing a post horn.

Sewing machines spring into action of their own accord.

As the coach and horses sped towards him in a thunder of wheels and hooves, Hocking slammed on his brakes and flung his arms over his head in an attempt to protect himself in the impending collision. However, the crash never happened, and the coach disappeared into thin air.

The stagecoach has since been identified as a mail coach of the type that was used in the eighteenth century. Such carriages had been introduced to Cornwall in 1796, as part of the nationwide stagecoach service, by a character called Walter Cross who was involved in a number of different activities, one of which was smuggling. Could it have been him at the reins of the coach, fleeing the law with his smuggler's booty? It is unlikely that we will ever find out, but we can be sure that the mysterious Cornish landscape, steeped in myth and legend, will continue to be haunted by the ghosts of its former inhabitants.

BATTLEFIELD GHOULS

Battlefields are the scene of murder, mutilation and mayhem, and so it is not surprising that they are some of the most common arenas for supernatural encounters. Resonances of the mutual hatred felt by opposing armies and the violence perpetrated still seem to echo around the scene of many conflicts. Innumerable visitors report strange phenomena, such as the eerie sensation of being watched, ghostly lights, mysterious cold pockets of air and sightings of the spirits of long-dead soldiers.

One of the most famous battlefields in British history is Culloden Moor in the Scottish Highlands, the site of the last battle to be fought on mainland British soil. The ferocious and bloody fighting that took place on that sodden day in April 1746 lasted a mere 40 minutes, but the effects of the slaughter abide to this day.

> Innumerable visitors report strange phenomena, such as the eerie sensation of being watched.

The battle was between the Jacobites, under Bonnie Prince Charlie, who were seeking to restore the Stuart monarchy to the throne and government troops, led by Prince William, the Duke of Cumberland. The Jacobites were exhausted, having spent many days marching back from an ineffectual mission to gather more troops and a failed surprise attack on the Duke's men. They were also vastly outnumbered and not suited to fighting on boggy moorland.

The battle commenced with an artillery exchange that decimated the Jacobite forces. Bonnie Prince Charlie was notably absent from the front line, so the men were left leaderless and hesitant, with no real battle plan. The slaughter intensified when they finally decided to charge, as those troops who had managed to survive the bombardment were then slain by a new, and highly successful, strategy employed by Prince William's troops.

This involved stabbing the Highlanders on the right hand side, and took the Jacobites totally by surprise. The government troops were able to inflict wounds on their enemy under the right sword arm, an area left unprotected because the small shield that they carried, known as a targe, was borne on the left arm.

Those who were not mortally wounded were cruelly slaughtered as they lay on the blood-soaked ground, and those who fled were hunted down and murdered without pity. Bonnie Prince Charlie managed to escape to Italy, but was never able to return to his native land.

Those who have visited the scene of this battle speak of numerous mysterious happenings, particularly on the anniversary of the action on 16 April. For example, they see the ghostly soldiers and hear the clamour of carnage and the clash of steel. Specific sightings of a tall, gaunt Highlander who utters the word 'Defeated' under his breath are described.

Others report coming across the spectre of a dead Highland soldier lying beneath a tartan cloth on one of the many burial mounds of the battle site. Birds are said to fall silent in the region of these mounds, and there are also numerous wells strewn across the area that are said to abound with the spirits of the dead, most notably St Mary's Well.

Also ripe with rumours of hauntings is Gettysburg, the site of one of the bloodiest and most infamous battles in the history of the United States. As the location of the turning point of the Civil War, which raged in the country during the nineteenth century, Gettysburg is of evident importance from a historical perspective. But could it also be of supernatural significance?

Visitors flock to the region every year, some simply to pay their respects to the huge numbers of men who perished there, and others in the hope of an otherworldly encounter. Countless reports of similar incidents in specific areas of the battleground seem to indicate that there may be some truth in the stories, and there is some photographic evidence to suggest that spirits may exist in the vicinity.

The battle, which took place from 1–3 July 1863, was fought between the Army of the Potomac, led by George Gordon Meade, and the Confederate troops, under General Robert E. Lee. A number of strategic skirmishes took place, the most famous of which was Pickett's charge, the Confederate attack against the Union troops.

It was the Union side, however, that was to attain victory in this encounter, which saw the staggering loss of 48,000 lives. When the fighting ceased, the battlefield was awash with blood and echoed with the agonized cries of

This monument to the many fallen men who perished on Culloden Moor serves as a reminder of past carnage.

mortally wounded men from both sides. Worse was yet to come, as huge hogs, let loose by the destruction of containing fences, gorged themselves on the bodies of the dead and dying.

Over the years, visitors to the site of the battle have reported curious occurrences, most notably in those areas of the field that saw the most intensive fighting, such as High Water Mark, Little Round Top and Devil's Den. They have spoken of face-to-face encounters with ghostly soldiers and recall feeling suddenly and strangely cold, as well as hearing the solemn beat of battle drums and the sound of men marching.

Electrical equipment also seems to register the potential presence of supernatural activity, as cameras and recording devices that previously were functioning perfectly normally inexplicably failed to work around the site of the battle.

It is not only on the battlefield of Gettysburg that mysterious happenings take place – local residents also seem to have had their fair share of ghostly encounters. Ghostly soldiers have been seen in those buildings that were standing at the time of the battle, where strange noises and spectral orbs are frequently reported.

In the Eisenhower Elementary School a man's boot prints repeatedly appear on the high ceiling of the first-floor bathroom. Noises are also heard in this room, and tiny green flashes are said to appear when the lights are extinguished.

Gettysburg College is also inhabited by supernatural residents dating from the Civil War. One of the most haunted buildings on campus, Pennsylvania Hall, was used as a hospital during the conflict and as such was inevitably the site of pain, suffering and death.

Students of the college have reported many strange happenings there – for example, the building's lift, rather than going to the selected storey, often inexplicably descends to the basement, where its occupants are, to their horror, suddenly confronted with a particularly gruesome hospital scene.

Others tell of a civil war soldier who is seen guarding the hospital from his position on the cupola on the roof of the building. Upon noticing the gaze of the living person looking at him, he is said to aim his rifle at the imagined intruder, before disappearing into thin air.

Culloden and Gettysburg are just two of the many battlefields to reverberate with the ghosts of fallen fighters. It seems certain that these sites of conflict will continue to fascinate us, as the extent of the suffering there makes them poignant, and ultimately deeply mysterious, places of pilgrimage for mortal man.

An illustration of the Battle of Gettysburg from 1884.

ALCATRAZ

Stories of incarceration, torture and thrilling escape attempts have long been associated with the world-famous prison of Alcatraz, nicknamed 'hellcatraz' by its unfortunate inmates. Besides these, however, many mysterious occurrences are reported to have taken place there, and we must ask ourselves whether anything more ominous than a bloody history lurks within its impenetrable walls. Could it be that the island is inhabited by malevolent powers?

Alcatraz – or 'The Rock' – was not always a prison. Many years ago, in the time of the Native Americans, this barren and remote island was known as the 'White Rock', because it was covered with white pelican droppings. It was avoided by local tribes, as it was thought to be the haunt of evil spirits and a possible portal to another, sinister, dimension.

When the Spanish came across the island in the seventeenth century they named it 'La Isla de los Alcatraces', or 'the Island of the Pelicans', but failed to recognize its importance as a strategic outpost. All this changed in the 1850s, however, when the excellent military defensive potential of the island was finally realized and it became home to a fortress for the purposes of guarding the Golden Gate.

Building work on the fort commenced in 1854. Unfortunately, planners had failed to take into account both the geographical and meteorological factors which were to prove so devastating for many of the construction workers. There was only one landing site on the island and access to this was restricted by strong currents and hazardous weather conditions,

Burt Lancaster in the 1962 film *The Birdman of Alcatraz*. This is just one of the films that have been made about the notorious prison, perhaps the most famous of which was *The Rock* from 1996, starring Sean Connery, Nicolas Cage and Ed Harris.

notably wind, rain and fog. Once on the island, there was no water or vegetation and, with the supply route being so hazardous, access to essentials from the mainland was severely limited. In spite of the subsequent building of a wooden town around the construction site as well as roads enabling better access, starvation and disease were rife, and huge numbers of workers died in the building of the fort.

Eventually work was completed, and in 1859 the first prisoners were sent to Alcatraz. By 1861 the fortress had been made the official military prison for the entire Department of the Pacific. Prisoners were confined in atrocious conditions, forced to lie head to toe in serried ranks on the hard floor with no sanitary facilities. Not surprisingly, the captives died in their scores from disease.

As time went on, the prison became increasingly notorious, housing military convicts and society's worst criminals. Thieves, thugs, rapists, murderers and escapees from other prisons were sent to the formidable fortress, where they stood little chance of escape. When the increasingly desperate prisoners tried to escape their horrendous conditions, it seemed as if nature was working against them, as fearsome currents would wash them back to the island, or cause them to drown in the icy waters.

By the 1930s Alcatraz had become a maximum-security prison, where only the most vicious and hardened criminals were sent. Men armed with machine guns stood on guard, although far more inmates met their death as a result of the conditions than through being shot. Once again, nature seemed determined to punish those kept within the prison walls. A cloying, dense fog enshrouded the fort, and icy winds cut through the otherwise impenetrable walls, causing inmates to feel perpetually cold and to fall ill.

Prisoners were confined in atrocious conditions, forced to lie head to toe in serried ranks on the hard floor with no sanitary facilities.

Prisoners also had to endure the mental anguish of isolation, which was only heightened by the fact that they could see the lights of San Francisco and hear party boats passing by the island. It was a harsh, brutal life, with violence constantly breaking out among the inmates, and any men who did survive an escape attempt were immediately executed.

The fort ceased to be a prison in 1969, after lying empty for some years, and it remains the property of the Golden Gate National Recreation Area. Every year it attracts thousands of visitors, lured by its brutal history of bloodshed, anguish and hatred. Increasingly, people are drawn to the island by tales of strange occurrences within its walls, many of them coming from officials who frequent the fort, and who are made eerily aware of the resonance of evil. They speak of feelings of dread and of being watched, tormented screams, inexplicable crashing sounds, and the sudden, mysterious closing of cell doors.

Of all of the seemingly haunted areas of the fort, it is cell block D that is the most frightening. This was formerly the solitary confinement area of the prison, and housed the most hardened criminals. Here, prisoners were forced to stand in naked isolation in the freezing darkness for days on end and, as if this was not bad enough, a ghostly presence was rumoured to stalk the area, attempting to strangle the unfortunate inmate.

The inexplicable death of one of the men seems to confirm these reports. This unfortunate prisoner's fate perplexed medical experts at the time, as the position of the bruises on his body revealed that it would have been physically impossible for him to have strangled himself. Could the evil spirit of a long-dead felon have been responsible? Whatever the reason, many inmates of cell block D continually screamed with terror and eventually went insane.

Today, many Recreation Area rangers refuse to go near this area, which is unnaturally cold and instills dread and horror in those who set foot there. One of the many psychics to visit the island claimed to have felt icy fingers around his neck in one of the cells of D block and he recalled that he was filled with a fear so intense that his hair stood up on end.

In other parts of the prison, sobbing is heard, and the ghosts of inmates appear before rangers and visitors. Sometimes, a strange whistling sound is heard, and the lighthouse, which was demolished many years ago, appears out of the dense fog, casting an eerie light over the troubled island.

Reports of such supernatural encounters are morbidly fascinating to the world at large, and many people continue to be attracted to the island, perhaps hoping to experience the paranormal for themselves. Whether or not the Native Americans were correct in their assumptions about the island being a portal to another world, the site certainly seems to possess considerable negative energies which hold all who visit in their thrall.

Visitors being shown around the prison after its closure in 1969.

Alcatraz **145**

PAST LIVES

Most of us are busy enjoying or enduring our everyday lives, too frantic to hear the quiet inner voice that speaks of another place, another time. But for a minority of people, details of a previous existence encroach on the present, making a strong case for the principles of reincarnation.

Several major faiths, including Hinduism, Sikhism, Jainism and others give credence to life after death. Buddhists have a similar but not identical philosophy of rebirth, although Tibetan Buddhists invest heavily in the idea of reincarnation in order to identify legitimate heirs to the role of Dalai Lama.

Tenzin Gyatso, today's Dalai Lama, is believed to be the reincarnation of his predecessor. Indeed, he was born in the same year his predecessor died (1935), to a peasant family in north-eastern Tibet. A Buddhist dignitary trying to divine the identity of the new Dalai Lama had a vision in which he saw a monastery. Aides were given detailed descriptions of the monastery and dispatched across the region to find it. They discovered one that fitted the description in Taktser. There they encountered a 2-year-old boy who demanded the rosary being worn by one of the party that had once belonged to the deceased Dalai Lama. When he correctly identified the men in the deputation by name and rank, it was deemed that he was the embodiment of the Dalai Lama. He was finally enthroned in 1940.

There is a growing body of evidence in the West to say that earthly life after death is a reality. Two methods have been used to gather examples of past lives: regression through hypnosis in adults and the spontaneous recollections of young children, whose previous lives remain fresh in their memories.

Psychologist Helen Wambach carried out a 10-year survey of past-life recollections among 1,088 subjects. With the exception of only eleven people, the descriptions given about minute details of past lives, including kitchen utensils, clothing and footwear, were uncannily accurate. She found that the majority of the lives described were in the lower classes, reflecting the appropriate historical distribution. She also discovered that 49.4 per cent of the past lives were female and 50.6 per cent were male, reflecting the correct biological balance. Although she started out as a sceptic, Wambach became convinced by the evidence in front of her. In 1978 she declared: 'I don't believe in reincarnation — I know it!'

Among the celebrities of today are several who are convinced they have lived before. These include Sylvester Stallone, who thinks he has been here no less than four times in the past, and

The Tibetan spiritual leader the Dalai Lama, who is believed to be the reincarnation of his predecessor.

was on one occasion guillotined during the French Revolution. He also claims to have been a boxer who was killed by a knockout punch in the 1930s. Actor Martin Sheen talked of being a cruel US cavalry soldier who was trampled to death by a horse. Today he has a loathing of horses, which might be linked to his past life experiences. Singer Englebert Humperdinck thought he once ruled the Roman Empire, while pop goddess Tina Turner has been told she is a reincarnation of the Egyptian queen Hatshepsut. Shirley MacLaine also claims numerous past lives, among them a Moorish girl living along a pilgrim trail in Spain. Under hypnosis, movie star Glenn Ford was able to speak fluent French, since one of his past lives was spent as a French cavalryman in the reign of Louis XIV.

The fact that hypnosis subjects are suddenly able to speak in a foreign language is one of the oddest and most compelling pieces of evidence about past lives. Other positive benefits such as the relief of long term illnesses, nightmares or phobias have been felt when the harm supposedly caused by past life injuries or experiences was addressed.

Opponents to hypnosis believe it is perilous and that beneficial results are unproven. They believe that symptoms people put down to past existences are more likely to be caused by inherited or suppressed memories. Hypnosis might even be making the problem worse by creating a multitude of personalities in a subject, rather than pinpointing true past life experiences.

The experience of a Colorado housewife who regressed into a supposed past life as Bridey Murphy of nineteenth-century Ireland was documented in a book. But the account was swiftly debunked when it was proved that no woman of that name was born in the year she had claimed. Nor was her death on record anywhere. Her command of the old Irish language and lifestyle was later deemed to have been learned through a close relationship with an Irish woman in her early years.

Still, the stories relating to hypnotherapy remain intriguing. In 1983, psychologist and former sceptic Peter Ramster featured in a documentary with four women who recounted their past life experiences. One woman remembered a life in Somerset, England, in the second half of the eighteenth century. When she was taken to the rural village in question – a place she had never visited before – she was able to find her way around and identify local landmarks, some of which had been long forgotten. Furthermore, it became clear that she had a thorough knowledge of local legends, dialect and families.

The fact that hypnosis subjects are suddenly able to speak a foreign language is one of the oddest and most compelling pieces of evidence...

For many, the coherent and cohesive descriptions of different environments recounted by very small children are altogether more persuasive. One benchmark case is that of Shanti Deva. In 1930, aged 4, Shanti told her parents that she had once lived in a place called Muttra, that she had been a mother of three who died in childbirth and that her previous name had been Ludgi.

Only when they were continually pressed by the youngster did the bewildered family from Delhi investigate. They discovered there was indeed a village called Muttra and that a woman named Ludgi had recently died there. When

Shanti was taken to the village, she lapsed into local dialect and recognized her previous-life husband and children. She even gave twenty-four accurate statements that matched confirmed facts, an impressive feat for such a young child, and one that it would be impossible to hoax.

Since 1967, psychiatrist Dr Ian Stevenson has pioneered the scientific study of spontaneous past life recollections among infants. Usually a youngster is aged between two and five years old when they describe what went on in a previous existence. In most cases, although not all, recall has faded by the age of seven.

Having interviewed thousands of children from all over the world, Dr Stevenson has discovered some interesting facets to the phenomenon. In some cases, the mother had experienced a prophetic dream, announcing or implying the past life identity of the child in her womb. Meanwhile, a number of children claiming a previous existence bore birthmarks that corresponded to wounds inflicted on them when they lived before. For example, a boy in India who was born without fingers on one hand remembered that in a prior existence he had put his hand into the blades of a fodder-chopping machine, amputating the digits. Dr Stevenson aimed to corroborate the verbal evidence of a child with relevant death certificates and interviews with witnesses to both existences.

Critics think the prophetic dreams are no more than wishful thinking. They credit Dr Stevenson with collecting anecdotal rather than scientific evidence.

Yet some of his cases are compelling and strangely thought-provoking. On one occasion, Dr Stevenson made an unannounced visit to a Druze village in Lebanon to see if any children there were subject to past life statements. He was immediately dispatched to the home of 5-year-old Imad Elawar, who had for several years been talking about another life in a different village some 40 km distant. Young Imad had even stopped a former neighbour in the street to share recollections about the life he once lived. His first words as a child were Jamileh and Mahmoud, the names of his mistress and uncle in his previous life. Stevenson noted more than fifty-seven separate claims by the child about his past life, the majority of which could be supported with evidence from elsewhere.

When Shanti was taken to the village, she lapsed into local dialect and recognized her previous-life husband and children.

While the study of reincarnation has leapt ahead recently, it is a subject that is by no means the preserve of the modern age. In 1824, a Japanese boy called Kastugoro recounted details of a village where he had once lived and the family that was once his own. Despite his tender age, the minutiae he recalled were sufficient to persuade investigators of the day that past lives were a reality.

Throughout the ages, belief in reincarnation has been powerful and widespread. Could it be that life is not as simple as we believe and that we are closer to history than we imagine…?

Seers and Oracles

The desire to predict the future is deeply rooted in human nature. People have always been fascinated by the art of prophecy and throughout the ages have attempted to discern what the future might hold for them. Many try to achieve this by consulting an individual who possesses the unique ability to see into the future – a seer or an oracle. There are many different methods of divination, which are practised by societies all over the world. Belief in the power of the prophet is strong, as case after case demonstrates that there is some truth behind this mysterious phenomenon.

EZEKIEL

The Holy Bible abounds with stirring tales of mankind's deeds, with stories of heroism, war and treachery figuring prominently. Above all, though, it is the prophetic word of God that can be found within its pages. The moral and religious messages of the Bible's many books are delivered for the most part through prophets of the Old Testament such as Ezekiel and Jeremiah.

The Bible contains several main prophetic books, and within each of these is a series of 'Oracles against Foreign Nations'. These highly stylized and poetic sections contain God's predictions about the fate of those nations who commit crimes against humanity and who sin against God. One of the most famous of these indictments can be found in the book of Ezekiel, and it is particularly notable because of the fact that it is dated, and so can be linked to the historical circumstances that surround both its pronouncement and fulfilment.

The oracle against the island city of Tyre, contained within Ezekiel 26, is from 586BC and was a result of the turbulent events in Israel that occurred around the late seventh and early sixth centuries BC. At that time, Babylon, under the awesome auspices of Nebuchadnezzar, was in the process of consolidating and expanding its empire in the Eastern Mediterranean, and was aiming to gain control of Egypt.

Israel, on the other hand, had become weak and vulnerable following the abortive attempts at reform by Josiah in 621BC. This had led to a succession of disorganized and godless leaders, who undermined the nation's commitment to God and made them deaf to the dire warnings of prophets such as Ezekiel and Jeremiah.

Ezekiel predicted that, despite its strong defensive position, Tyre and its land-based 'daughter' villages would be totally destroyed.

Israel was the stepping-stone between Babylon in the east and Egypt in the west, and so invasion was inevitable. It happened in 606BC when Israel became a vassal state of Babylon. Discontent and nationalism brewed as a result and eventually surfaced as a full-scale rebellion against the Babylonian forces. This was quickly quashed, however, and many of the Israeli ringleaders, including Ezekiel, were deported in 598BC. A few years later, just before the destruction of Jerusalem by the Babylonians, Ezekiel made his now famous oracle against Tyre.

The city of Tyre, situated very close to the shore of what is now Lebanon, was a significant

Phoenician seaport, which linked shipping routes from all over the Mediterranean with land caravans from Arabia, Babylon, Persia and India. Ezekiel predicted that, despite its strong defensive position, Tyre and its land-based 'daughter' villages would be totally destroyed. He prophesied: 'For thus says the Lord GOD: Behold, I will bring upon Tyre from the North Nebuchadnezzar king of Babylon, king of kings, with horses and chariots, and with horsemen and a host of soldiers … He will slay with the sword your daughters on the mainland.'

These predictions did, in part, subsequently unfold. Historical records, including those written by the Jewish historian Josephus Flavius, relate that Nebuchadnezzar did demolish the mainland parts of the city and lay siege to the island for thirteen years. Although this was unsuccessful at the time, Tyre did eventually become a vassal of Babylon as a result of a negotiated settlement.

The overthrow of Jerusalem and the undermining of power in Tyre were viewed as divine retribution by Ezekiel and Jeremiah. In their eyes, the state of Israel had wavered in its faith and failed to serve God, and thus deserved punishment at the hands of Nebuchadnezzar. In turn, it seemed the Babylonians were being rewarded for their punitive actions by allegedly achieving their ambitious invasion of Egypt.

Although many of the specifics of Ezekiel's oracle may not have come to pass exactly as predicted, its message remains abundantly clear, with the factual details taking on a comparatively reduced significance. The fact that Tyre was eventually demolished many years later, in 332BC, by

Ezekiel prophesying after his deportation by the Babylonians.

Alexander the Great gives the oracle against Tyre an enduring resonance, and is further evidence of the amazing power of prophecy.

THE *I-CHING*

The *I-Ching* or *Book of Changes* remains as important today as it was when it first appeared between five and eight thousand years ago. Containing the founding principles of Chinese philosophy, this book, together with the Bible and the Koran, is one of the most studied works in the world and is revered for the great insights held within its pages.

By interpreting the I-Ching, key decisions about war, love, business and many other personal and political issues can be made.

The *I-Ching*, which represents a guide to divination and moral counsel, is central to Chinese and other Asian cultures. The study of this book and the basic Taoist principles that underpin its philosophy also form a major part of the study of *feng shui*, Chinese medicine and most martial arts. By interpreting the *I-Ching*, key decisions about war, love, business and many other personal and political issues can be made.

Taoist principles dictate that within the universe there exists the unknown – this is called the Tao and is represented by a symbol that incorporates the basic universal polarity of the yin and the yang. These two universal forces are united in a perpetual motion of change, and represent the notion that duality and polarity are constantly in flux – nothing is either solely good or solely bad, and all things are in continual motion.

For the Taoists, true virtue arises as a result of a balance and harmony with the universe, a notion that is also evident in Buddhist beliefs. The *I-Ching* derives its form and usage from these principles of yin and yang, the yin being represented by two short lines, the yang by a longer, more solid line.

The earliest records of the practice of 'wisdom divination' in China involved not only the reading of cracks on bones that had been cast into a fire, but also the interpretation of the pattern of cracks found on a tortoise shell. These cracks contain parallels with the arrangement of the yin and yang lines, and on the first tortoise shell the layering of these lines formed eight trigrams.

These trigrams are representative of the eight primal forces of the universe. When multiplied by eight, they represent all possible interactions of these forces with each other. These sixty-four line figures, representing reality on all levels, are known as *kua*. The *I-Ching* contains a chapter for each of these possible outcomes, explaining the meaning of the patterns and providing an insight into the future.

Some believe that the first person to recognize and understand this 'line symbol system' of eight trigrams on the shell of a tortoise was Fu Hsi, the legendary first emperor of China. Other stories relate that Fu Hsi first noted this system, not on a tortoise shell but on the side of a dragon horse as it rose out of the Yellow River. The markings were recorded as the Ho Tu, or 'Yellow River Map', and interpreted according to an early symmetrical arrangement of the eight trigrams. This system then went on to be modified by another mythical emperor, Yu, after seeing a similar pattern on the shell of a tortoise in the Lo River. This 'Lo Shu' map was then interpreted according to a later asymmetrical system that incorporated the four seasons and five elements, and refers to the order of change in the manifest world.

Whichever is correct, both stories agree that the next modification of the system occurred in the Shang dynasty, between 1766–1121BC. Wen Wang, usually referred to as 'King Wen', was a powerful feudal lord who was sentenced to death and imprisoned by the Shang Emperor, Chou Hsin. While languishing in prison, he is said to have studied the trigrams and combined them to form hexagrams and the *kua*. He then named and organized the sixty-four hexagrams into their present arrangement, and provided much of the accompanying explanatory text.

Following his release after a year in prison, King Wen revealed his findings and modifications to his son, the Duke of Chou. These were later added to by the Duke, who eventually became ruler and founder of the Chou dynasty following the overthrow of Chou Hsin. For this reason, this version of the book is usually referred to as the

Chinese divination bones from the Shang dynasty.

Chou-I, or the 'Changes of Chou'.

The final modification and resulting present-day name occurred during 5BC. Kung Fu-Tze (Confucius) studied the *Chou-I* and added further philosophical commentary, so overlaying the Taoist principles with Confucian ideas.

Careful manipulation of the straws produces a pattern that denotes a sequence of hexagrams.

Although some controversy surrounds the two systems because of the fact that they give vastly differing distribution patterns for the yin and yang lines, both techniques are respected and widely used as methods of divination and guidance.

The *I-Ching* was first introduced to the West in 1882, when James Legge provided the first English translation. Legge, however, did not approve of the oracular function of the book, and it failed to arouse any significant interest until Jung brought his attention to bear on it.

Jung discovered that consultations with the oracle...resulted in consistently meaningful and startlingly accurate insights.

There are two principal methods of reading the *I-Ching*, both of which have their basis in the random generation of binary choices. The traditional method is a complex process involving the manipulation of fifty dried yarrow straws, whereby the resultant patterns denote a certain sequence of hexagrams.

The simple, more commonly used method involves the casting of coins. The side which is uppermost when the coin has fallen relates to the drawing of a yin or yang line, which in turn constitutes the sequence of hexagrams.

Jung discovered that consultations with the oracle on a wide range of topics resulted in consistently meaningful and startlingly accurate insights. He subsequently recorded these findings in an introduction to a German translation of the book in 1929. When it was finally translated into English, under the title of The *I-Ching* or *Book of Changes*, in 1949, it was received with great enthusiasm and is still widely used and studied.

Today, the *I-Ching* continues to be held in high esteem all over the world as a result of its remarkable powers of prophecy and guidance. Although debate surrounds some of its early history, this has not affected its popularity, and it seems likely that this ancient Eastern oracle will continue to be consulted for the mystical wisdom it contains for many years to come.

THE ORACLES OF BALAAM

One of the most controversial seers of the Old Testament is Balaam, the barbaric prophet whose name means 'devourer of people'. Although reviled and often attached to the epithet rasha, 'the wicked one', in Rabbinical literature, this mythical figure attained a level of exaltation among the heathens that is sometimes equated with that achieved by Moses among the 'chosen' people.

While some sources proclaim Balaam to be one of the seven heathen prophets, among which his father Job was numbered, others state that his lineage stemmed from Beor, and that he lived in Pethor in Mesopotamia. The prophet is often depicted as being blind in one eye and lame in one foot, with his followers distinguished only by merit of possessing the three morally corrupt qualities of an evil eye, haughtiness and greed.

Balaam started his career as an interpreter of dreams, before becoming a magician and finally a prophet. This gift of prophecy enabled him to predict the exact moment at which God's wrath would occur, and thus his powers could be extremely valuable to the world at large. So great was his reputation as a reliable oracle, that people far and wide asserted 'he whom thou blessest is blessed, and he whom thou cursest is cursed'.

Anxious to secure Balaam's services, Balak – a worshipper of the god Baal and king of Moab, a heathen state embroiled at that time in a bloody battle against the Israelites – sent messengers to summon the infamous soothsayer. Balak, whose name means 'the devastator', had assumed his position of power in Moab after the destruction of the Amorites during the time of Moses.

Balaam, however, having consulted with God and been forbidden to return with Balak's messengers, refused to go. The king, desperate to gain Balaam's assistance in overcoming the Israelites, tried once more, sending further emissaries with promises of riches and power.

> The gift of prophecy enabled Balaam to predict the exact moment at which God's wrath would occur.

Balaam was tempted by Balak's enticing offer, and again consulted with God. This time, he was granted permission to return with the messengers, provided that he promised to do only as God commanded. Balaam agreed to this and set out on an ass on the journey to Moab.

An illustration of a prophet from the period in which Balaam made his predictions.

According to the story, God was angered by Balaam's motives of greed, and suspected that he would not obey his decree. An angel of the Lord, invisible to the human eye, was sent down, and the ass, which was able to discern the heavenly body, refused to move. At this, Balaam became incensed and proceeded to thrash the animal, but to no avail. The ass was then bestowed with the gift of human speech, reproaching the prophet for his actions. In response, Balaam claimed that, if he had the means, he would kill the ass.

At this point, the angel made himself visible. Balaam bowed down before the divine messenger, confessed his sins and offered to return to his homeland. The angel responded by saying that he could continue his journey, but only if he honoured his promise to the Lord.

Balaam agreed and continued on his journey to Moab. Here, in response to God's instructions, he ordered Balak to offer sacrifices of seven oxen and seven rams on seven altars positioned on high ground overlooking the land of Israel. Balak did so and, accordingly, the two men travelled together to Bamoth-Baal, from where most of Israel could be seen. Here Balaam, obedient to God, delivered the first of the four famous oracles in favour of Israel.

Balak, expecting Balaam to pronounce a curse rather than blessing on his enemy, was annoyed by what he had heard. Nevertheless, he journeyed with the seer to the second of the high places, Mount Pisgah, from where all of the Israeli encampment was visible.

To Balak's increasing vexation, Balaam again spoke in favour of the Israelites, this time praising them even more highly. He compared their might to that of a lion, saying: 'Behold, the people riseth up as a lioness, And as a lion doth he lift himself up; He shall not lie down until he eat of the prey, And drink the blood of the slain.'

Upon hearing this second prediction, Balak begged the prophet to say no more. Balaam, however, maintained that he must fulfil his promise. The pair then journeyed to Mount Peor, which again overlooked the Israeli encampment, and here Balaam delivered his third pronouncement, which predicted the sustained fertility of Israeli soil.

At this point, Balak became enraged, and attempted to dismiss the seer, but was thwarted when Balaam delivered the last and most portentous of his prophecies. In this, he spoke of the rise of the Israelites and their subsequent victory over Moab and the neighbouring states of Edom and the Kenites. Shattered by what he had heard, Balak allowed the seer to return to his home country, where, at the age of 33, he was stoned, burned, strangled and decapitated for his many wicked deeds.

At the age of 33, he was stoned, burned, strangled and decapitated for his many wicked deeds.

As a result of what he had been told, Balak ceased his aggression against the Israelites. Despite this, Balaam's prophecy later came true, as Moab fell into the hands of King David of Israel. Not only was Balaam's prediction entirely accurate, but also his remarkable abilities had shown themselves to be so powerful that they had fundamentally influenced the actions of one of the world's most potent leaders.

THE DELPHIC ORACLE

Throughout history, the role of the oracle has figured prominently, as it has in numerous tales of classical mythology. Of all the famous oracles, perhaps the best known and respected was that found at Delphi in Greece.

The oracle at Delphi was at the shrine of Apollo, the Greek god of fine arts and prophecy. Set high on the hillside of Mount Parnassus, it occupied a prominent position, reflecting the esteem in which it was held in Greek culture.

According to legend, Apollo took control of Parnassus when he was a child, by killing Python, a huge dragon snake, in the battle between the gods of the sky and the earth. Apollo then assumed the form of a dolphin (*delphis* in Greek, from which the shrine derived its name) and journeyed out into the ocean to capture some sailors who were appointed his first high priests.

Apollo delivered his prophecies at Delphi through various prophetesses, or sybils. The sybil, who was always a mature woman who had lived a pure life, would take on the name Pythia upon

Depicted in a stone carving, suppliants queue to consult the oracle at Delphi.

being appointed, after the python slain by the young Apollo.

When the prophecies were made, Pythia would enter a trance before delivering her predictions in riddles. These were then translated and interpreted by the high priests and then they would be relayed to the waiting suppliants.

Upon arriving at Delphi, these suppliants registered and paid a fee to make an appointment. They would then have been required to purify themselves in the Castalian spring, where a bathing trough still exists, and travel up the Sacred Way to the shrine. A sacrificial offering of a sheep or goat would have been made and the entrails examined for omens by priests. When the pilgrims finally reached the sybil, they were allowed in, one at a time, to ask for her predictions.

The Delphic oracle was visited over a period of almost 2,000 years, during which time countless prophecies were delivered on subjects ranging from wars and matters of state to personal affairs, births and deaths. The suppliants came from almost every level of society, a factor that demonstrates the regard in which prophecy was held in the everyday life of those times. The power and influence of the oracle can also be seen in the art and literature of the period. Not only does it figure in Virgil's *Aeneid* and Homer's *Odyssey*, but in Sophocles' story of Oedipus, the oracle predicts to the King and Queen of Thebes that their son Oedipus would kill his father and marry his mother. As the dramatic events unfold, the prophecy is fulfilled, evoking questions about fate and morality that are relevant to this day.

NOSTRADAMUS

The words penned by Nostradamus during his many years as a seer have been translated, pored over and debated. Still, no one is sure how much weight to lend them. While some of his predictions appear wildly speculative and never came to pass, others seem to have neatly summed up events with spine-chilling clarity.

Nostradamus was born Michel de Nostradame in St Rémy de Provence on 14 December 1503. He was from a prosperous middle-class family and his father is generally described either as a

While some of Nostradamus' predictions appear wildly speculative and never came to pass, others seem to have neatly summed up events with spine-chilling clarity.

lawyer or grain merchant. Young Michel proved to be a brilliant young scholar, showing particular skill for languages and the sciences. He also read voraciously. The family had recently converted from Judaism to the more prevalent Roman Catholic faith, so Michel grew up with a thorough knowledge of both belief systems.

However, Nostradamus' first passion was medicine, and at the age of 18 he entered the University of Montpellier to train as a physician. He was able to put his new-found expertise to good use, since the bubonic plague, or the 'Black Death' was ravaging medieval Europe, and doctors were in great demand At the time his approach to patients was radical. Donning the protection of a rudimentary mask, he treated people using good hygiene and herbal poultices rather than the barbaric practice of 'bleeding' patients that brought them to the brink of death.

Nostradamus married and fathered two children, but his medical skills were not sufficient to save his young family from the clutches of the Black Death. After the death of his wife and children, the bereft Nostradamus became a wandering scholar, travelling throughout southern France and Italy.

It was while he was in Italy that the first sign of his future career became apparent. He came across a group of Franciscan monks herding cattle and had a strong premonition of the future, which led him to kneel down and address one of the monks as 'Your Holiness'. Years later the monk, Felice Peretti, became Pope Sextus V (1520–1590).

When Nostradamus reached the age of 44, he ended his itinerant lifestyle and settled in the Provençal town of Salon. He married a wealthy widow and began his career in prophecy in

Nostradamus (1503–1566) couched his prophecies in a mysterious combination of French, Latin, Greek and Italian, in order to avoid condemnation by the Catholic Inquisition.

earnest. His aim was nothing less than to prophesy the future of mankind, and eight years later he produced the first of more than a dozen books of predictions. The books are called *Centuries* because each is made up of a hundred verses, or quatrains.

Nostradamus was a devout man, but he saw no conflict between his religion and his prophecies. However, he knew that others would not share this open-minded attitude. This was the age of the Inquisition, and anyone suspected of anti-Catholic sentiment was mercilessly punished. The art of peering ahead in time would certainly not sit well with the cruel monks who led the Inquisition. So he set about disguising his predictions by couching them in a mysterious combination of French, Latin, Greek and Italian. Furthermore, he used metaphors and anagrams to produce baffling and impenetrable riddles. He did this, so he told his son, so that the enlightened folk of the future could decipher his messages. But as yet, the generation he was pinning his hopes on has not emerged.

Despite the mysterious nature of the predictions, Nostradamus' *Centuries* became popular reading material, particularly amongst nobility and royalty, and his reputation grew ever greater. During his lifetime, he came to prominence for one prediction in particular, which gained him both friends and enemies.

> The Young Lion will overcome the older one
> on the field of combat in a single battle,
> Inside a cage of gold his eyes will be put out,
> Two wounds made one,
> He dies a cruel death.
> (*Century 1*, Quatrain 35)

Just four years after this prophecy, King Henri II died during a joust when a lance pierced his gilded visor and caused two mortal injuries. Many believed that Nostradamus had caused the death of the king, and demanded that the prophet be tried for heresy. Fortunately for Nostradamus, the king's widow, Catherine de Medici, did not share their view. She was so impressed by his powers that she hired him as physician to her son and heir.

But Nostradamus was not only adept at predicting events during his own lifetime. After his death in 1566, one prophecy in particular appears to have pinpoint accuracy:

> The blood of the just will be demanded London,
> Burnt by the fire in the year 66,
> The ancient Lady will fall from her high place,
> And many of the same sect will be killed.
> (*Century 2*, Quatrain 51)

This seems to refer to an event that was to rock Europe exactly a hundred years after the death of the seer. In 1666, the Great Fire of London destroyed much of the city, including St Paul's Cathedral. This prediction is particularly striking because it includes a date. Unfortunately, many of the others do not, but in translation they do seem to jigsaw with history.

> That which neither weapon nor flame could accomplish will be achieved,
> By a sweet-speaking tongue in a council,
> Sleeping, in a dream, the king will see the enemy not in war, Or of military blood.
> (*Century 1*, Quatrain 97)

This prediction seems to have a particular resonance with the fate of King Henri III of France. The king, who was on the throne during

Nostradamus alarms Catherine de Medici, Henri II's queen, with his predictions.

Nostradamus' lifetime, survived wars and jousts, but in the end he fell victim to a treacherous monk. Just three days prior to his death, he had a premonition about what would happen in a dream.

> The rejected one shall at last reach the throne,
> Her enemies found to have been traitors,
> More than ever shall her period be triumphant,
> At seventy she shall go assuredly to death,
> in the third year of the century.
> (*Century VI*, Quatrain 74)

Surely this refers to Queen Elizabeth I of England, who was the least favoured of her father's children. But when she finally ascended the throne in 1558, in the face of Catholic opposition, her reign was indisputably glorious. She did indeed die aged 70, and the year was 1603.

One premonition that he got exactly right was his own death.

Although many of Nostradamus' predictions tally with historical events to a startling degree, others are tantalizingly vague and they are not in chronological order. Sceptics have drawn attention to the prophet's ambiguous language, and the fact that he is thought to have copied other prophecies current in his era. The subject matter he chooses is invariably war or natural disasters, and these will always be a feature of history. The critics claim that if the cryptic messages of Nostradamus can be applied to real events, then it is nothing more than coincidence. Take, for example, the quatrain thought by many to refer to the coming of Hitler:

> Beasts wild with hunger will cross the rivers,
> The greater part of the battlefield will be against Hister,
> He will drag the leader in a cage of iron,
> When the child of Germany observes no law.
> (*Century II*, Quatrain 24)

Incredibly, this quatrain does at first seem to sum up the events of the Second World War during Hitler's dictatorship and to allude to the savage Nazi troops swamping Europe and humiliating conquered leaders. However, Hister is also the exact name of an area close to the Danube river. So the prediction can be read with two meanings, although with historical hindsight, it makes better sense when Hister is read as Hitler.

Some of Nostradamus' prophecies have been wrong, most spectacularly the one that implied a catastrophic war would break out in July 1999. Yet despite the ambiguity that surrounds his predictions, thousands of people give due respect to Nostradamus, believing his case has been proven at least in part. With long grey hair and a beard, he certainly must have looked the part of an accomplished seer. Whilst other prophets of a similar kind have been forgotten, the reputation of Nostradamus has flourished through the centuries since his death. And since his predictions continue until 3797, he still has plenty of time to be proved right.

One premonition that he got exactly right was his own death. 'You will not see me alive at sunrise,' he told his assistant on the evening of 1 July 1566. True to his word, by the following morning he was dead.

THE BRAHAN SEER

Deep in the mists of the folklore of the Scottish Highlands lies the character of Coinneach Odhar, the 'Brahan Seer'. An enigmatic figure, his uncannily accurate powers of prophecy and eventual trial for witchcraft made him renowned across the land.

With little in the way of written evidence about the seer, his actual identity is unclear. Indeed, many of the tales about him have been preserved through oral tradition alone. The only official documents uncovered to date that might relate to this figure are two Commissions of Justice ordering the prosecution for witchcraft of a Keanoch Owir in 1577. However, this date is almost a century earlier than the period described in more traditional tales of the seer's prophesying, and seems unlikely to relate to the same man.

Local legend identifies the seer as Kenneth Mackenzie, a labourer born in Baile-na-Gille on the Isle of Lewis in around 1650. It is said that he lived at Loch Ussie in Ross-shire, where he worked on the Brahan estate, the seat of the Seaforth chieftains, from about 1675. As the last, and most famous, of his fulfilled predictions specifically relates to this family, it seems likely that Mackenzie was the true Brahan Seer.

Many of the prophecies made by this figure related to the geographical region in which he lived, where the fulfilment of his predictions can

be seen to this day. As many as 150 years prior to the construction of the Caledonian Canal, Coinneach Odhar is reported to have told a listener: 'Strange as it may seem to you this day, the time will come, and it is not far off, when full-rigged ships will be seen sailing eastward and westward by the back of Tomnahurich, near Inverness.' As, at the time of the premonition, the area in question consisted of rolling hills, the listener deemed what he had heard to be so preposterous that from that point on he ceased all contact with the seer.

Another visible example of the seer's prophecies lies in the parish of Petty, where a huge stone once marked the boundary between the estates of Culloden and Moray. In 1799 this colossally heavy stone inexplicably moved some distance into the sea. How or why this occurred remains a mystery, but whatever the cause, the event was specifically foretold by the seer, who predicted: 'The day will come when the stone of Petty, large though it is, and high and dry upon the land as it appears to people this day, will be suddenly found as far advanced into the sea as it now lies away from it inland, and no-one will see it removed or be able to account for its sudden and marvellous transportation'.

The seer seems also to have been adept at predicting numerous important events in the history of Scotland, such as his premonitions of the carnage wreaked at the famous Battle of Culloden. While walking in the vicinity, he is said to have stated: 'The bleak moore shall, ere many generations have passed away, be stained with the best blood of the Highlands'.

He also accurately foresaw the demise of the clan Mackenzie of Fairburn and its sixteenth-century Fairburn Tower, which stands high on the ridge between the Orrin and Bonon river valleys. At the time at which the prophecy was made, the Mackenzie clan, presided over by a rich and powerful chieftain, was enjoying success and stability. Nevertheless, the seer made the now famous claim: 'The day will come when the Mackenzies of Fairburn shall lose their entire possessions; their castle will become uninhabited and a cow shall give birth in the uppermost chamber'.

Unthinkable as this may have seemed at the time, this prophecy has since been fulfilled to the letter. A few generations after the prediction was made, the family lost its power and wealth, and the tower was eventually abandoned, fell into disrepair and was taken over by a farmer, who used the upper floor for storing hay. One day, according to numerous eyewitness reports from 1851, a pregnant cow followed a trail of dropped hay up the precarious staircase to the upper level. Having become stuck, the cow gave birth to her calf right there on the top floor, just as the seer had predicted.

This was not the only fall from greatness accurately predicted by Coinneach Odhar, since he foretold the end of the male line of the Seaforth clan as a result of the premature deaths of all four sons. He also stated that all of the last lord's possessions would be 'inherited by a white-coiffed lassie from the east and she is to kill her sister'.

And so it happened that, upon the death of the last Lord Seaforth, the estate was passed to the eldest remaining daughter, Mary, who was

A sailing vessel on the Caledonian Canal, which was completed in 1887, 150 years after the seer's prediction.

married to Admiral Hood and lived in the East Indies for many years. Upon the admiral's death, Lady Hood returned to her family home wearing a white coif, a traditional Indian mourning garment. Some years later, she lost control of the pony carriage in which she and her sister were travelling, and her sister died.

Coinneach Odhar did not live to see the fulfilment of this prediction. Over the years, suspicion about the seer had grown, with his mysterious powers being linked with witchcraft and the dark arts. His fate was sealed when he told Countess Isabella Seaforth, wife of the third Earl of Seaforth, that her husband was having an affair with a Frenchwoman. This news apparently so enraged Isabella that she ordered that he be tried for witchcraft. At the end of his trial the Countess had claimed that, in view of his powers

of witchcraft, the seer's soul would not be fit for heaven. Upon hearing his sentence, the Brahan Seer had responded with one final prediction. He declared that upon his death, a dove and a raven would meet in the air above his ashes and would alight on them. If, he said, the raven alighted first, then the Countess would be correct. However, if the dove should alight first, then his soul would go to heaven, while hers would go to hell. He was found guilty and executed by being pitched into a barrel of burning tar. According to legend, the spectators were astonished when the two birds did appear above his ashes, and awestruck when the dove alighted first.

Many more of the Brahan Seer's predictions have since been proved accurate. Whatever his real identity, it would seem that he really did possess truly mysterious powers of prophecy.

THE UNKNOWN PROPHET

Early in the First World War came the discovery of a man who was remarkable for his powers of prophecy, making a series of astoundingly accurate predictions about events that would occur during and after both World Wars. Very little is known about this individual, other than that he was French, and he appeared to be a holy

man. Whoever he was, his unique gifts have baffled experts for many decades.

In 1914, two German soldiers captured a lone Frenchman in the Alsace region of France. They imprisoned and questioned him, and it was during this interrogation that the extraordinary predictions were made. One of the soldiers,

Adolf Hitler in 1941, addressing a crowd at a rally.

Andreas Rill, was so amazed by what he had heard that he wrote detailed accounts of the incident in letters to his family.

The unknown prophet predicted not only that the war was going to last for five years, but also that Germany would lose. There would then be a revolution, followed by a period of great prosperity in which, amazingly, money would be flung out of windows to lie untouched on the ground.

He said that, during this period, an Antichrist would be born, who would begin a nine-year reign of tyranny in 1932, passing new legislation and secretly impoverishing the people of Germany. Preparations for a second war, that would last three years, would commence in 1939, and this time Italy would be allied to Germany, rather than fighting against it as it had in the previous conflict. Despite this, however, Germany would again lose. The German people would then rise up against the tyrant and his followers, and 'the man and his sign would disappear'. In a year containing the numerals '4' and '5', Germany would be surrounded by its enemies and destroyed.

History proved the amazing veracity of these predictions. The First World War, in which Italy fought against Germany, did last five years, and Germany did lose. This was followed by inflation in which the German currency became so devalued as to be worthless.

Adolf Hitler's rise to power began during the 1920s, and in 1933 the National Socialist German Worker's (Nazi) Party commenced its oppressive reign, with Hitler at the helm. The Nazis then passed the Enabling Act, allowing

Hitler to pass any new law he so desired, thus effectively signalling the demise of democracy and the dawn of dictatorship.

Preparations for the start of what was to be the Second World War began, as predicted, in 1939 when Germany invaded Poland. This conflict lasted until 1945, when the Germans were surrounded and forced to surrender. Hitler committed suicide and the arrival of the Allies resulted in the end of the reign of the Nazi party.

Rill was amazed to watch history unfold in line with the prophet's statements and, as time went by, the letters to his family became famous for their contents. Indeed, at one point they almost resulted in Rill's internment in a concentration camp due to their predictions about the imminent rise of a dictator.

The letters then lay dormant during the turbulent years of the Second World War, surfacing only briefly in 1950 when they appeared in a mission journal, published by a Father Frumentius Renner. This publication passed almost unnoticed and no attempts were made to check the authenticity of the letters or establish the identity of the unknown prophet.

The letters then arrived at the Freiburg Institute for Border Areas of Psychology and Mental Hygiene. Here, the accuracy of their contents provoked such suspicion that forgery was suspected and the documents were subjected to extensive testing and scrutiny by a team of expert criminologists. The results proved that the letters were the genuine documents that Rill had sent home to his family back in 1914.

It was then decided to try to locate the mysterious seer, not an easy task as Rill had died.

Professors Hans Bender and Elber Gruber traced Rill's movements in an effort to establish the locality in which the man had been arrested. They conducted interviews with Rill's family, learning from his son that the visionary had apparently been a rich man who had given his wealth away so he could join a holy order. His son also remembered that his father had himself attempted to locate the nameless prophet in 1918, while posted in the town of Colmar. Upon arriving at the nearby monastery in Sogolsheim, he was reportedly told that the man had died.

The results of these interviews and their own painstaking detective work led the two professors to believe that this monastery had indeed been the last residence of the prophet.

After consulting monastery records, they established that he may have been Frater Laicus Tertiarius, who had died in 1917, not long before Rill's visit. This man seems to have stayed at the monastery as a guest rather than as a monk, which supports the theory that he had indeed been a rich man and consequently would have been barred from joining the brotherhood.

While it is true that this prophet did make some predictions that were not eventually realized, this may have been the fault of inaccurate recollection of the details by Rill, or even to linguistic errors on the part of the Frenchman while speaking German.

Overall, the accuracy of his predictions is astonishing, especially since they concerned events that would only take place decades after his death.

How this anonymous seer achieved his prophetic visions is a mystery, and can only be attributed to the incredible powers of foresight.

TITANIC PREDICTIONS

The sinking of RMS *Titanic* is such a dramatic story that it is still being told today, all over the world. Most people are aware of the main causes of the tragedy – the freak iceberg and the shortage of lifeboats – but very few realize that, fourteen years prior to the accident, a book was published that set out almost the exact details of the entire incident.

The Wreck of the Titan, or *Futility*, written by a little known author, Morgan Robertson, was printed in 1898. Receiving little attention, the book tells the story of a 70,000 tonne 'unsinkable' ocean liner named the SS *Titan*, which hit an iceberg on its fourth voyage across the Atlantic. The ship, bearing a number of wealthy and powerful dignitaries, was equipped with fewer than half the necessary lifeboats, and consequently more than two-thirds of the 2,500 passengers on board perished in icy waters when the liner sank.

The parallels with the true story of the RMS *Titanic* are immediately apparent. Moreover, there are further, uncanny, similarities between the fictitious and real vessels, in details such as the weight of the ship, the nationality of the principal shareholders involved, the time of the impact and the number of lifeboats on board.

Incredibly, this was not the only time that a prediction was made about the fate of the *Titanic*. A few years prior to the publication of *The Wreck of the Titan*, a similar story had appeared in a newspaper article. A prophetic note by the editor at the end of the piece warned that 'this is exactly what might take place, and what will take place, if liners are sent to sea short of boats'.

In a chilling irony, this editor was one of the very passengers who perished when the RMS *Titanic* sank beneath the waves twenty years later.

Could this really be merely a cruel twist of fate, or was some higher power at work?

The GREATEST WRECK in HISTORY
THE LOSS OF THE WHITE STAR TITANIC
THE LARGEST SHIP IN THE WORLD, WHICH SANK ON ITS MAIDEN VOYAGE WITH A LOSS OF 1635 LIVES

An article from 1912, depicting lifeboats being lowered after RMS *Titanic* struck an iceberg.

THE HITLER HOROSCOPES

Countless history books have recorded, analysed and discussed the events that occurred before, during and after the Second World War, but, of these, few mention the significant part that astrology and prophecy played in determining the course of history. It is now known that both Stalin and Hitler frequently consulted seers and mind readers, even though, officially, they had forbidden the employment of such mysterious powers. In Nazi Germany, in particular, occultists suffered harassment and persecution, in common with all other minority groups.

Prior to the outbreak of war, a prophet and astrologer, Karl Ernest Krafft, was gaining great respect in Germany among his contemporaries. Born in Basle in 1900, Krafft was highly numerate, especially in the field of statistics, and was also passionate about astrology. However, it was the publication of his book, *Traits of Astro-Biology*, that was to raise him to such an extent in the estimation of fellow prophets and occultists. In this work, Krafft expounded his theory on predicting the future, which he termed 'typoscomy'. Essentially, this maintained that a person's destiny could be predicted on the basis of his or her personality.

When the war commenced, Krafft's privileged position was placed in peril. However, his life changed dramatically when a remarkably accurate prediction about Hitler brought him face to face with leading members of the Führer's command. Krafft foresaw that Hitler's life would be in peril at some point between 7 and 10 November 1939. In fact, he was so sure of this that on 2 November of that year he wrote to Dr Heinrich Fesel, a close acquaintance of Himmler, warning him of Hitler's impending fate. Fesel, not wanting to be associated with the prophet, filed the letter away without mentioning it to Himmler.

Essentially, typoscomy maintained that a person's destiny could be predicted on the basis of his or her personality.

On 8 November a bomb exploded in the Munich beer hall just 27 minutes after Hitler had left the building. When the story became known, Fesel immediately supposed that Krafft must have been involved in the plot to kill the

Führer, and so gave the letter to Hitler's right-hand man, Rudolf Hess.

Krafft was immediately arrested by the Gestapo, but they found him innocent of conspiring to kill Hitler. At this point, word of Krafft's remarkable powers reached the ears of Josef Goebbels, head of the Ministry for Propaganda, who had recently become fascinated with the works of Nostradamus. Goebbels ordered that Krafft be employed to decipher Nostradamus' complex quatrains and extract any references which could be inferred as good omens for the Third Reich and which could be used for propaganda purposes.

Then, in 1940, Krafft was called to give a horoscope reading for Hitler. In this, he advised that a planned attack on the USSR be postponed until a later date. In spite of the fact that he had not actually met Krafft personally, Hitler followed his recommendation and waited until the following June before launching Operation Barbarossa. The success of the attack on the USSR in the early days of the offensive seemed to prove Krafft's prediction to be correct, although this ultimately proved unsustained.

Krafft then insisted that it was imperative that Germany secured victory by 1943 at the latest, or else the war would be lost. Although history was to reveal the accuracy of this prophecy, the result for Krafft was that he was imprisoned. Hitler was enraged by his prediction, and cited it as the reason for the sudden defection of Hess in 1941. As a result, all occultists and astrologers were rounded up and put in prison.

Upon his release in 1942, Krafft was ordered to study the horoscopes of Allied leaders in order to

The wreckage of the Munich beer hall, following the explosion on 8 November 1939.

provide his leaders with vital information about the enemy. Among his many readings was his divination that Montgomery would prove a stronger enemy than Rommel, an insight which proved to be correct.

His final, accurate, premonition – that a bomb would destroy the propaganda ministry in Berlin – resulted in Krafft being tried for treason. After languishing in prison for several years, he eventually contracted typhus and died in 1945.

The remarkable accuracy with which Krafft made his predictions seems undoubted proof of his oracular powers. In fact, Krafft's abilities so impressed the Allies that they attempted to find a seer of comparable skill to assist them in much the same way as Krafft had helped the Nazis. The fact that they were unable to do so demonstrates how rare and precious Krafft's talent really was.

THE SANGOMA

Deep in the heart of southern Africa there lives a tradition of healing and divination that is integral to African culture, and is as respected today as it was thousands of years ago. The extraordinary powers of Sangomas, or diviner priests, are a revered alternative to more modern medicine, and their predictions are remarkable in their accuracy. It is estimated that around 200,000 such diviners are practising today, helping more than 84 per cent of the southern African population.

It is believed that the ancestors are messengers from the higher power.

The role of the Sangoma varies and can be divided into two primary categories, although these are by no means rigid. The principal kind of Sangoma is the ancestrally designated diviner who communes with the ancestors, usually by entering a trance, to predict the future. The second type of Sangoma is the herbalist or doctor, who uses traditional methods to cure the sick and has not been called by the ancestors. However, these boundaries are often blurred, as the ancestrally designated diviner is often also a herbalist, consulting the ancestors for guidance on treatments and cures.

Novices (*thwasas*) begin their training by enduring and surviving an 'initiation illness' (*ukuthwasa*). This signals that the ancestors, or deceased spirits, have called them to their vocation. The relationship between the novice and the ancestors is forged during the recovery from the illness, and the person assumes a new identity and role in life.

The ancestral link is crucial to the cures and readings that will be made by the Sangoma, as it is believed that the ancestors are the messengers from the higher power, or 'Supreme Being', acting as a link between deity and man. The Sangoma, in turn, provides a mouthpiece for the oracles, and carries out their instructions, in much the same way as the sybils of Roman times delivered prophecies from Apollo.

The deliverance of these oracles fulfils a major social and political function, as the prophecies provide an acceptable arena for debate about issues that may otherwise be taboo. Predictions are made on subjects ranging from the state of the crops and the weather to personal problems and health issues. Sangomas maintain that illness can be attributed to one of three main causes — the ancestors, witchcraft and 'pollution' (for example, menstruation or miscarriage). Once the root of the problem has been established, the process of healing can begin.

The trance state entered by the diviner is usually central to the process of delivering the oracle. This condition is achieved through a wide variety of ritualistic methods, including rhythmic drumming, clapping and dancing, the inhalation of herbal medicines (*muti*) such as snuff, and the burning of incense (*indumba*). The attire of the Sangoma is also very important, and he will often wear elaborate ostrich feather headdresses, and tie rattles and beads to his body.

Upon entering the trance, the Sangoma often starts to shake, and his breathing becomes more erratic. The rhythmic rituals result in hyperstimulation of the body, while the irregular breathing brings on hyperventilation, both of which are said to 'open' the body and mind to allow access to the ancestors. The men then use 'bones' (shells, coins, dice and twigs) as part of the divination ritual, which are thrown onto an impala skin. The position and alignment of the scattered objects are then interpreted, providing the Sangoma with the information required to deliver the oracle or to cure the patient.

The predictions provided by these revered men have become such a part of everyday life in these regions that their magical elements tend to be overlooked. In Western culture, however, the repeated fulfilment of the Sangomas' prophetic pronouncements and incredible cures continues to baffle and astound.

A potential customer examines a Sangoma's wares, which include bones and herbs.

Paranormal Powers

Within human society there are groups of people whose remarkable talents and abilities set them apart from the crowd. This is because they are able to break the rules that bind the rest of us — sometimes crossing the divide between the worlds of the living and the dead, or transcending physical constraints through their healing powers. Various terms are used to describe these people, such as mediums, psychics, telekinetics, or healers and there are innumerable examples of the amazing feats that they have achieved throughout history.

MADAME BLAVATSKY

Madame Helena Petrona Blavatsky was a figure as controversial as she is remarkable, and her writings, views and predictions arouse heated debate and astonishment even today. To many she is considered a powerful psychic, a cultural messenger and even a prophet. As with all controversial figures in history there are those who attempt to debunk her incredible achievements and abilities, but when faced with the evidence, it is particularly hard not to believe that she was genuinely psychic. During her lifetime a wealth of literature by her and about her was created, and she brought about a revolution in Victorian spiritual thinking that affects us all today.

She brought about a revolution in Victorian spiritual thinking...

Madame Blavatsky was born in 1831 to a family of aristocrats in Dnepropetrovsk, Ukraine, although she spent most of the rest of her life travelling. The staff and servants of her family home later recalled how unusual she was as a child and how they credited her with possessing powers spoken of in their ancient rustic superstitions. She was reported to be a strange and troubled child, prone to sleepwalking, fits and headaches, all of which are common symptoms amongst those who have experienced visions or otherworldly communications.

By the age of 18 Blavatsky was married to a man much her senior, but she quickly grew tired of him and embarked on a life of adventure and travel, leaving her family and country behind. There are numerous versions of Blavatsky's life story, especially concerning the less documented part of her early years. In this time she was alleged to have borne an illegitimate child and to have been the mistress of numerous men. However, despite this behaviour, which was utterly scandalous for the era she lived in, Blavatsky still achieved great fame and respect in society.

Blavatsky spent most of her sixty-year life travelling over huge expanses of the globe, studiously absorbing the culture and spiritual thinking of various different sections of humanity. Among the countries she visited were lands as diverse as Canada, Mexico, the West Indies, the USA, Japan, Egypt, Tibet and India.

Many of the skills she acquired while on this enlightening world tour were to have a bearing on her later life. She worked at one point with a circus and at another as an assistant to a medium who performed seances. However, it was her work alongside Eastern spiritualists that she claimed was the most influential force in her life.

Blavatsky told of how she spent several years in both Tibet and India, studying as the student of great spiritual masters. She claimed that several 'mahatmas' took her into their trust, and that she became their apprentice. Her unique abilities were recognized by these great mystics and she was granted unprecedented access to ancient mystical secrets reserved only for the initiated.

These Eastern travels were a crucially important aspect of Madame Blavatsky's life and have left us a legacy of knowledge even today. She stated that it was here that she acquired the most important knowledge of her life. With this spiritual learning as her base, she introduced the first real taste of the wisdom and understanding of Eastern religions to the Western world, in particular ideas of karma, reincarnation and the hidden higher powers of the mind.

On her eventual return to the West after her spiritual apprenticeship, Blavatsky propounded the idea of reincarnation – a concept that was totally alien to Western Judeo-Christian spiritual thinking. She explained how she believed in the spiritual journey of the soul through many different bodies on the road towards perfection. She did not believe in humans reincarnating as animals, but rather that the human soul slowly evolves, improving itself until it can gain extraordinary superhuman powers.

She maintained that a small number of these highly evolved superhuman beings existed in Tibet and India and that they were guiding the fate of the world. The mythical Tibetan paradise of Shambala is said to be inhabited by these luminous superhuman beings who have attained greatness after many reincarnated lifetimes.

Madame Blavatsky in pensive mood.

Blavatsky stated that they were the sole possessors of the hidden 'ancient wisdom' that originated from highly advanced human civilizations of the past.

The nature of what she described endorses certain aspects of Tibetan and Hindu philosophy. Both Tibetan monks and Indian yogis attempt to reach a higher state of consciousness through dedicated training and the application of their minds through meditation. Many such monks and yogis are capable of extraordinary superhuman feats as a result of the mystical power they have cultivated within themselves.

Blavatsky was later to crystallize her view of this Eastern spiritual thinking, and combine it with her own sense of mysticism, into a system called the 'Theosophical Movement', which she founded with a number of her followers in 1875. The teachings of this movement are still adhered to by a number of people around the world today. According to Blavatsky herself: 'The chief aim of the … Theosophical society [was] to reconcile all world religions, sects and nations under a common system of ethics, based on eternal verities'.

In some of her demonstrations she was said to have materialized objects such as a cup and saucer.

Blavatsky's aim was unity. It seems that she was seized with a kind of moral fervour, recognizing the inherent wisdom of this ancient and peaceful school of thinking. She realized that for any change to come about in wider society she must publicize this wisdom as much as possible. There is no doubt that this mission benefited greatly from all the publicity she received from her psychic displays.

In some of her demonstrations she was said to have materialized objects such as a cup and saucer. On other occasions she produced written words that were said to originate from the spirit world. The nature of her displays would vary hugely, demonstrating her array of skills and powers. Blavatsky claimed to be able to communicate with her distant Eastern masters by a kind of spiritual telepathy. At one stage she explained how she had seen visions of a tall Hindu who actually materialized before her in Hyde Park, and then became her personal guru and teacher.

Some of this has been dismissed by the sceptical as trickery and stage-play, especially as she may have learnt various 'magic' tricks from the performers she worked with. However there is plenty of other evidence of her abilities that is not quite so easy to dismiss. For instance, her writings contained new explanations of world history that differed massively from the accepted view, and predictions for the future that appear to have the essence of truth within them. Despite seeming outlandish at the time, many of her assertions have been proved true.

Blavatsky explained to her Victorian audience that much of the 'ancient wisdom' professed by her Eastern teachers actually originated from the great lost civilizations of the past, such as Atlantis. She first mentioned the lost city of Atlantis in her 1877 book *Isis Unveiled*, which sold out on the day of its publication. In the decade following this, the mystery concerning Atlantis became the talk of the Victorian world, with other authors and thinkers such as Ignatius Donnelly approaching the subject with intense intellectual curiosity. Even today there are scientists and explorers searching for traces of this mysterious lost culture.

In 1888 Blavatsky went into even greater detail in her next book *The Secret Doctrine*. In this book she displays a thorough knowledge of the deep-sea floor, describing details which were far beyond the known science of her day. Notably she asserted that the recently discovered mid-Atlantic ridge continued under Africa and into the Indian Ocean. This has since been proved true, as the ridge is the boundary of a tectonic plate. What makes this so remarkable is that the Victorians had no idea of plate tectonics, and no means of verifying what she said.

Although this information may seem unrelated to her other teachings on theosophy, it is actually tied in completely with her general world view. All that Blavatsky had learned from her masters in India and Tibet was from a store of lost knowledge she referred to as the 'great ancient secrets', which had originated from lost civilizations such as Atlantis (see page 272) or Lemuria, and had been guarded for millennia. Only the initiated were allowed access to this knowledge. Blavatsky claimed that the philosopher Plato himself was an initiate of this secret advanced brethren, which is how he knew about the existence of Atlantis.

Blavatsky's prophecies of events that will befall our own culture make chilling reading. She predicted that there will be: 'a world destruction as happened to Atlantis 11,000 years ago … instead of Atlantis all of England and parts of [the] NW European coast will sink into the sea, in contrast, the sunken Azores region, the Isle of Poseidonis, will again be raised from the sea'.

When predictions of doom come from a character as peculiarly convincing as Madame Blavatsky they cannot be ignored. What is more, scientific revelations and discoveries in the fields of climatology and meteorology have revealed the possibility that she may be right. At present the global climate is warming more rapidly than at any point in history. If this causes the polar ice caps to melt completely it could cause global sea levels to rise by several metres and low-lying areas of land, such as England or Holland, would be inundated, fulfilling the prophecy.

Blavatsky's predictions for the Azores also have definite potential to be fulfilled. The Azores is a particularly active geological area, with plenty of volcanic and tectonic activity. Although we still cannot say that Blavatsky is correct, she managed to pick one of the places in the world where the land is most likely to rise from the sea.

When individuals possess knowledge that is in advance of the science of the day, inevitably questions are posed about its origins. It becomes even more intriguing if they claim that this knowledge originates from a time before civilization is even believed to have existed.

She predicted that there will be 'a world-destruction as happened to Atlantis 11,000 years ago …

There is much about Madame Blavatsky's life and achievements that it seems impossible to explain fully. Yet there is the unmistakable ring of truth in much of what she said. The peaceful pursuit of meditation and spiritual advancement in Tibet still amazes many in the West, just as it did the audiences of Madame Blavatsky in the 1800s. Scientific predictions for the future seem to concur with some of her more doom-laden prophecies, and many of her assertions were proved true after her death, leaving us to wonder how she came to know such details. Lack of a better explanation means we must accept that she possessed these 'ancient secrets', and that she was one of the most amazing and mysterious characters in recent history.

R. J. LEES

While the horrific murders of Jack the Ripper were bloodying the neighbourhood of Whitechapel, Victorian London was paralysed with fear. The police force was under intense pressure to arrest the perpetrator and bring him to justice, but they had very few clues to go on. One man believed he held the key to the gruesome outrages. The age of the 'psychic sleuth' had dawned.

In this case, it was an unexpected 'psychic detective' that put himself forward to aid police in their investigations. Robert James Lees was born in 1849 in Leicestershire, England. He was a discreet and devout man, not at all the type to seek the limelight or newspaper headlines. In many ways he was the last person to seek the kind of controversy that is attached to serial killers. Yet his conviction about the existence of a powerful spiritual world never wavered, and was closely linked to his intense religious beliefs.

Debate about the Ripper killings still rages today. What is known for sure is that a killer stalked the deprived back streets of east London, securing the services of prostitutes and then butchering them. His crimes were typified by his cut-throat methods and the horrific practice of disembowelling his victims, often decorating the vicinity with inner organs. Five deaths were put down to the Ripper, although there may have

been more. (One killing that took place in New York has even been attributed to him.)

His confirmed victims were Mary Ann Nichols, Annie Chapman, Elizabeth Stride, Catherine Eddowes and Mary Jane Kelly, who were all killed between 31 August and 9 November 1888. Stride and Eddowes were killed on the same night, an occasion that became known as the 'double event'.

The police were baffled by the murders. Lacking the scientific know-how that we use today in criminal investigations, they were nevertheless subject to fierce scrutiny by the press, and under real pressure to solve the case. A sense of melodrama surrounded the manhunt, as the perpetrator stole away from the scenes of carnage like a phantom. Later, he apparently went so far as to send taunting letters and body parts to the police.

The facts surrounding Lees' involvement in the Ripper case are by no means certain. It seems that one day, soon after the 'double event', Lees had a sudden vision whilst travelling with his wife on a London bus. He became sure that one of the other passengers was the Ripper himself. Despite his wife's desperate objections, Lees followed the man and made a note of his address.

When he took his information to the police, he was greeted with derision. In October 1888 he wrote the following in his diary: 'offered services to police to follow up East End murders, called a fool and a lunatic.' The police refused to listen to him until he apparently quoted the contents of one of the letters sent in the name of the Ripper. There was, of course, no way that he could have

Robert James Lees was a studious and devout character, not at all the type to seek the limelight by claiming to have identified Jack the Ripper.

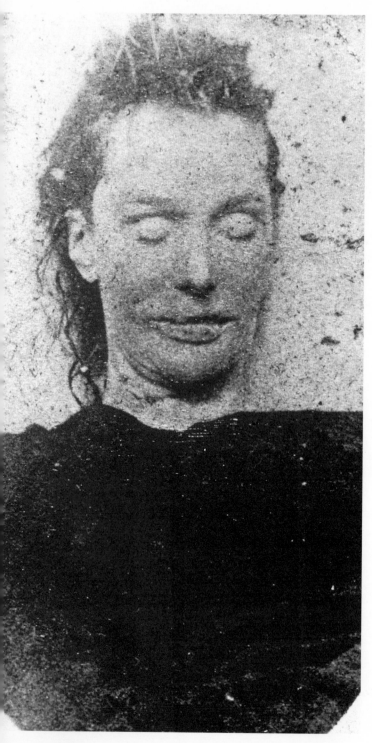

known what was in the communication, and the police began to take note. They already knew that the address pinpointed by Lees, 74 Brook Street, belonged to an eminent doctor, Sir William Withey Gull. The respected professional seemed at first to be beyond suspicion. Yet Dr Gull's wife told the police that recently he had been subject to violent rages and had even disappeared at the time when the notorious murders were taking place.

It emerged that the doctor was already ill, and he progressed to an asylum where he later died. Following his incarceration the murders halted.

It is this explanation that has earned Lees the reputation of being the man who captured the Ripper. But although the killer clearly had some anatomical interest or knowledge that might link him to the medical profession, there is actually scant evidence to endorse the tale. Lees barely spoke about the incident. Nor did he include details of the experience in his copious diaries, although it was highly sensitive information and he may have omitted it as a matter of discretion. Much later Lees' daughter revealed that her father had known something of the Ripper case, but she would say no more than that. Observers have both verified and denounced the story of the psychic vision on the bus, and ultimately the police refused to give him official credit for solving the case.

So why was there so much doubt about the outcome of the case? In the year preceding the murders, Dr Gull had suffered a stroke.

Jack the Ripper victim Elizabeth Stride, photographed after her death in September 1888. Unlike the other victims, Stride had not been mutilated, and her only wound was her slit throat.

Although it left him in a weakened physical state, one supposition is that the stroke might have altered the balance of his mind, perhaps rendering him capable of heinous acts. However, there is another, even more sensational theory. Gull was a loyal royal physician and there has been considerable speculation that the killer was royalty, specifically Prince Albert Victor, Duke of Clarence. He was son of the Prince of Wales, grandson to Queen Victoria. He was a self-indulgent, wayward young man, and certainly bisexual. Could it be that the prince himself was the real Ripper, and Gull's obvious anxiety was caused by the duty of protection he felt towards him?

Of course, Dr Gull and the Duke of Clarence were not the only two suspects in the case. Barrister Montague John Druitt was in the frame, especially since he committed suicide shortly after the final Ripper murder. However, there was nothing to suggest that he had the medical know-how to carve up the corpses.

Aaron Kosminski, a Polish Jew who lived in Whitechapel, was also of interest to the police. They noted that the killings stopped when he was committed to an asylum, where he died in 1919. Being poor and Jewish, Kosminski would have been a convenient scapegoat.

The case against two other doctors has been examined. Dr Francis Tumblety, who collected women's uteruses in jars, fled to America where he was popularly believed to be the Ripper. He died of old age in 1923. Dr Thomas Neil Cream had been convicted for two other killings, and implicated himself as he stood on the gallows with the noose around his neck. As the trap doors opened he cried: 'I am Jack the…!' However, he failed to finish the sentence and is widely believed to have been (belatedly) playing for time. Crime writer Patricia Cornwell strongly believes that the artist Walter Sickert was the Ripper, not least for his offensively detailed pictures of mutilated prostitutes. Yet others theorize about a Masonic link.

He was a self-indulgent, wayward young man, and certainly bisexual.

So what became of Robert Lees? Quite apart from the furore surrounding the Ripper case, he was a well-respected spiritualist in an age when mediums were often exposed as fraudulent. He is even believed to have held seances with Queen Victoria so that she could contact her late and beloved husband Prince Albert. There are claims that he helped police identify the Fenians, an Irish patriotic group who were plotting to blow up the Houses of Parliament.

As a healer, he is credited with curing Leona Petherbridge of South Devon, who was suffering from a mental affliction linked to an eating disorder. The case was widely reported, and his reputation spread.

Perhaps Lees' most remarkable psychic feat was a trilogy of books revealing the secrets of life after death. Bizarrely, Lees claimed no literary credit for these books, which he claimed were dictated to him over years by 'Fred' in the next world. When he died in 1931, Lees was a psychic of great reputation, but he left behind many secrets and remains a fascinating enigma to this day.

RASPUTIN

The story of Rasputin is a remarkable one, with the events of his life exceeded in peculiarity only by the truly inexplicable circumstances of his death. During his time he was a healer and self-proclaimed holy man, as well as the most unlikely of statesmen, enjoying incredible influence over the rulers of Russia. The reason for his achievements is still not fully understood, but the most likely explanation seems to be that his powers lay within the realms of the paranormal.

The real name of the man who came to be known as Rasputin (the word means 'debauched' in Russian) was Grigory Yefimovich Novykh. Born in 1865 into a typical Siberian peasant family, he could never have envisaged, in his early years, how much he would go on to accomplish in his life. When he was about 18, Rasputin underwent a religious experience and decided to enter the monastery at Verkhoture, where he stayed for some months. Despite his famous soubriquet of 'the mad monk', however, Rasputin never actually became a genuine monk, perhaps because he was illiterate and unable to read the scriptures for himself.

While at this monastery, Rasputin became familiar with the Khlysty religious sect – which mixed its own brand of mysticism with a degree of sexual hedonism not often found in the Church, and which had actually been banned in Russia on heretical grounds. In spite of the fact that he was married, Rasputin launched himself into this world of fornication with considerable enthusiasm, even holding orgies in the marital home. At this time he was beginning to be aware that he might possess some unusual powers, and believed that these could be directly attributed to his sexual indulgences – for this reason he took part in these excesses at every opportunity.

Rasputin went on to father three children by his wife, and probably many more by other women. Yet a family was not enough to keep Rasputin in one place and he wandered far and wide, slowly gathering a reputation as a healer and clairvoyant. He had developed an unusual ability to cure ailments without even having to make a diagnosis, almost as if he detected the nature of the problem through psychic means alone. He travelled as far as Mount Athos, in Greece, and Jerusalem, where he demonstrated his skills to the religious dignitaries, to great acclaim. And so he established his reputation as a 'staretz' (the term for a self-proclaimed holy man and faith healer). Rasputin was not the first illiterate man devoid of formal religious training to follow this path, but he was remarkable in the level of the success he enjoyed – which was probably the result of the force of his personality and the incredible results he achieved. Needy people would travel great distances to meet him, rewarding him for his services with gifts or money.

After some time spent travelling, Rasputin returned to his family village where his fame had spread far across the region. It was here that he experienced the vision that was to alter not only the course of his own life, but arguably would have an enormous influence on the history of the whole world. While working in the fields one day, Rasputin apparently saw an apparition of the Holy Mother, who spoke to him and said it was his duty to help to save the life of the young Tsarevich (the prince) Alexis.

The Tsarevich was suffering from haemophilia, which can cause fatal bleeding from even a small cut, as it prevents the blood from clotting. This hereditary disorder – common among the European royal families because of their history of intermarriage – had no known cure, and the Tsarevich was in very grave medical danger.

Rasputin travelled to St Petersburg to carry out this mission, although it was to be a while before his influence was felt. By this time, Rasputin had come to the attention of the nobility, some of whom recognized him as a man of God and a person of considerable and inexplicable personal power. Others, however, despised him for his lewd conduct, and considered his claim to be a holy man as nothing short of scandalous.

Rasputin lived in St Petersburg for two years before he came to meet the royal Romanov family. He had by now become famous for his lechery, and was extremely popular with Russian noblewomen, with whom he enjoyed many scandalous liaisons. Nonetheless, his success as a powerful religious healer became known to the

Rasputin as he appeared in 1910.

Tsar and the Tsarina, and in 1906 they summoned him to see them, hoping that he might be able to cure their sickly son. They had to take Rasputin into their personal confidence, for the Tsarevich's illness was shrouded in secrecy because it might have threatened the prince's right to succession if it ever became known to the public.

The decision by the Tsar and his wife to invite Rasputin into their lives cannot have been taken lightly, but was to prove fruitful. Through methods impossible to understand, Rasputin appears to have successfully brought to a halt the bleeding of the Tsarevich. This amazing feat rendered him indispensable to the royal family and it would eventually make Rasputin one of the most powerful men in Russia. On leaving the palace after healing the young prince, Rasputin gave one of his famous predictions. He warned that the destiny of the Romanov family was irrevocably linked to that of his own, a prophecy that, with hindsight, turned out to be perfectly correct.

The Tsarina Alexandra grew increasingly close to Rasputin, feeling indebted to him for the

The extent of Rasputin's personal power within Russia was to reach its peak in the years before the First World War.

service he had performed in healing her young son. She was convinced that his power was a gift from God, and that he had been sent in answer to her prayers. This seems to have been corroborated by Rasputin's own account of his vision. Meanwhile, Rasputin's affiliation with the royal family was causing his influence within the church to grow. After a while, he came to enjoy such power that he was able to replace those who were against him with his own supporters, gradually eroding his opposition.

Yet Rasputin's support was far from universal. The predilection for alcohol and sexual deviancy that had earned him the name 'Rasputin' had also earned him enemies, since many Church members and noblemen were absolutely appalled by his behaviour. They were also very concerned about the growing influence exerted by Rasputin over the Tsarina, and the rumours that the pair had become lovers – as was Tsar Nicholas himself.

Yet the Tsarina would hear nothing against Rasputin. As far as she was concerned, he was just an illiterate peasant who had succeeded where everyone else, royal doctors, holy men and healers alike, had failed. Little is known about exactly how Rasputin healed the sick child, although many have surmised that it may have been through a form of hypnosis.

The extent of Rasputin's personal power within Russia was to reach its peak in the years before the First World War, and from 1911 onwards he was permitted to appoint his own ministers within the Imperial government. At this time, the Romanov family was becoming dangerously detached from the Russian people, and was shielded by the nobility from the pre-revolutionary feeling that was brewing in the country.

In 1915 Tsar Nicholas took personal control of the Russian armed forces that were fighting in the First World War. Tsarina Alexandra was left in sole command of the country and she immediately appointed Rasputin as her personal advisor. This made Rasputin the effective leader of Russia, an incredible feat for a man who was born a Siberian peasant. Could this have been due simply to the magnetism of his personality, or was Rasputin in possession of psychic powers that enabled him to rise to power in this way?

The evidence certainly seems to suggest that Rasputin had powers that were well beyond the abilities of most people. In addition to his well-documented and proven healing ability, there is evidence of his remarkably accurate predictions for the future. He even managed to successfully foresee his own murder, although he was unable to prevent it.

A group of disaffected aristocrats who deeply resented the power that Rasputin had acquired were intent on killing him and returning power to the nobility. The group of conspirators was led by Prince Felix Yossupov, who invited Rasputin to his home under the pretext of meeting his wife Irina, a woman famed for her beauty. Rasputin accepted the invitation and travelled to the palatial home of the prince, where he was warmly received. The conspirators planned to poison Rasputin with cyanide, which they concealed in some cakes and Madeira wine. Cyanide is one of the deadliest substances known to mankind, and its effects are almost instantaneous. However, these men soon discovered that the extent of Rasputin's powers was greater than anyone could have imagined.

Prince Felix engaged Rasputin in conversation, and persuaded him to try some of the cakes. Although Rasputin's preference was for wine, out of politeness he ate a couple, washing them down with a good measure of Madeira. The prince watched in amazement as Rasputin appeared to shrug off the effects of enough poison to kill six men. At this point, the prince withdrew temporarily to confer with his fellow conspirators who were all mystified by Rasputin's apparent resistance to poison. Prince Felix was then presented with a pistol, and told to shoot his unsuspecting guest, whereupon he returned and shot Rasputin in the chest from point-blank range.

Believing Rasputin to be dead, the conspirators gathered over his body to observe their handiwork. At this point, Rasputin is said to have been roused from apparent death and forcefully grabbed hold of them. The men had to beat and stab him in order to free themselves. Amazingly, Rasputin is said to have pushed them off and attempted an escape. He was then shot a second time before being bound with ropes. To be sure they had killed him this time, the assassins then dragged him to the icy Neva river and threw him in.

> The prince watched in amazement as Rasputin appeared to shrug off the effects of enough poison to kill six men.

The Tsarina was distraught by the loss of Rasputin and she demanded that a search be carried out. When his body was recovered, an autopsy was performed, which established that the cause of his death had been drowning. However, it appeared that, remarkably, he had managed to break his bonds and so, no doubt, had come very close to escaping from the river.

This kind of resilience seems beyond human comprehension. Rasputin was poisoned, shot, beaten, stabbed and drowned. Any one of these acts would have been enough to cause the death of a normal man. Surely this was irrefutable evidence of Rasputin's mysterious powers?

To further add to the intrigue and provide yet more proof of Rasputin's extraordinary abilities, it was discovered that he had predicted his own demise in a letter to the Tsarina, a communication that also contained a dire prophecy for the Romanov family.

In the letter, dated 7 December 1916, Rasputin stated that he did not expect to live to see the

New Year, a prediction that proved to be correct, for he was murdered only nine days later. The letter also specified that, should he be killed by a common man, then the family of the Tsar would survive, but – chillingly – should he die at the hands of a nobleman, the Tsar's family would all be dead within two years and, furthermore, that no nobleman would live in Russia for at least twenty-five years.

Only a few months after the death of Rasputin, the Bolshevik revolutionary forces overthrew the Romanov family and the entire system of Russian nobility. Within less than two years, the entire royal family had been assembled and killed, providing absolute and bloody proof that

Rasputin's last prediction had come true. The Bolsheviks also desecrated Rasputin's grave and burned his corpse, such was the strength of feeling he had generated in the country.

Although Rasputin is now famous only for his association with the Tsar and Tsarina, it should be remembered that he achieved that position as a result of his great success as a healer. What lay at the root of his amazing powers is still unclear – Rasputin himself claimed that his abilities were religious in origin, but his personal conduct would seem to suggest that they were simply an innate gift of his own. Whatever the explanation, this colourful Russian figure looks set to remain a source of intrigue for the foreseeable future.

Tsar Nicholas II, his wife Tsarina Alexandra and their haemophiliac son, the Tsarevich Alexis.

JEAN DIXON

Jean Dixon was a psychic, clairvoyant and astrologer who, during the course of her life, made a large number of predictions, with varying degrees of accuracy. One prophecy about which she was entirely correct, however, was her foretelling in 1956 of the assassination of President Kennedy, several years before it actually happened. It was only after this event that the world really started to pay attention to her remarkable psychic abilities.

Dixon was born in 1918 and, long before her famous prediction, had been working in the realms of the paranormal, using her powers to prophesy world events. She would foretell the future by means of dreams, in which spirit helpers would impart information to her. This method of prophecy is not uncommon, having been shared by a number of psychics over the years, but it is not the most reliable means of predicting the future as there can be confusion over the interpretation of certain visions.

Dixon's prediction of the Kennedy assassination was, indeed, initially vague – in fact, she did not at first actually name Kennedy as the victim. However, in subsequent predictions, she added more details: she foretold that a Democrat (which Kennedy was) would win the election and that Kennedy would either be assassinated or would die in office. Moreover, she backed up these predictions with a timescale that also proved to be correct.

Although Dixon is best known for her pronouncement on the Kennedy assassination, this was not the only event that she accurately foresaw. She also predicted other notable historic happenings, such as the Soviet Sputnik launch in 1957 and the Apollo rocket disaster that killed several American astronauts in 1967. In addition, she foretold that in the spring of 1989 the world

Jean Dixon in Miami, 1976.

President John F. Kennedy and his wife in the motorcade, moments before his assassination.

would witness a shipping accident – and the Exxon Valdez oil disaster did occur at this time.

Some of Dixon's other prophecies were not quite so accurate. She wrongly predicted, in line with early thinking, that the Soviets would land on the moon before the USA, but of course the reverse happened. She also mistakenly foresaw an apocalyptic 1980s, in which a devastating meteor would strike the earth.

Occasionally, Dixon made a prediction that came very close to being reality, such as her prophecy that a third world war would commence in 1958. Although such a conflict did not actually take place, this period of our history was overshadowed to a large degree by the imminent threat of nuclear war.

Dixon also told of a plague that looked likely to descend on the USA during the late 1970s – while this was of course inaccurate, some have suggested that she may have been catching a future glimpse of the arrival of AIDS in the Western world and its devastating effects on public health.

Many have wondered whether it is possible to credit Jean Dixon with psychic abilities when the verity of her predictions has varied so much over time. Her advocates would argue that the future does not actually run along a set course, but is flexible, and that there are numerous possible realities. Dixon, they maintain, simply presents us with one of these potential scenarios. If this is the case, then it would certainly go some way towards explaining how she was so very nearly correct in her predictions of a third world war.

It is certain that debate will always surround figures such as Dixon, because of the inexplicable nature of their amazing powers. Believers will see patterns of truth in the psychic's predictions, while sceptics will continually point out their inaccuracies or ambiguities.

As long as mankind exists, there will be a desire to know the future before it actually happens, and it seems that certain special people, of whom Jean Dixon is one, will be able to divine these truths, defying the very laws of time in order to do so.

EILEEN GARRETT

Eileen Garrett was one of the most respected mediums of the twentieth century, who possessed remarkable psychic abilities. In one particular seance, she astounded those present – and made headlines around the country – with her uncannily accurate observations. Garrett is also renowned for the assistance she gave to the scientific community in the investigation and explanation of paranormal powers.

Born in 1893 in Beauparc, County Meath, Ireland, Garrett's early years were troubled, as is often the case among those with psychic abilities. Shortly after she was born both her parents committed suicide, leaving the infant Eileen to be adopted and raised by her aunt and uncle. Her gifts became apparent from a very young age. Not only was she able to see auras of light and energy around living things during her childhood, but she also had a large number of imaginary playmates, who took on a very physical appearance to her.

It seems that at this time Garrett was also visited by visions of the dead. She later described the first of these occasions, in which she observed one of her aunts, who lived some distance away, walking up the pathway towards her house with a baby in her arms. The aunt told her that she had to go away and that she was taking the infant with her. The following day it was discovered that this aunt had died in childbirth, along with the baby. Such communication with the dead proved to be an increasingly frequent occurrence throughout Garrett's life.

Having contracted tuberculosis as a child, a condition that was to affect her repeatedly for the rest of her days, Garrett moved to the milder climes of England at the age of 15. Before long, she was married to her first husband, Clive, and she bore him four children. Tragically, her three sons all died very young, two of them from meningitis. Her daughter survived, but by this stage the marriage had ended in divorce.

> She also had a large number of imaginary playmates, who took on a very physical appearance to her.

During the First World War, Garrett met a young officer through her work at a hospital for wounded soldiers and subsequently remarried. Shortly after he left her to join the fighting at the front, she was visited by a vision of her new husband. Two days later she was informed that he had been killed in action at Ypres.

Amazingly, until this point Garrett had not investigated her remarkable powers to any real

French firemen holding up a Royal Air Force flag found among the wreckage of the R101 airship.

extent. However, another period of ill health afforded her the time to consider her unusual abilities and she began to attend seances and table-rapping sessions.

She later recalled that it was at one of these events that she started to feel overwhelmingly drowsy and drifted off into slumber. When she awoke, she discovered that she had actually entered a trance, and that during this state her body had been used by the dead as a means of communicating with living people in the room. Shortly after this she made her first contact with the spirit of Uvali, a fourteenth-century Arab soldier who was to become her primary contact with the spirit world at future seances.

After a while Eileen's growing reputation as a psychic brought her to the attention of a well-known psychic investigator, Harry Price. In October 1930, Price arranged for Garrett to be present at a special seance at the National

Laboratory of Physical Research. It was hoped that she would be able to contact the spirit of the famous writer, Sir Arthur Conan Doyle, who had recently died. In preparation, Price arranged for both his secretary and a journalist, Ian D. Coster, to be present to authenticate and document the findings.

It was, therefore, initially disappointing for all concerned when Garrett failed to make contact with Conan Doyle, who had been a spiritualist himself. However, their disappointment soon gave way to astonishment when Garrett proceeded to bring forth the spirit of Flight Lieutenant H. Carmichael Irwin. It slowly dawned on those present at the seance that this man had been an officer on the R101, Britain's largest airship, which had crashed in France two days earlier, killing 48 of its 54 passengers.

Subsequent news reports of the seance came to the attention of a Mr Charlton, who had been involved in the construction of the airship. Intrigued by what he read, he then asked to see the notes of the seance proceedings. These filled him with amazement, as it transpired that, while in a state of trance, Garrett had produced more than forty specific pieces of highly technical, confidential information. It would have been impossible, he maintained, for Garrett to have had prior knowledge, or understanding, of such matters.

Charlton was so impressed by these discoveries that he alerted his superiors at the Ministry of Civil Aviation, after which it was decided to hold another seance with Garrett. This time, Major Villiers from the Ministry was in attendance while very specific technical questions were put to Garrett to try to gain further information about the air accident. Detailed answers to these questions were relayed through Garrett, who was

She merely provided the opportunity to speak with the deceased.

able to pinpoint the exact cause of the disaster, even naming the very girder that had failed.

The official court of inquiry examined all of the evidence produced by Garrett during the seance and concluded that it was genuine. Experts declared that it would not have been possible for her to be aware of such precise information about the crash, and that the only explanation was that she had, indeed, communicated with the spirit world. The whole incident was widely taken as proof that such extraordinary powers do definitely exist. This was seen as a real vindication for the spiritualist community, who were often denigrated rather than supported by the establishment.

Garrett differed from many of her fellow mediums in that there were never any overtly theatrical physical manifestations at her seances. Rather than perform table-rapping or materializations, for example, she merely provided the opportunity to speak with the deceased. It was perhaps this simplicity of her approach that caused the establishment to support, rather than condemn, her activities, with many scientists risking their reputations to do so.

Following this widespread acceptance of her abilities, in 1932–33 Garrett agreed to participate in extensive psychoanalytical experimentation at the New York Psychiatric Unit and John Hopkins University, USA. In so doing, she revealed her open-minded attitude towards the human need to understand and explain the workings of the paranormal, which she embodied and, indeed, she had a very personal desire to gain a greater understanding of her own abilities. She lectured widely, founded the Parapsychology Foundation in 1951, and contributed her thoughts and findings to several publications, including the *International Journal of Parapsychology*, in 1959.

By the time of her death in 1970, Eileen Garrett was held in high esteem, not just for her skill as a medium, but also for her personal qualities. If she were alive today, she would no doubt continue to be as mystified as the rest of the world as to the precise nature of her psychic powers which, in spite of extensive investigations, remain within the realms of the unexplained.

NINEL KULAGINA

During the Cold War, each side conducted extensive secret research into any area that might give them an advantage over the other. With no subject deemed too unusual to be exploited, both the CIA and the KGB investigated the possibility of using paranormal powers, such as telepathy, for intelligence-gathering purposes. Anyone demonstrating special psychic abilities was seized upon and exploited in the quest for victory.

Ninel Kulagina was one such character. She was a housewife from St Petersburg who was studied by the Soviets for more than ten years because of her paranormal abilities.

During this time she revealed her amazing powers of telekinesis – the ability to move objects by the power of the mind alone. The fact that Kulagina was investigated for such a long period of time seems to indicate that she was nothing other than entirely genuine.

Film footage still exists of Kulagina causing a compass needle to move by focusing energy through her fingertips. Another of her displays of telekinetic ability was to move matches across a table, or to cause a pile of them to collapse purely by the power of a concentrated stare.

But it is the later displays of her remarkable talent that reveal why the authorities were so interested in her powers. In one experiment, an egg was cracked into a saline solution, and she proceeded to separate the yolk from the white by her powers of kinesis.

In another demonstration which was particularly sinister, Kulagina is said to have stopped the heart of a frog from beating, purely by the power of her mind. To the Cold War scientists, this must have been an incredibly exciting breakthrough in human mental ability and this aptitude would have presented all sorts of horrific possibilities to men who were determined to emerge victorious from this most sinister of global conflicts.

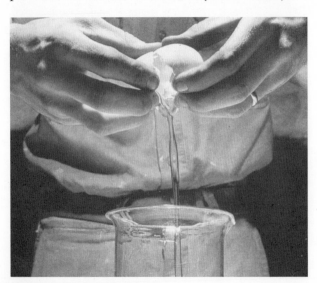

During one of Kulagina's most famous feats, an egg was cracked into a saline solution and she separated the yolk from the white by kinetic energy.

Performing these incredible feats took a serious physical toll on Kulagina, and it is this that apparently persuaded the Soviet doctors of the authenticity of her feats.

After she had demonstrated her telekinetic prowess, she reported having experienced a sense of hot energy running up and down her spine and emanating from her hands. During this time, her pulse would apparently race to over 200 beats per minute – the equivalent of doing strenuous exercise, and she is even reputed to have lost weight through such a display. The activities would also affect her blood pressure and she spoke of feeling dizzy and exhausted for several days afterwards, experiencing headaches and blurred vision. Eventually, she was forced to end her involvement with the research after suffering a heart attack, no doubt brought on by her exertions.

Sceptics have argued that all the evidence that exists about Kulagina could have been nothing more than a huge conspiracy on the part of the Soviet powers to alarm the Western world, especially as, during the Cold War years, each side went to a great deal of effort to deceive the other over the extent of the scientific progress being made. Perhaps this is just one more example of such an attempt.

It is impossible to know for sure what secret scientific discoveries were actually made during the era of the Cold War, but there is certainly some very convincing evidence to suggest that Ninel Kulagina was possessed of very remarkable, and mysterious, powers.

DANIEL DOUGLAS HOME

Daniel Douglas Home is considered by many spiritualists to be one of the most gifted mediums of all time. During his unusual career, he demonstrated his psychic prowess on countless occasions and is remarkable for the incredible range of his ability. Whereas most spiritualists tend to specialize in the demonstration of a particular type of paranormal activity, nothing seemed beyond the reach of Home's amazing powers.

Home was born in 1833 in Edinburgh, Scotland and, in common with many spiritually gifted people, his talents first manifested themselves during his childhood. His aunt described how, even as an infant, his cradle could be seen to rock itself, unassisted. As a child, he experienced some significant psychic events, and at one stage is said to have seen a vision of his mother that coincided with her death in another city.

Such powers could not protect him from illness, however, and he was a very sickly child. At the age of 9, he moved to Connecticut, USA,

Sir William Crookes, the eminent scientist, who put Home's abilities to the test.

to live with his aunt, and it was here that he was diagnosed with tuberculosis.

One of the results of this condition was that Home's childhood was a particularly solitary one, during which time he came to believe that he was surrounded by the spirits of the dead. In fact, he would maintain throughout his life that he was supported by certain spiritual benefactors, and that it was these beings that were responsible for his paranormal displays.

The young Home's fascination with the supernatural and the strange happenings of his early years worried his God-fearing aunt, who believed that he must be possessed by the devil. She was unable to come to terms with his activities and, while he was still in his mid-teens, she cast him out of her house. From this time on Home was forced to seek his fortune in the only way he knew how – by working as a professional medium. He would often be offered board and lodging by a patron in exchange for the performance of seances and rituals, at which he would demonstrate his impressive abilities.

Home's repertoire was huge – apart from communicating with the deceased, he would also conjure up from nowhere whole arrays of spectral lights and music. Another of his skills was his extraordinary ability to shrink himself in size, or elongate his body, a phenomenon that was witnessed, and verified, by several people at once.

It was perhaps his displays of telekinesis, though, that were the most remarkable. At several seances, Home caused tables and chairs to move of their own accord and on one occasion he was able to levitate a table to such a height that he could walk beneath it. He maintained, however, that these demonstrations could not actually be classed as telekinesis, for the actions stemmed not from the power of his own mind, but from the actions of friendly spirits with whom he was able to converse easily.

Home made it publicly known at this time that he believed the vast majority of mediums to be fraudulent, and so he took measures to prove that, unlike them, he was genuine. In contrast to other practitioners of the time, Home would conduct his seances in well lit rooms, or even out of doors. When he demonstrated his ability to move items of furniture, he would challenge the audience to take hold of his hands and feet to prove that he was not touching anything. Many found his displays utterly convincing, particularly those in which he would summon up spirit hands that would then either touch members of the seance, or write out personal messages for them.

Despite such public demonstrations of his talents, it was not until 1852 that Home's career, quite literally, took off. In a display that seemed to set him apart from his fellow spiritualists,

Home showed how he was able to levitate off the ground for a prolonged period of time. According to the account of a journalist, F. L. Burr, who witnessed the event, Home levitated no fewer than three times, and on the last attempt actually rose up to touch the ceiling. Home later asserted that the levitation should be attributed to the power of his spirit companions, who had chosen to lift him into the air in this way.

Home's fame spread far and wide, and he set off on a European tour, eventually reaching Russia, where he married. During his travels, he performed seances for some of the leading figures of the day, notably Emperor Napoleon III of France and the Empress Eugenie. Both were amazed by his abilities. At one stage, Home even appeared to make contact with the deceased Napoleon Bonaparte, who signed his name on paper. The Emperor was enormously impressed by this, announcing to all that the handwriting was genuinely that of Bonaparte himself.

Arguably the most famous and impressive of Home's feats was performed in London, at the home of Lord Adare, in 1866. Apparently without warning, Home slipped into a trance and began to levitate. He then proceeded to float out of one of the open windows before drifting back in through another. This demonstration ensured Home's popularity and fame, especially as the assembled audience was possessed of considerable credibility and influence.

What is clear is that Home was a supremely talented individual. Some sceptics have asked, however, whether his skills as a medium were genuine or whether his abilities lay more in the area of deception. It has been suggested that Home may have induced some powerful kind of mass hallucination in his audiences through the power of suggestion.

Nevertheless, taking into account the consistency of his displays, the numbers of people convinced of his authenticity and the lack of any evidence to the contrary, it seems highly unlikely that Home was anything other than a true psychic.

Home was so confident of his own abilities that he agreed to subject himself to some rigorous investigations. Sir William Crookes, a well-known scientist of the day with a particular interest in spirituality, studied Home's activities

Many found his displays utterly convincing, particularly those in which he would summon up spirit hands.

over a two-year period. During this time, Home apparently managed to make an accordion play while it was sealed inside a cage which had been specially designed by Crookes to block out the magnetic energies that he believed were the root of Home's power.

Finally, Crookes was forced to admit that he could find no scientific explanation for Home's remarkable powers.

At this point, his recurrent tuberculosis forced Home to retire. His powers had not only been displayed and witnessed, but they had been inspected scientifically and there is still no explanation that is more plausible than his own. He was indeed a uniquely gifted individual, and an astonishing manifestation of the latent powers of human consciousness.

JOSE ARIGO

During his lifetime Jose Arigo became renowned for his inexplicable psychic talents, which he used to great effect in healing the sick and injured. Indeed, many of his actions were even proclaimed as miracles by his admirers. Sadly, however, his attempts to use his amazing healing powers for the good of mankind were eventually cut short by his imprisonment, when the authorities ruled that his activities were contrary to the law.

Born in 1918 into the peasant class of Brazil, Arigo could never have anticipated the level of international fame he would eventually enjoy as a result of his unusual gifts.

He first became aware of his abilities while visiting a dying relative; the whole family had assembled to bid their farewells to the woman who was suffering from a life-threatening tumour. However, as the priest read out the last rites, Arigo recounted how he felt strangely compelled to take action. Seizing a knife from the kitchen, he cut into the woman and removed the tumour on the spot. Amazingly, she made a rapid recovery, and it was after this that Arigo's community realized that they had a remarkable psychic healer in their midst.

Such was the poverty in Arigo's neighbourhood that there was very limited access to doctors and medicine. It was not surprising, therefore, that the news of his healing ability spread rapidly, and soon he was being asked to treat large numbers of people. Although initially reluctant to put others at risk by operating on them, Arigo quickly discovered that he was able to repeat the success of his first operation on numerous occasions.

Seizing a knife from the kitchen, he cut into the woman and removed the tumour on the spot.

Although such healers have been known to exist in other communities, particularly in the Philippines, rarely has this talent been used with such success, or without recourse to hidden methods. Many of these healers have claimed that they are somehow blessed, often seeing themselves as conduits for the Holy Spirit. In contrast, Arigo's explanation for his healing powers was an unusual one, as he attributed his skills to the fact that when he was operating he would become possessed by the spirit of a deceased German physician, Dr Adolphus Fritz.

It is difficult to find an alternative explanation for Arigo's remarkable abilities, since he was very poorly educated and certainly had no medical knowledge whatsoever. The only other possibility is that Arigo invented the story of Dr Fritz in order to deflect attention away from the incredible powers that were actually entirely his own. Whatever the truth, Arigo continued to credit the success of his work to the spirit of Dr Fritz throughout his entire life.

Arigo had practised his healing on many people before he came to the attention of the authorities. The medical establishment had serious concerns about the unsanitary nature of his operations and his lack of medical qualifications.

Eventually, in 1936, he was arrested for the illegal practice of medicine, fined and sentenced to eight months in jail. The establishment was not prepared, however, for the huge level of public support for Arigo – the extent of which eventually caused the President of Brazil to step in and offer him an official pardon.

Almost thirty years later, however, in 1964, Arigo was not so lucky, and he was forced to face his sentence. Although the prosecuting judge, Filippe Immesi, was amazed by a demonstration of Arigo's powers, he was forced to conclude that Arigo was nevertheless breaking the law and sentenced him accordingly. While in jail, Arigo continued his healing practices, believing that it was his mission to help as many people as possible.

Some time later, Judge Immesi visited Arigo in jail, where the ensuing episode impressed him so much that he subsequently wrote an account of what he witnessed. He described how he had seen Arigo perform a cataract operation on a woman's eye with a pair of nail scissors. Despite the fact that the operation was conducted while the patient was fully conscious, she displayed no signs of pain. No type of disinfectant or antiseptic was used, Arigo merely wiped the

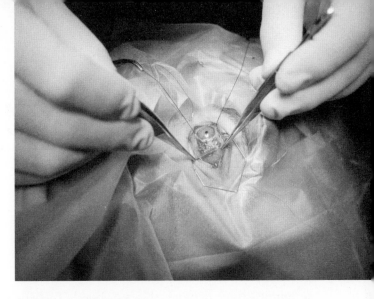

Conventional methods of modern eye surgery require specialized instruments and a sterile environment.

scissors on his shirt before cutting into the woman's eye. After he had performed the operation, Arigo said a short prayer before pronouncing that the woman was cured.

Arigo died following a car accident in 1971. In the course of his lifetime, he had healed many thousands of people who, without his intervention, would surely have died.

Modern science is unable to offer an explanation as to how Arigo was able to practice with such an astonishing degree of success.

One suggestion is that he might have been using the placebo effect on his patients in the same way as that practised by African witch doctors. These remarkable people trick patients into thinking they have been healed and, because the patients' belief is so strong, they go on to make a full recovery.

However, this method could not explain the incredible level of success that Arigo managed to sustain over so many decades. Belief in his power of healing will take many years to fade.

MATTHEW MANNING

Matthew Manning's life story might resemble a strange combination of *Harry Potter* and *The X Files*, but there is nothing fictional about the scientific data on his extraordinary powers. For almost three decades, this remarkable British healer and psychic has worked with some of the world's leading academics as they try to explain the inexplicable.

Manning first came to public prominence in 1974, following his appearance on a BBC prime-time show *The Frost Interview*. He caused a national sensation with a display of automatic writing – apparently transcribing messages from the dead – which accurately diagnosed health problems suffered by members of the audience. However, for his family, friends and former schoolmates, this feat was unsurprising compared to some of the extraordinary displays of Manning's past.

In his autobiography, *One Foot in the Stars*, Manning tells how his family first experienced poltergeist activity in February 1967, at their 1950s-style home in Shelford, near Cambridge. Events began unremarkably when a silver tankard threw itself off a wooden shelf overnight, and progressed to the daily movement of everything from ashtrays to armchairs. Eventually, Manning's father contacted George Owen, Professor of Genetics at Trinity College, Cambridge, and the world's leading authority on poltergeist activity.

Professor Owen assured the family that they were experiencing a natural, though unexplained, phenomenon that would eventually pass, and for a time it seemed he was right. But in the autumn

In a single week, no fewer than 503 signatures, including the names of deceased locals, appeared on the walls of the house.

of 1968, when 12-year-old Manning and his family moved to Queens House, an eighteenth-century home in nearby Linton, the poltergeist returned with a vengeance. In one incident, which Manning describes as 'worthy of a horror film', he watched a bedroom wardrobe inching towards him – then he felt the bed itself vibrate, hover about 15 cm above the ground and then reposition itself.

The following morning, the family went downstairs to find that the kitchen, sitting room and lounge had all been completely ransacked. Over the next few months, dozens of similarly bizarre events occurred, which included random scrawling on walls inside the house and water appearing out of nowhere. At one point, Manning's mother suggested they leave a paper and pen in a locked, empty room to see what happened. A few minutes later they returned to find the words 'Matthew Beware' alongside a Leo sign.

Three years later, the extraordinary goings-on at Queens House had increased yet further in intensity. In a single week, no fewer than 503 signatures, including the names of deceased locals and the dates of their deaths, appeared on the walls of the house.

At first Manning's father, a particularly level-headed architect, tried to find rational explanations for what was going on. But after witnessing so many paranormal events, he grudgingly accepted them as fact. When his son started boarding at Oakham School in Rutland, Manning Senior warned the headmaster, John Buchanan, about what might happen. It was just as well he did.

In his book, Manning recounts some of the weird, wonderful and frightening incidents witnessed by pupils and teachers at Oakham School – many of which easily compare with Harry Potter's supernatural experiences at Hogwarts. Beds moved around as their occupants tried to sleep. Nails, glass and bone-handled knives materialized and flew about. Wire coat hangers squashed themselves into small balls and glowing lights appeared on dormitory walls.

In desperation, Manning's house tutor took him to see an occultist to learn a 'banishing ritual'. Unfortunately this did not work, and within two weeks terrified pupils were massing

Manning is a renowned healer, and has treated tens of thousands of patients for everything from toothache to secondary cancer.

in their matron's sitting room. Later that night, she watched wood chippings, pebbles and shards of glass falling from nowhere into her lap. Incidents such as these became a feature of Manning's school life, although with time, more 'sophisticated' psychic skills began to emerge.

Despite general agreement among staff that Manning was hopeless at art, he began producing outstanding 'automatic drawings' in a variety of styles. Among them were pictures supposedly originating from dead masters such as Paul Klee, Thomas Rowlandson and W. Keble Martin. Later, Manning produced work resembling that of Picasso, Goya, Beardsley and Durer, and

Manning was correct eight times out of ten in each of three separate runs – far beyond the realms of chance.

sometimes his feats were witnessed by teachers from beginning to end. His housemaster Roger Blackmore later told how he had watched Manning at work and questioned him. 'He could answer quite happily', recalled Mr Blackmore. 'He would talk about the period in which the drawing was based. He didn't appear to be in a trance. He was working as a normal artist of considerable talent.'

Throughout this period, Manning was also producing messages from apparently dead people in widely differing handwriting styles. During the summer holidays of 1971, one of his most regular otherworldly correspondents was a certain Robert Webbe, who seemed to be a previous

owner of Queens House (and spoke as though he still was). The following year Manning, concerned about his sick grandmother, established a dialogue with a physician called Thomas Penn, whom he found could be summoned at will. It was Penn whose diagnoses later captivated David Frost's audience in 1974.

The media frenzy that followed *The Frost Interview* turned Manning into an international celebrity overnight. He wrote a bestselling book entitled *The Link* and travelled the world promoting it. But he also tried to satisfy the curiosity of mainstream science, by submitting to a seemingly endless series of tests under laboratory conditions. From late 1976, he toured university campuses in the United States, starting at the University of California and the Washington Research Institute in San Francisco.

His experimental successes were many and varied. They included the ability to influence an electrical impulse on the skin of a frog, sedating or rousing a subject sitting in a separate room, influencing a coin to land heads or tails, and predicting which of ten canisters held water or ball bearings. In this last ESP (extra-sensory perception) test, Manning was correct eight times out of ten in each of three separate runs – far beyond the realms of chance. One experiment in California even showed that he could improve the yield of commercial grass seeds by holding a vialful in his hand and concentrating.

Perhaps Manning's most astounding result came the following year at the Mind Science Foundation in San Antonio, Texas. Here, a team led by psychologist William Braud sought to establish whether psychokinesis (using psychic

power to make things move) could influence human biological systems. His experiments with Manning on slowing the abnormal degeneration of red blood cells suggested that it could.

Braud later observed Manning attempting to destroy cancer cells. Manning operated under strict laboratory conditions and a control subject mimicked his every move. The control failed to

Matthew has demonstrated that he can influence cancer cells.

have an impact on any of the cells. Manning succeeded in twenty-seven out of thirty attempts, increasing the number of dead cancer cells by anything between 200 and 1,200 per cent. This was a ground-breaking result. Braud concluded: 'What Matthew has demonstrated is that he can influence cancer cells. There may be para-psychological factors involved that could be used to heal oneself or heal others.'

The rest, as they say, is history. These days Manning focuses his powers on healing, and since the 1980s he has been consulted by tens of thousands of patients, including the likes of Prince Philip and Pope Paul VI. Despite many documented successes – from back pain to secondary cancer – Manning rejects any suggestion that he is special and describes himself as 'proudly irreligious'. He does not claim to understand how his powers work, only that they do.

Manning has come a long way since the first poltergeist visits in the 1960s. He has collaborated with the world's leading scientists to try and discover how healing power works.

Matthew Manning 205

Religious Phenomena

Spirituality may seem out of sync with our hectic and consumer-driven society, yet there are millions of faithful – of many religions – all over the world. Many believe in miracles, whether it be crying statues, visions of religious figures or angels coming to the rescue in the nick of time. And recently, research into the enduring mysteries of biblical history has shed light a time-honoured subject, exciting global debate. Contrary to what we might expect, our belief in the miracles and mysteries of religion seems to be growing.

SHAMANISM

The mystical figure of the shaman has existed in human culture for thousands of years on almost every continent of the world, and yet the nature of shamanic powers remains largely unexplained. Widely dismissed by the scientific community, the fact remains that shamanism has played a powerful role in both healing and divination, and continues to do so today in some remote parts of the world such as the Amazonian rainforests and in tribal areas of Mongolia.

Shamanism has played a powerful role in both healing and divination, and continues to do so today...

Although the word 'shaman' is derived from the Tungus language of Siberian Russia, the practice of shamanism extends far across the globe. Separate disciplines can be classified as Turkic, Mongolian, Manchu-Tunguz, Korean, Japanese, Finno-Ugrian, American-Indian, Celtic and African, all of which are modelled on the same basic principles.

Now perceived as being similar to a witchdoctor, the shaman enjoyed a role in ancient society as a healer and counsellor, and was in many ways a kind of primitive psychotherapist.

People would consult the shaman to be healed of their physical, mental or emotional ailments, or to discover secrets from the future or the past. The shaman was able to perform these roles by acting as a psychic bridge between this world and the next.

Central to the principle of shamanism is the concept of 'soul flight'. Any medicine man or woman whose practice revolved around the flight of the soul was classed as a shaman. These people believed that a portion of the human soul could readily leave the body – for example, when in a dream state. In order to help others, the shaman first had to set about releasing his own soul, in the process achieving what has been described as 'a state of ecstasy'.

This state of altered consciousness could be brought about by a number of means, which are often combined, such as repetitive chanting, drumming and meditation. Shamans had an extensive knowledge of nature, particularly botany and would also use hallucinogenic plants or fungi, such as mushrooms, to induce their dream state. These substances were often extremely poisonous, so the shaman was at risk of coma, collapse or even death.

Once in this trance-like condition, the shaman would then be able to commune with the hidden spirit world. Believing that knowledge is contained in nature itself, he would consult the rocks, trees and soil, and would also speak with the powerful animal spirits to divine useful wisdom.

Power animals are spiritual guardians that watch over the souls of all people.

This belief in power animals was integral to shamanic practice. In a concept that is similar to that of a guardian angel, power animals are spiritual guardians that watch over the souls of all people. The shaman believed that each person has their own spirit animal, the characteristics of which manifest themselves in personal attributes. For instance, a bear spirit lends a person bear wisdom, which is recognizable from his or her behaviour.

Having consulted the land or animal spirits, the shaman would then be able to help people with a particular problem or cure them of their ailments. If a man required advice on a difficult decision, the shaman could consult with his personal animal spirits. If there was a blight on the land, or a disease, the shaman would be asked to commune with the land to find the reason and the cure. In the case of some illnesses, such as depression or coma, the shaman would attribute this to the fact that a portion of that person's soul had become lost. It would be the shaman's task to enter the spirit world and guide the soul back safely.

A modern shaman in a trance after inhaling strong hallucinogenic powder.

The notion of 'soul flight', so fundamental to shamanism, is not an uncommon one. For example, the idea that it is wrong to wake a sleepwalker dates back to the pagan belief that their soul has become separated from their body and, if the sleepwalker is woken prematurely, that soul will be unable to locate its rightful owner in order to return. Interestingly, accounts of near-death, or out-of-body experiences are often described in terms of the soul leaving the body. Individuals who have had such experiences frequently relate their feelings of being physically divorced from their bodies, before being eventually reunited with them once the episode is over.

The shaman may have had some kind of psychic link with the earth that is unknown to the modern world.

When the shaman's communications with the spirit world have ceased and he has awoken from his trance-like condition, he shares the experience with his tribe through song, dance and storytelling. If he has eaten hallucinogenic mushrooms, the shaman might sometimes decide to involve others in their experience in a rather unusual way. As the active ingredient of this potent fungus cannot be broken down by the human body, it would be passed in his urine, which the shaman dilutes and passes to other members of the tribe. In this way, everyone can experience a portion of the 'ecstasy' felt by the shaman.

Some believe that the role of the shaman can be compared to that of the faith healer, with the patients believing so utterly in the mystical power of the shaman to cure them that they would, in effect, make themselves better – in other words, a kind of self-hypnosis would take place. Others maintain, however, that maybe it is time to reassess the power of our ancestral knowledge in light of the incredible success of the shaman over thousands of years. Surely, they argue, this is based on something more solid than mere psychosomatic superstition?

It has been suggested that the shaman may have had some kind of psychic link with the earth that is unknown to the modern world. Shamanic practices were prevalent in hunter-gatherer societies, among people who lived close to the natural order, and whose lives were regulated by the natural rhythms of the seasons.

With the advent of agriculture, man became able to control certain aspects of nature, such as the crops, and once this happened there was less fear and superstition concerning the ultimate power of nature. It could be that, in breaking our link with nature, we have lost a vital store of knowledge that was well known to the shaman, wherever in the world he happened to be.

From whatever source the shamans derived their remarkable gifts, it is true to say that there are many today who believe strongly in their psychic abilities, and in the power manifest in the spirits of the natural world.

If we cast our eyes back to the past, rather than fixing them on the future, we may discover that our ancestors were not really that primitive after all.

STIGMATA

The grievous injuries suffered by Jesus on the cross included bloodied hands and feet, a spear wound in the side and sharp scratches around the brow from his crown of thorns. Followers of Christ have been known to exhibit some of the same wounds, a mysterious phenomenon known as stigmata.

The wounds, although not necessarily permanent, tend to defy treatment by doctors and are never prone to infection. Often, they do not have the same odour that might emanate from other long-running sores, and there are even some reports of them radiating a perfume. The belief, as yet unproven, is that the holy wounds allow Christ's blood to come forth rather than that of the sufferer.

> His hands and feet appeared to be pierced with black nails of flesh, bent backwards.

In addition to the bloodied patches, there might be lash marks and shoulder scars. These seem to mimic the wounds inflicted on Jesus when he was whipped and beaten before hauling his cross-beam to Golgotha. And the pain endured by stigmatics is not confined to external injuries. They also suffer acute feelings of hopelessness, desperation and sorrow.

About three hundred cases of stigmata are on record, a staggering ninety per cent of which occurred in women. Sixty-two saints have been afflicted. The first stigmatic on record is Stephen Langton who, in 1222, appeared to suffer all the hallmark injuries. No one knows how his condition was investigated, but his claims were swiftly dismissed as a hoax. It is surely not coincidence that the iconic emblem of Jesus on the cross had just become widespread in Europe at this time.

Just two years later, St Francis of Assisi (1181/2–1226) was revealing signs of the crucifixion on his withering body. The son of a merchant, St Francis had turned his back on a comfortable middle class existence to champion the poor, following a series of dreams that beckoned him to his faith. He went on to live a spartan existence in Italy in prayer and solitude. Not only did he bear the wounds of Christ, but he also exhibited the strangest of stigmatic symptoms: his hands and feet appeared to be pierced with black nails of flesh, bent backwards.

In the following centuries a number of holy figures were stigmatics, including St Catherine of

Siena in the fourteenth century, St John of God in the sixteenth century and St Mary Frances of the Five Wounds in the eighteenth century.

The most famous stigmatic of the twentieth century was Saint Pio of Pietrelcina, better known simply as 'Padre Pio'. Born in Italy in 1887, he became a Capuchin monk called Brother Pio at the age of 15. In 1910, a year after his ordination as a priest, he noticed the first signs of the condition that would come to dominate his existence. A red mark about the size of a penny appeared on each of his palms, causing him some pain. The left hand, he reported, hurt more than his right, and he felt the same sensation in his feet.

But it was not until 1918 that the full-blown symptoms of stigmata afflicted Padre Pio. He wrote to his mentor about the experience, which occurred just after he had celebrated Mass. 'I yielded to a drowsiness similar to a sweet sleep. All the internal and external senses and even the very faculties of my soul were immersed in indescribable stillness. Absolute silence surrounded and invaded me. I was suddenly filled with great peace and abandonment which effaced everything else and caused a lull in the turmoil. All this happened in a flash.'

He described how a man whose hands, feet and side were dripping with blood appeared before him. When the vision disappeared Pio discovered he had similar wounds, with blood pouring forth. For the next fifty years he bore the injuries that imitated those of Christ, and bleeding from the side wound was especially severe between Thursday and Saturday, the days that led up to the crucifixion of Jesus.

Padre Pio won a reputation as someone who could read souls, foretell the future and heal the sick. Thousands of people flocked to see him, convinced that he possessed divine gifts passed on from Christ himself. Their faith was further confirmed when, on his death in 1968, all signs of stigmata had vanished. Flesh in the affected parts had healed without leaving scars. Padre Pio had predicted this would occur.

Self-inflicted stigmata could be an attempt to attract attention, or an example of what is known as a 'pious hoax', one carried out with the sole intention of shoring up people's faith.

Stigmatics, including Padre Pio, are renowned for their frugal lifestyle. Therese Neumann, (1898–1962), another twentieth-century stigmatic, apparently lived for thirty-six years on nothing more than a daily communion wafer. She also eschewed sleep for most of her life, concentrating instead on her visions. Despite significant blood loss, St Pio also managed to survive on minimum sustenance.

In 2002 Pope John Paul II elevated Padre Pio to sainthood. All doubt about the authenticity of his wounds was officially banished by this decision. Yet, for the impartial or sceptical observer, there is an obvious difficulty in believing the accounts of stigmatics. How can we be sure that the wounds were not self-inflicted? Only 24-hour surveillance could eliminate doubts about that possibility. Self-inflicted stigmata could be an attempt to attract attention, or an example of what is known as a 'pious hoax', one carried out with the sole intention of shoring up people's faith.

There have been numerous examples of frauds, notably Magdalena de la Cruz (1487–1560) who confessed before death that she had injured herself in order to duplicate Jesus' wounds. Many people believe injuries like this could be incurred through self-hypnosis.

The issue has been further complicated by the enduring enigma of the Turin Shroud (see page 228). The shroud clearly indicates that the body supposedly wrapped in it suffered wounds to the arm rather than the hands. Indeed, modern research into ancient execution methods tells us that those who were crucified were pinioned between the radial and ulna, two wrist bones, rather than nailed through the palms. This distinction is not made in the depiction of traditional crucifixes. If the stigmata signs were really a heavenly miracle, ask sceptics, why do puncture marks always appear on the palms, and not on the wrist?

Whatever questions are raised, mystery still surrounds stigmata, which is often accompanied by other mysterious phenomena. Padre Pio was seen with Pope Pius XI at the Vatican at the same time he was reportedly taking Mass in his church in San Giovanni Rotondo. He later explained that bilocution (being in two places at once), was an extension of his personality. What is more, images of Padre Pio in the sky allegedly deterred pilots in the Second World War from emptying their bombs on his home town.

St Francis of Assisi showed one of the earliest recorded cases of stigmata in the Middle Ages. He has become a spiritual icon for believers all around the world.

The bodies of stigmatics are frequently found to be incorruptible after death, that is, they do not deteriorate in the usual way. Four days after Therese Neumann died, for example, there was no sign of rigor mortis. It seems that the bloody signs of stigmata are parts of a much larger puzzle, divine or otherwise, that has yet to be solved.

APPARITIONS OF THE VIRGIN MARY

Religious visions have been witnessed by many people over hundreds of years. Some of these apparitions have been actively endorsed by the Church, and have even had the power to make sceptics think twice.

On some evenings, the full figure of the Virgin Mary would be visible, whereas at other times only her head could be seen.

In 1968, in Zeitun, Egypt, more than one million people were stunned to witness an apparition of the Virgin Mary hovering above the town's church. The visitation was visible for varying durations of time, sometimes even for several hours at once, and continued to happen for almost a year.

The actual form of the apparition varied from night to night, reducing markedly the chances that the vision could have been the result of some kind of deception. On some evenings, the full figure of the Virgin Mary would be visible, whereas at other times only her head could be

seen. On several occasions, she would be accompanied by a number of birds, which were taken to be doves of peace. These were seen to move around and were controversially photographed flying in the formation of a cross – although close inspection of the photographs has proved that they were live birds rather than part of the apparition. A number of observers sent from the Egyptian Coptic Church also claimed to witness plumes of fragrant purple smoke coming from the church during the apparitions.

Word spread about the remarkable occurrence and pilgrimages were made from miles around. Large numbers of miraculous healings were reported, such as cripples finding that they could walk and the blind regaining their sight. Of all the miracles achieved by the apparition, however, perhaps the greatest of these was the sense of common destiny that it fostered among many peoples of disparate religions. In a region such as Egypt, where conflict has existed between different creeds for hundreds of years, it was amazing in itself for all people to agree that what they were seeing with their own eyes seemed indeed to be a religious miracle, and could not be explained without God. Muslims who saw the vision chanted passages from the Koran, such as: 'Mary, God has chosen thee. And purified thee; He has chosen thee. Above all women.' If there were any celestial message implicit in the apparition, it was one of unity and tolerance, as was displayed before the vision.

The apparitions attracted a high level of public attention, and were not only photographed, but also broadcast on television. The fact that there were so many witnesses, combined with the high level of public acceptance of the phenomenon, served only to increase the validity of the apparition. The Egyptian president himself, Gamel Abdul Nasser, a lifelong Marxist with nothing to gain by acknowledging the event, witnessed and verified the apparition.

The authorities, however, believed that the vision was the result of an elaborate hoax.

Accordingly, the police carried out an exhaustive search over a 25 km radius for any evidence of foul play, but were unable to find anything.

Everyone was asking one question – was the apparition genuine and, if so, what was its significance? Opinions on a subject such as this will always be staunchly divided. There is always the possibility that the vision was the result of unscrupulous activities and that the whole event was staged for some ulterior motive.

Alternatively, there are people who claim to have been cured of lifelong afflictions by coming into the vicinity of the beatific presence, although this could perhaps be attributed to the strength of their beliefs rather than to divine intervention.

It is unlikely that the world will ever know the answer to the question of the vision's validity, leaving it a resounding mystery to all.

Crowds watch 14-year-old Marie-Bernarde Soubirous (later to become St Bernadette) experience a vision of the Virgin Mary in the grotto of Massabielle in Lourdes in France.

TALKING IN TONGUES

The practice of 'talking in tongues' (glossolalia) has existed in many forms in different cultures and religions all over the world. Over the last century it has become well known to Christianity, especially within the Pentecostal Church movement. Although its validity has been questioned by many within mainstream religion, the practice of glossolalia nevertheless has many adherents.

'The faithful talking in tongues were taken by the bystanders for being drunken men, but intoxicated men do not talk in languages of which they are normally ignorant'.

Essentially, 'talking in tongues' describes the uttering of words and sounds that are unintelligible to all except those gifted with the power of translation. Christian Pentecostalists believe that the sounds made are actually a manifestation of the Holy Spirit entering the mind and body of the faithful, and communing with the world. Similar to glossolalia is xenolalia, the name given to speaking in a language that is foreign to the speaker, and yet is known and understood by others.

Many references to both types of phenomena, occurring separately or even together, can be found within the pages of the Holy Bible, especially in the descriptions of the Day of Pentecost, from which the Pentecostal Church derives its name. The instance is described by Luke: 'the faithful talking in tongues were taken by the bystanders for being drunken men, but intoxicated men do not talk in languages of which they are normally ignorant'.

The Pentecostal movement appears to have been born in around 1900 following an episode of 'talking in tongues' and subsequent interpretation at the church of a preacher named Charles Fox Parham. Following one of Parham's sermons, a member of the church, Agnes Ozman, stunned listeners with a revelatory outburst, which was in essence an example of spontaneous glossolalia. Parham declared that the utterance was a 'Pentecostal blessing', and this branch of the Church has been in existence ever since.

Certain elements of 'talking in tongues' seem related to the practice of hypnosis and the religious or supernatural belief in possession. Indeed, adherents within the Pentecostal Church believe that those who speak in this way are being possessed by the Holy Spirit. Before the utterances are made, a trance-like state of ecstasy occurs in the believers. Interestingly, this higher

A woman possessed by a spirit at a Pentecostal service in Nigeria.

state of consciousness is common in many other rites and rituals that attempt to form connections with other worlds.

At seances, for example, mediums usually need to enter a trance before they can contact the spirits of the deceased. Similarly, a shaman needs to go into a state of ecstasy before he is able to commune with his spirit guides. It seems that certain individuals really do have the ability to experience some form of communication with the spirit world when they are in such a state of trance. The difference in this case is that, with glossolalia, another party is required to actually interpret the language as it is heard.

While the practice of 'talking in tongues' has many believers around the world, it has nevertheless aroused much doubt and suspicion. Many of the instances of glossolalia that have been judged as blessings could just as easily, in other religions, have been deemed to be curses, or evidence of demonic possession.

Perhaps, however, it is neither possession nor blessing, but is in reality something more basic. It could be that the utterings are no more than the result of the trance-like state itself, very similar to the vague mutterings of a person who is fast asleep. After all, the state of trance is similar to that of sleep, in many ways. The strange outbursts of glossolalia could be little more than a primal mental process at work.

There are many who would argue, though, that the mystery lies not in how the utterances are produced, but in how their meaning comes to be deciphered.

In the practice of xenolalia, although the speaker has no knowledge of the language in which he is speaking, at least his words are intelligible to those listening.

In glossolalia, however, there is no real possibility of proving what is being said and so the potential for an unscrupulous preacher to deceive a congregation in this way should not be overlooked. This is probably the main reason why the practice of 'talking in tongues' continues to be viewed with suspicion by a large part of the Church.

Others would argue, though, that this practice is a prime example of an alternative method of communication about which the world still has much to learn. It looks as if the mystery will continue.

THE HOLY GRAIL

It may take the form of a chalice, a stone, a herb or even a woman. The Holy Grail has been the subject of treasure hunts, violent quests and detective work down the centuries since the death of Christ. Yet even today, no one knows its true identity or the extent of the spiritual powers it possesses.

For many years the Holy Grail was thought to be the cup used by Jesus at the Last Supper. It was allegedly taken by Joseph of Arimithea to the crucifixion and was used to catch the blood spilling from Jesus' wounds. He later retrieved Jesus' body, and for that he was apparently imprisoned for a number of years. Only the chalice kept him alive during those harsh times, as it had life-giving properties.

Later he travelled to England and put the prized chalice into a well at Glastonbury, where he had started one of the early Christian churches. Even today, this well is a place of pilgrimage for the faithful.

The story sounds feasible and it has obvious significance as regards the Eucharist (Holy Communion), one of the foundation stones of today's Christian practice. But in reality, this is only one of many tales surrounding the Holy Grail. No one knows which, if any, is true.

Prior to the era when Christianity dominated, there were similar tales about an object – usually a cauldron – that was imbued with life-giving properties linked to a named hero. Like so many

Joseph of Arimithea, having travelled to England to found a church, is said to have secreted the legendary Grail at the bottom of this well in Glastonbury.

pagan traditions, it was appropriated by Christians and duly tweaked to suit the faith.

Grail stories that emerged in the Middle Ages frequently had an Arthurian angle to them. Among the most eminent authors of such stories are Chretien de Troyes and Robert de Boron in the twelfth century and Wolfram von Eschenbach who wrote slightly later. It is not known if they were acquainted with a single source or legend regarding the Grail, or if they were party to different inspirations. It was Wolfram who lent the interpretation of the Grail as a stone, although he may have been speaking allegorically.

The Grail is also sometimes thought to be a herb, mandrake, which is a member of the nightshade plant family. Some believe this herb was administered to Jesus on the cross so he could feign death and 'return' to life some time later. Until the later twentieth century, however, it was the cup theory that prevailed.

If the Grail really was an artefact directly linked to Jesus, could it have survived to the present day? Archaeology has produced numerous vessels of that age or older. There are even Grail claims attached to some cups on display today, including one in Valencia Cathedral. Another in Genoa was also highly regarded until, after being dropped two centuries ago, it was found to be decorated with glass rather than emeralds.

Perhaps the Grail was kept in the safe hands of guardians to ensure its survival. One popular current theory is that it was in the possession of the Knights Templar, a sect of chivalrous warriors of the twelfth and thirteenth centuries, finally destroyed by an envious French king and a manipulated pope in the early fourteenth century.

Before then, it might have been in the hands of the Cathars, a heretical group living in France who, by the fourteenth century, had also been eradicated. But the location of the Grail in the centuries prior to the Middle Ages is entirely unknown. The medieval period was marked by a roaring trade in religious relics throughout Europe and the Holy Land and it is fair to imagine that many of these were forged.

Critics argue that a true relic from the time of Christ could never have survived centuries of religious war and pillage. Yet there is a good case for the existence today of part of the Titulus, the inscription that was pinned to the cross upon which Jesus died. Indeed, it is said the entire cross was rescued from the execution site firstly

Critics argue that a true relic from the time of Christ could never have survived centuries of religious war.

by early Christians and then, in AD326, by the Empress Helena, mother of the Christian emperor Constantine the Great (AD280–AD337). It was Constantine, of course, who did much to ensure that the entire Roman Empire converted to Christianity, in accordance with his own beliefs.

Faced with three similar crosses, Helena watched as a gravely ill woman was placed on each. When the woman showed signs of recovery after a spell on the third cross, it was deemed to be the relevant one. Helena, later made a saint, brought the cross to Rome and during the

Crusades it was carried with Christian armies. Much later it was apparently captured by a Muslim army and dragged by a horse through the streets of Jerusalem, splintering along the way.

However, part of the Titulus was apparently secreted in the Church of Santa Croce Gerusalemme built by Helena in the grounds of her palace – probably at a time when Rome was enveloped in riots – to be discovered during renovations in 1492. The lettering running from right to left in Hebrew, Greek and Latin lends it credibility, although it could nevertheless be a clever forgery.

There is a rival theory that has recently gained ground, which claims that the Holy Grail is not a cup, but a woman.

If this section of the Titulus is genuine, then it seems more likely that a durable relic such as a gem-encrusted chalice would survive. But there is yet another rival theory that has recently gained ground, which claims that the Holy Grail is not a cup, but a woman.

In short, the theory maintains that Jesus did not die on the cross but lived, married Mary Magdalene and fathered at least one daughter and possibly other children. Both the womb that carried Jesus' offspring and the bloodline descended from him are known as the Holy Grail.

This highly controversial notion has been explored at length in *The Holy Blood and the Holy Grail* by Michael Baigent, Richard Leigh and Henry Lincoln, first published in 1982, when its conclusion was so radical it caused the suicide of at least one monk. The theme was further popularized in a recent novel called *The Da Vinci Code* by Dan Brown, which has been made into a film. Acres of newsprint have been devoted to this debate and yet still we are no nearer to uncovering the truth.

The clues are tantalizing, among them the fact that the word grail appears to come from the adaptation from Old French and Latin for plate, *graal*. Remarkably, the translation for Holy Grail is *san grial* while the phrase for royal blood is *sang rial*. One alternative name for the Holy Grail that has endured down the centuries is the *Sangreal*, implying a close relationship with the blood of Jesus. So what is the real meaning, plate or blood? It is all inspirational material for the conspiracy theorists, who believe that the real intention of Jesus was to revive a royal house in Jerusalem and that eventually the bloodline went to France with Mary Magdalene.

The time when religious bigots could pick a theology that best suited their needs, and tell the populace what to believe, is hopefully far behind us. To accept that the Holy Grail might be a person turns hundreds of years of received wisdom on its head and dislodges the cornerstone of a widely-held faith. The edifice of the Christian faith is holding firm in the face of this onslaught, with its supporters calmly refuting what once would have been branded heretical notions. However, until the Holy Grail – in whatever form – is presented for public scrutiny, speculation will abound.

The recent controversy surrounding the Holy Grail has centred on the figure of Mary Magdalene.
Could she have been the mother of Christ's children?

THE ARK OF THE COVENANT

The discovery of the Ark of the Covenant, considered the greatest of all hidden treasures, would provide indisputable proof that the Old Testament is hard fact rather than embellished fable. Its recovery remains the goal of every modern archaeologist and adventurer but, despite having pieces of the Ark puzzle readily to hand, this great prize has so far eluded everyone.

Although no one is sure where the Ark is, there is plenty of information about its physical appearance in the pages of the Bible, where it is called the Ark of the Testimony, the Ark of the Testament, the Ark of God and the Ark of the Lord. It is better known these days, though, as the Ark of the Covenant.

The purpose of the Ark was as a container for the Ten Commandments given on stone tablets by God to Moses on Mount Sinai. These were the laws by which the Israelites would live, having escaped from servitude in Egypt and headed for the Promised Land.

In Exodus, the second of the Old Testament books, a description of the Ark reveals that it was made of shittim wood (something similar to acacia), that it was gold-covered inside and out and was topped by a mercy seat comprising two cherubs, also made of gold. It was carried by parallel shittim wood staves, coloured in gold. So it would have been a valuable and extremely distinctive construction.

The size of the Ark was considerable, at two and a half cubits in length and a cubit and a half in width. A cubit reflected a half-arm length, from the tip of the middle finger to the elbow. It is better expressed today as between 43 cm and 56 cm, which would make the Ark itself about 0.75 m by 1.25 m.

However, the Ark was more than just a receptacle for God's laws. It was intended to be a symbol of God's presence in Israel among his chosen people. It was even believed to have supernatural powers, not least because it appeared to have caused the death of one ill-fated man called Uzza. He died when he attempted to steady the Ark, as the oxen hauling the cart that held it stumbled. Just a single touch of the sacred object was enough to arouse God's anger, according to the account of Uzza's death given in the Chronicles.

The Ark was credited with bringing down the walls of Jericho during one battle and showering misfortunes upon the Philistines after they captured it in another.

There is no shortage of references to the Ark on the pages of the Bible until the time of Solomon. After that, word of the sacred vessel is sparing, which has fuelled speculation that it was taken from Jerusalem during the rule of Solomon. The prime suspect for taking the Ark at this point is Menelik I, by tradition the son of Solomon and the Queen of Sheba, who took charge of it following a visit to his father's kingdom.

If this were the case, then it lends credibility to one theory concerning the present day whereabouts of the Ark. For Menelik I was reputedly the founder of Ethiopia, and it is in this unlikely corner of Africa that some believe the Ark resides. The precise location is Axum, a city holy to the enduring Ethiopian Orthodox faith.

Today, the Chapel of the Tablet, where the Ark is allegedly closeted, has a somewhat shabby appearance. Local clergy who have access to the room that houses the Ark (known to them as the Tablet of Moses) are unable to give a full description to curious Westerners, as it is veiled at all times. Its power is respected, if not feared. Legend has it that a seventeenth-century ruler of Ethiopia called Iyasu was so wise and good that he could peer inside the Ark and seek wisdom from it. Iyasu could, it is said, trace his lineage back to King David. The implication is that others less worthy will perish if they try to handle the venerated artefact. Unfortunately, all attempts to establish a scientific examination of the object have so far been rebuffed.

The supernatural powers of the Ark are reputed to have brought the walls of Jericho tumbling down.

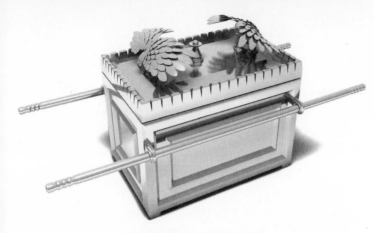

The description of the Ark in the Old Testament reveals that it was made of shittim wood and embellished with gold.

But it is possible that this is not the real Ark. Solomon lived and died in the latter half of the tenth century BC. If his son Menelik I really made off with the Ark, he cannot have taken it directly to Axum, since the city did not come into existence until the third century AD. In another region of Ethiopia, locals insist the Ark remained in a tent on the banks of a lake for 800 years, until the first Christian king of Axum commandeered it. But even if this were true, there is still a chronological gap in the story that remains unexplained.

Solomon is also the starting point for a rival theory that places the Ark firmly in Jerusalem. He is supposed to have built a marvellous temple there that became the home of the Ark. All was well until 587BC, when Nebuchadnezzar's marauders destroyed the temple and perhaps everything in it. The assumption is that the second temple, existing in Herod's time and destroyed by the Romans in AD70, was built on top of the site of the first. So if the lost Ark was placed in the bowels of the first building, then there is plenty of stonework lying on top. Or perhaps Jewish authorities managed to hide the

Ark elsewhere in Jerusalem, maintaining the secrecy of its whereabouts to their deaths.

While some heavyweight scholars think Jerusalem the most likely site for finding the Ark, its existence cannot be proven until extensive excavations have been carried out. Given the city's sensitive political balance and religious divisions, this kind of work is unlikely to occur in the foreseeable future.

One claim says the Ark is housed in Jesus' burial chamber, although this notion is fraught with uncertain scholarship. The whereabouts of the Ark prior to the crucifixion and how or why it was transported to the site are entirely unknown.

While it will take a shrewd operator to find the Ark, it will need a brave or even foolhardy person to open it...

Another possibility is that Jordan is the modern home of the Ark. This has been inspired by the discovery of the Dead Sea Scrolls in Jordanian caves during the 1940s and 1950s. If items of religious value like the scrolls were placed there for security, is it not possible that the Ark would have been hidden there too? But scrutiny of the caves has not turned up the Ark.

So the hunt for the Ark continues. The prospect of finding God's words carved in ancient Hebrew is certainly an alluring one. Yet while it will take a shrewd operator to find the Ark, it will need a brave or even foolhardy person to open it, challenging centuries of superstition concerning its mysterious powers.

BIBLE CODES

When author Dan Brown sought to add intrigue to a claim that the bloodline of Jesus continued today, he looked towards another of history's most enigmatic figures to flesh out the tale – Leonardo da Vinci (1452–1519), artist, scientist and visionary. But did da Vinci really include compelling clues in his work about great strategic truths that would affect the faith of millions?

Dan Brown would have us believe that the truth about Jesus is concealed in da Vinci's great religious works. He states, for example, that in *The Last Supper*, painted in the late fifteenth century, the figure generally taken to be John the Evangelist is in fact Mary Magdalene. She and Jesus are dressed in mirror image colours and appear to be joined at the hip, perhaps a clue that

Da Vinci's famous painting of the Last Supper is now the subject of a heated debate. Did the artist include symbolism that could change the course of history?

they were a couple. As they lean away from one another they produce a V-shape, representative of the chalice or Holy Grail (see page 218) so closely connected with stories of the Last Supper, but absent from the table. The symbol-seeking protagonists of Brown's book uphold that this was da Vinci's way of saying the chalice was Mary's womb. Furthermore, Peter's hostile hand illustrates his antipathy to Mary as Jesus' chosen successor. Brown was inspired to this controversial theory about the painting by Lynn Picknett and Clive Prince's book *The Templar Revelation*.

> As they lean away from one another they produce a V-shape, representative of the chalice or Holy Grail...

But facts about *The Last Supper* stop far short of establishing the code that Brown and his millions of readers long to see. Da Vinci was experimenting with an oil and tempera mix, which meant he could make swift changes as he worked. He did not realize that the colours would degenerate quickly, and despite several renovations, it remains difficult to say how the Mary/John figure originally appeared.

Critics of the novel's assertion of a true-life da Vinci code believe the artist had chosen to depict the last supper according to the gospel of St John, which did not mention a chalice at all. What is more, there was an artistic convention that frequently saw John painted in feminine form.

Other paintings by da Vinci, including the *Virgin of the Rocks*, are said to be littered with clues that in essence debunk some aspects of biblical history. Defenders of the faith point to the fact that many of da Vinci's original scenes have vanished under subsequent layers of paint.

Da Vinci was certainly a complex and intelligent man, more than capable of threading themes into his work for the benefit of future generations. He enjoyed mirror-writing and often indulged in riddles and wordplay. Like other artists, he worked with the threat of heresy looming large. It is surely possible that he used encrypted messages to convey his own point of view at a time when he was unable to speak freely about his thoughts and beliefs for fear of hideous punishment by the Church.

But belief in the possibility of a da Vinci code is also fuelled by mankind's enduring fascination with codes and their use to convey esoteric knowledge. The theory that codes exist within the Bible is a topic that perplexes biblical scholars and mathematicians alike.

The words handed down from God via Moses have always been sacred to the Jewish people. If the ancient texts such as the Torah possessed hidden words and phrases it would make them even more potent than previously imagined.

In medieval times, students of the Torah began looking at it in a new light. Within the words they saw codes that brought forth new messages, which they believed were issued directly from God. Bachya ben Asher, a fourteenth-century Spanish Rabbi, became the first on record to announce his belief that a code lay within the words of the Torah. However, it was not until the twentieth century that serious study of messages embedded in the Torah began again.

This time it was Rabbi Michael Dov Weissmandl (1903–1957) probing the theory of Torah codes. In short, he discovered that the Hebrew spelling of Torah could be found in at least three books of the Torah by using a particular formula. Inspired by his findings, Israeli schoolteacher Avraham Oren toyed with the codes until his work attracted the attention of the Hebrew University of Jerusalem.

Three men are credited with more in-depth work on the Torah codes. Eliyahu Rips, Doron Witztum and Yoav Rosenberg succeeded in uncovering the names and dates of thirty-four great Rabbi sages within the confines of Genesis. There was, they believed, only a remote possibility that the names and dates occurred by chance. They had their study published in the peer-reviewed *Statistical Science Journal*, lending it significant credibility. This fostered international interest – and a degree of sensationalism – at a time when computers meant Torah investigation was a simpler process than ever before.

Soon everybody was using code-breaking techniques to find hidden messages in both the Hebrew text of the Torah and in the Bible. There were rumours of predictions that had come to pass and prophecies as yet unfulfilled. Supposedly encoded warnings about the advent of Hitler and the assassination of Israeli premier Yitzhak Rabin were just two of the topical subjects that made banner headlines around the world.

The messages were deemed proof that God existed and that his words revealed a pre-planned scheme for human existence that is still unfolding.

So what is the key to the Torah code? It is a fundamentally simple system called Equidistant Letter Sequencing, or ELS. First the code-breaker runs all the sentences of the literature together so there are no spaces for punctuation and no significance for capital letters. The code begins with a given letter, skips a certain number of letters then alights on another before making the same skip forwards to the third letter.

> *To find the word 'codes' in the phrase 'can you endorse this?', take a letter and miss three until the word 'codes' emerges.*
> C A N Y O U E N D O R S E T H I S

Code-breaking takes another leap ahead when the words are arranged in matrices, with messages reading forwards, backwards, up or down.

While the biblical word searches presented an intriguing puzzle, there were many Jews, Christians and secular academics who doubted the premise that God had hidden messages to mankind in this way. After all, there are different versions of both the Hebrew Torah and the English Bible. Witztum and company used the Koren version. But had the Codex edition been selected as an example, then entirely different results would have been yielded. Idiosyncrasies surrounding the Hebrew language further complicate the issue. During the thousands of years they have been in existence, both the Torah and the Bible have evolved and do not mirror the original words allegedly delivered by God to Moses.

Yet despite the difficulties, biblical codes are back in fashion. Enthusiasts the world over are working to decrypt divine mysteries, inspired by such theories as the da Vinci code. The complex abundance of holy texts and revered artwork will surely keep them busy for a long time to come.

THE TURIN SHROUD

For countless thousands, the Turin Shroud is the holiest of relics. They believe it is the shroud in which Jesus was wrapped following his death, and that the image of a face and body imprinted in the cloth are those of the Saviour himself. But others dispute the age of the shroud, and believe it is the work of an artful medieval hoaxer. Conclusive proof of its authenticity has been hard to come by.

There are some things we know for certain about the shroud. Today, it is housed in the Cathedral of St John the Baptist in the Italian

> There is visual evidence on the shroud of bodily wounds consistent with a crown of thorns and with the torture of crucifixion.

city of Turin. The cloth measures 4.4 m in length and is 1 m wide. The first reliable records of it appeared in France in 1357, and we know that in 1532 it was damaged in a fire. The markings – which appear to be a man's face with shoulder-length hair, a middle parting and a beard and moustache – are etched into the cloth. The image is both three dimensional and photonegative, although no one knows exactly how it was made.

These few facts are probably the sum total of what can be said with certainty about the Turin Shroud. Almost everything else concerning it is the subject of conjecture and controversy.

There is visual evidence on the shroud of bodily wounds consistent with a crown of thorns and with the torture of crucifixion. Yet while some scientists have said that there is blood on the shroud others have disagreed, pointing out that the fragile quantities of DNA have brought forth inconclusive results.

The cynics have insisted that the features on the shroud were painted on by a talented artist in the Middle Ages. This was a time when the Church badly wanted to focus the faithful on convincing relics and deflect their attention from rampant disease and poverty. But in turn, their opponents have claimed that there is not a trace of paint in evidence.

Some scholars of the shroud – known as sindonologists – have recently come to believe that coins once covered the eyes of the dead man and are still visible on the imprint. At least one of the coins is said to be a lepton, produced in the Roman Empire at the time of Christ. But others have been unable to identify the coin marks at all. They point out that, in any case, it was not the Jewish custom to cover the eyes of the dead with coins at that time.

The shroud is housed in Turin Cathedral, although because it is so fragile a replica is usually on display for visitors.

Even the height of the body supposedly kept within the shroud is a source of disagreement. One study claims he stood at 1.8 m while another puts him closer to 1.9 m tall.

Modern scientific methods might well clarify some of these hotly debated issues if only they were applied to the shroud. But its great age and sacred value mean that the Catholic Church is reluctant to permit wide-ranging experiments.

Sceptics thought the long-running debate was nailed in their favour when radiocarbon testing carried out in 1988 put the age of this intriguing cloth firmly in the Middle Ages. To be precise, the findings of researchers at Oxford University, the University of Arizona and the Swiss Federal Institute of Technology put its creation at somewhere between 1260 and 1390, some twelve centuries after the era of Christ. The revelation led the Cardinal of Turin, Anastasio Alberto Ballestrero, to admit publicly that the shroud was a hoax. This was particularly embarrassing for the Catholic Church given that, eight years earlier, Pope John Paul II had reverently kissed it, clearly believing it to be genuine.

However, two factors now point to the carbon test result being flawed. The material taken for testing was removed from the corner of the shroud where repairs were evidently made following a blaze. For the purposes of scientific analysis, the repaired material would not yield accurate results.

Perhaps more significant still were the findings of Swedish textiles expert Dr Mechthild Flury-Lemberg who announced the seams on the shroud were of a style used in the first century AD or before. She caught sight of the seam during a restoration project that took place in 2002.

The findings of a botany professor just prior to the millennium have lent greater weight to the argument for the authenticity of the shroud. Avinoam Danin, of the Hebrew University in Jerusalem, looked not at the cloth but into the minute evidence of plant life upon it. The pollen and the imprints of thorns, said Professor Danin, indicated that the shroud originated in the Middle East. Together with colleagues, he identified the bean caper plant, the Rock rose and Goundelia Tournefortii tumbleweed, an unlikely combination anywhere else in the world other than the Holy Land.

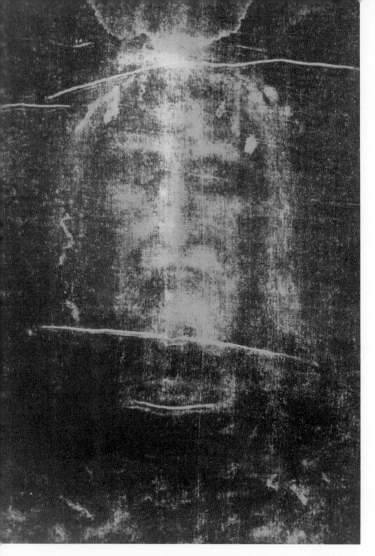

A close-up of the shroud shows the face at the centre of the debate. Could this be the face of Jesus himself?

body was kept in the shroud before his execution and that chemical reactions caused the imprint of his face and body on the cloth.

Leonardo da Vinci is another possible contender for the face of the shroud. The artist and inventor may have been attempting photography using a *camera obscura*, the most rudimentary instrument upon which to secure an image. But, quite apart from the fact that the kind of camera necessary has proved difficult to construct even now, the shroud was reportedly in existence before da Vinci. There is no doubt that if da Vinci could have imprinted his image on the shroud he would have done so, and enormously enjoyed the ensuing furore, but the theory is tenuous.

If the shroud is genuine, the presumption is that it was taken by one of Jesus' disciples and presented to King Abgar V, who ruled from Edessa (in present day Iraq) and was in correspondence with Jesus. Much later it would have found its way to Constantinople – known today as Istanbul – and was stolen when the city was ransacked in the Fourth Crusade early in the thirteenth century. Following this, the French knight Geoffrey de Charny put the relic on display in Lirey, France, and pilgrims flocked to see it. In 1578 it moved to Turin, and it has been there ever since. Surprisingly, the shroud was owned by the House of Savoy (European royalty) as recently as 1983, when it finally became the property of the Vatican.

There is one credible indicator to suggest the shroud is not history's greatest art forgery, and this is the twin wrist wounds visible on the cloth. The bloody spots are definitely visible on

There are several theories in existence that claim the face belongs to someone other than Jesus. Jacques de Molay, the leader of the powerful chivalric sect of the Knights Templar, is one name in the frame. The Knights Templar were persecuted after 1307 by the French king who sought to control their mighty wealth and de Molay was tortured before being burnt at the stake. The contention is that his badly battered the wrists rather than the palms. In the Middle Ages it was assumed that the crucifixion of Christ entailed his hands being nailed into position and so presumably, any belated (fake) representation would have been made that way. But recent research has revealed that nailing through the hands would not be sufficient to keep the human body upright during crucifixion and the victim would have died relatively quickly from suffocation via a collapsed chest. Nails through the two major bones above the wrist would have kept the victim vertical, and denied them such a quick death. It is these grisly details that constitute the best proof of the shroud's authenticity.

In 2004 researchers discovered a second, much fainter face on the opposite side of the shroud, which corresponds exactly to the face on the front. This second image is superficial, meaning that it has not soaked through from paint or some other substance on the front. This finding lends weight to the theory that a chemical reaction between body and cloth implanted the image on the shroud, and it makes the idea of a faked image implausible. Of course, it tells us no more about whether the body in question belonged to Jesus.

Expect a respite in the Turin Shroud debate for a few years. The elusive garment is not scheduled to be seen again in public until 2025, when the controversy will surely be ignited once more.

ANGELS

When a crisis is looming, panic sets in and the heartbeat starts to race. But suddenly a stranger appears out of nowhere to offer a helping hand,

A survey concluded that as many as one-third of Americans had actually seen an angel.

and disaster is averted. A coincidence, perhaps, but many believe such timely intervention is the work of angels sent to guide and protect us.

All the major faiths embrace the existence of angels. Indeed, the Koran, the Bible and the Torah are littered with references to them.

Nor has belief in angels waned in recent times. Eight out of ten Americans questioned for a Fox News poll in 2005 admitted to believing in angels. (The precise breakdown was 86 per cent of women and 72 per cent of men.) A different survey concluded that as many as one-third of Americans had actually seen an angel. So what proof is out there for such widespread conviction?

Author Joan Wester Anderson relates one compelling story concerning her son Tim. On

Christmas Eve, 1983, he and two friends were making their way back from college in Connecticut to her Chicago home. Weather conditions were atrocious and there was a widespread freeze. Having dropped one friend off in Indiana, Tim was driving on a rural road when his car spluttered to a halt. Tim and his friend Jim looked at each other in terror as the voice of the radio announcer – warning against anyone stepping outside into a dangerously icy wind – echoed between them. There was not a house or another car within sight and all around the

> As they battled to stay calm and ward off the cold, they suddenly became aware of headlights flashing…

countryside was cloaked in darkness. As they battled to stay calm and ward off the cold, they suddenly became aware of headlights flashing in the rearview mirror. There was a knock on the window, followed by a cry: 'Need to be pulled?' The voice belonged to a tow truck driver who hitched up the car so they could return home.

When they arrived at their destination, Tim dashed into the house, asking for cash to repay the debt they surely owed to their rescuer. But outside the truck had vanished, along with its driver. Even more mysteriously, they could find only one set of tyre marks in the snow on the road, those belonging to Tim's vehicle.

If the truck had not arrived and towed them, the two young men would undoubtedly have frozen to death. Tim and his mother Joan remain convinced that an angel heard his prayers for help on that Christmas Eve of 1983, and intervened to prevent disaster. The story is among many featured in Joan's book *Where Angels Walk*.

Tales of angel encounters are by no means rare. One magazine entitled *Angels on Earth*, which has a 600,000 circulation, receives about a thousand submissions a month, mostly from Americans. Nor is interest in angels solely a North American phenomenon. Theology graduate Emma Heathcote-James was intrigued by the strong presence of angels perceived among Americans and wondered if the same was true in Britain.

After putting out a plea for personal stories in the media, she was overwhelmed with the response. She received more than a thousand written testimonies from UK residents who believed they had had some kind of angelic encounter, and set about analysing the data. She found that 'people from all cultures, backgrounds and faiths were relating the same types of experience, so (angelic encounter) has a multi-faith and cross cultural element.' The results were published in 2001 in her book, *Seeing Angels*, which is one of many publications on the subject.

Angel reports claim that the heavenly visitors are tall, clad in black or white, male, female or without gender, and are often bathed in light. Apparently they can be cherubic, jovial or serious. Some talk while others are silent. Occasionally, their presence is sensed rather than seen. Often, witnesses draw a distinction between different types of angels, including archangels, messenger and guardian angels.

So anecdotal evidence about the existence of angels is not hard to come across. Pinning that evidence down to specific events poses a harder challenge. The response from cynics is that belief in angels represents a comfort zone that is frequently lacking in the stressful lives of today's citizens. Encounters may have occurred because a generation largely brought up without religion is now urgently seeking spiritual fulfilment. The onset of a new millennium may also have revived long-buried religious feelings in a secular society. Alternatively, events can be explained away as intuition or coincidence. Angelic encounters often take place in hospital and therefore, say some observers, they could simply be a side effect of prescribed drugs.

In Birmingham, England, Muslim accountant Anver Hajee was in hospital suffering from chest pains. His mind was centred on his father and brother, both of whom had died prematurely from heart disease, and on his disabled daughter. Then, Anver saw a figure that he has since presumed to be his guardian angel. 'He was tall, about 7 ft [over 2 m tall], with very good cheekbones and pink cheeks. I felt a warmth coming off him. He touched me and said something like, "You'll be fine."'

Anver insists the incident had nothing to do with the medication he had been prescribed. He kept the experience quiet until he heard a radio programme about angels. Only then did he feel confident to make his spiritual experience public.

Children seem especially prone to seeing angels and there are numerous reports from bewildered parents about angel incidents. This is believed to be because children's minds are uncluttered by preconceived notions and are consequently more open to extraordinary sights and sounds. It is tempting to believe that childrens' reports of encounters with fairy godmothers and invisible friends are in fact all about guardian angels.

The following account provides a poignant example of a child's encounter with angels. When his grandfather was admitted to hospital suffering from terminal cancer, 5-year-old Bryan Simmerman, from New Jersey, told him: 'It's ok Pop-Pop, you can rest now. The angels are with you.' The dying man responded: 'I know, I can see them.' The story is remarkable as the pair came from a non-religious family. And joint testimony about a single incident is all the more persuasive. It is for this reason that the story of an angel appearing before scores of witnesses during the Battle of Mons in the First World War has maintained currency for so long.

The skies allegedly opened up to reveal a winged figure with two others, witnessed by scores of soldiers on the battlefield.

On 23 August 1914, British forces were facing annihilation by the Germans in Belgium. As the outlook grew ever more bleak, the soldiers began to lose all hope of survival. However, at this crucial moment, the skies allegedly opened up to reveal a winged figure with two others, witnessed by scores of soldiers on the battlefield. Together the figures appeared to hold back the Kaiser's men while the British soldiers escaped the onslaught. The combined testimony of those present was so convincing that eminent historian

A.J.P. Taylor accepted the account as fact even as late as 1963.

Since then a shadow of doubt has been cast upon the tale. It was, some scoff, an illusion inspired by fear, which was exaggerated by the authorities to put a favourable spin on the conflict at home. The angelic figure was even taken to be Saint George of England accompanied by armoured figures or a row of bowmen. Furthermore, the story is similar to a fictional one written by Arthur Machen and published in September 1914. It was this, sceptics claim, that seeped into the consciousness of many, influencing their experience. Curiously, though, there are a few letters home from the front which appear to verify the story, pre-dating Arthur Machen's story. And other sources have been found to support the angel accounts. The following paragraph appeared in The *Observer* of 22 August 1915.

'The Rev. A.A. Boddy, Vicar of All Saints' Sunderland, who has just returned home after two months ministerial work at the front, says he had several opportunities of investigating the story of the vision at Mons. The evidence, he says, though not always direct, was remarkably cumulative, and came through channels which were entitled to respect.'

However, as the veteran soldiers from the terrible conflict aged and died during the twentieth century, the potency of the story seemed to ebb away. While angel sightings by individuals appear to be many and frequent in the twenty-first century, it seems that mass visions belong to a different era. But perhaps it is mankind who is changing, not our guardian angels...

MAITREYA AND THE CRYSTAL TEARS

In 1996 an incredible event took place that stunned the world, for it defied any kind of medical explanation. As if this were not remarkable enough in itself, it was also accompanied by numerous religious visions of the mystical figure of Maitreya, a teacher and saviour of mankind.

The strange events started in March of that year, when a 12-year-old Lebanese girl, Hasnah Mohamed Meselmani, was amazed to discover that solid crystals of glass were emerging from her eyes several times a day. These crystals were sharp enough to cut paper, and yet their appearance did not seem to be causing her any

Crystal is one of the hardest and sharpest types of rock existing on earth.

pain. The process continued over a period of eight months, during which time she produced an average of seven crystals a day.

He told her that he was a messenger from God and that he had been responsible for the phenomenon of the crystal tears.

Shortly after it began, Hasnah's worried father took her to the city of Chtaura to visit an ophthalmic expert, Dr Araji. The doctor was amazed by what he saw, and certified that the crystals were real, and that they were definitely forming in Hasnah's eyes. He could find no scientific explanation for the mystery and declared that it must be an act of God.

The phenomenon attracted huge publicity. Journalists and television crews arrived in droves to report what was happening. In order to dispel any doubts, Hasnah and her family allowed the process to be filmed in close-up, at the moment at which a crystal actually appeared from within her eye. Religious authorities competed with

scientific figures to offer a plausible explanation to the public, and to capitalize on the event.

An unexpected explanation was offered by Hasnah herself, however, who described how she had witnessed a vision of the mystical figure of Maitreya. She told how a figure dressed in white and sitting upon a white horse had beckoned to her as she lay in bed at night. He told her that he was a messenger from God and that he had been responsible for the phenomenon of the crystal tears. She asked whether the tears would stop and Maitreya had replied 'When God wills.' Hasnah's brother had apparently heard his sister speaking to someone in this way, but had been unable to see who that person was.

The psychic Madame Blavatsky told of the coming of Maitreya.

The arrival of a great saviour or teacher has been long awaited by many of the major world religions. Although he is known by different names, his function is thought to be the same, whatever the nature of the religion. His coming is expected to be presaged by miracles and visions, such as those that befell Hasnah, and he is thought of as a kind of messiah.

Buddhists call this teacher Maitreya Buddha, the fifth Buddha. Hindus expect the arrival of Krishna, who will arrive as the Kaki-avatar. Christians are waiting for the return of Christ, while Jews anticipate their Messiah. Muslims also await the arrival of their Messiah, Imam Mahdi.

A stone relief of the Maitreya Buddha in India.

In her *Theosophical Glossary*, the famous psychic Madame Blavatsky (see page 178) told of the coming of Maitreya. She wrote about the legendary Persian saviour, Sosiosh, who appears on horseback, predicting that: 'Sosiosh, the Mazdean Saviour, who, like Vishnu, Maitreya, Buddha and others is expected to appear on a white horse at the end of the cycle to save mankind.' Interestingly, in common with both Madame Blavatsky and Hasnah, almost every civilization to have predicted the arrival of Maitreya describes him in the same way – clothed in white, and riding a white horse. Unsurprisingly, he is often referred to as 'The White Knight'.

This mystical teacher, who appears to unite the various disparate elements of world theology, has been sighted on numerous occasions all over the globe. The sightings have been followed by a series of predictions – all delivered by a British author and lecturer, Benjamin Crème – to the effect that the teachings of Maitreya will inspire humanity to forget its differences and work together to share and support each other. Crème claims to have received these utopian visions by a process of 'spiritual telepathy'.

These assertions have generated controversy – can the proclamations of one man be relied upon as evidence of this global unifying force, or are Crème's apparent visions a more calculated attempt to draw people together?

Hasnah's personal accounts would certainly seem to support Crème's claims, and the remarkable existence of the crystals still remains to be explained.

Hasnah went on to declare that she had conversed with the figure of Maitreya on several occasions, during which she had received important advice from him. At one point, he had predicted that a misfortune would befall her family, and advised them to all leave their home temporarily. The whole family obeyed, except for one of her brothers; the next day, the young man was involved in a car crash, from which he was fortunate to escape alive.

Hasnah claims that, later that night, she was reprimanded by Maitreya, who insisted that the family should all have left home together, as he had instructed.

No-one has been able to explain the appearance of the crystal tears – this is a medical mystery in its own right.

This case has baffled many people all over the world. Inevitably, it has also attracted numerous allegations of fraud, and certainly Hasnah's far from affluent family benefited financially from all the surrounding publicity. It should be remembered, however, that no-one has been able to explain the appearance of the crystal tears – this is a medical mystery in its own right. When taken in conjunction with the visions, it really does seem that a remarkable phenomenon took place at this time.

Perhaps we should just accept that there are some occurrences in this world that we cannot explain. Maybe time will provide an answer to the questions raised by this particular case, but in the meantime we should try to be open to the possibility that miracles can, and do, occur.

Disappearances

That people and things go missing without trace is almost beyond our comprehension. Individuals, communities, even whole cities have vanished, seemingly into thin air. When a person in the public eye disappears, such as Lord Lucan or Agatha Christie, the case grips the public imagination and speculation abounds. Often, however, extensive efforts to solve disappearances are futile and we are left baffled. Unless new evidence comes to light, such mysteries will remain unexplained, haunting reminders of our own precarious existence.

THE LOST TREASURE OF THE AZTECS

The legend of the wealth of the Aztecs has been in existence ever since civilization was found on the continent. The original Spaniards who set sail from Cuba to explore the coast of Mexico had the pursuit of riches firmly fixed in their minds. When the first of these Spanish explorers returned to Cuba with finely worked gold, it did not take long for them to return in greater numbers to investigate further.

> When the Spanish arrived in Mexico with finely crafted glass beads, the inhabitants were only too glad to trade their gold for these strange new objects of beauty as they had an entirely different monetary value system.

It is hard to tell whether the great trove of treasure actually existed, or whether it was simply a product of the different values of the two colliding cultures. The Meso-Americans valued gold for its beauty and did not revere it in the same way as the European invaders. Gold ornaments were worn freely by the native people, who appeared to prize it no more highly than items such as beautiful feathers.

When the Spanish arrived in Mexico with finely crafted glass beads, the inhabitants were only too glad to trade their gold for these strange new objects of beauty as they had an entirely different monetary value system. When the Spanish saw the native people handing over their gold with such ease, they began to believe that in this land gold must be incredibly abundant for it to be distributed so freely.

To a certain extent the Europeans were right – at that time the untapped mineral wealth of the country was very great, as they quickly realized when they began to mine the resources of the Americas. The ease with which they acquired the gold from the Aztecs must have fired both their imaginations and their greed. Thus it did not take long for the legend of El Dorado, the city of gold, to take shape and develop.

When Montezuma, the king of the Aztecs, realized that the invaders were eager to acquire gold, he bestowed lavish gifts upon them, hoping to satisfy their needs. The giving of gifts was a polite ritual for the Aztecs, and the Spaniards in turn gave gifts of cloth and beads, which were, in truth, of little value to them. As the Spaniards pushed ever further inland towards his city in an insatiable quest for more gold, the Aztec king grew increasingly desperate, almost emptying the royal coffers in order to please the Spanish.

The Spaniards misinterpreted this generosity as a sign of even greater wealth. Surely, they thought, if the king could afford to give away such valuable gifts, he must have vaults absolutely brimming with gold. The invaders sent much of this gold back to Spain, as a gift to their own king and as a bid for more support, fully expecting to discover more riches when they conquered the city of Tenochtitlan.

On this point, however, the conquistadors were sorely mistaken. When they took command of the city, they found that the hoard of gold was much smaller than expected. On discovering this, they demanded that all citizens hand over every item of gold they possessed. Once this had been amassed, the conquistadors were more satisfied, but it was around now that events began to turn against them.

Angry at being invaded and plundered, the natives turned against the Spanish. A great battle ensued and the Spanish were driven from Tenochtitlan, over the long causeways crossing the lake that encircled the city. The Spaniards were outnumbered by more than one hundred to one, and although they attempted to carry their hoard of treasure out with them on mules, they were unable to protect it and the majority was lost in the lake. Many men drowned because they were laden down with so much precious metal.

The ancient structure of Montezuma Castle in the Verde Valley, Arizona, which was built by a western Anasazi tribe and misleadingly named after Montezuma.

If these stories are true, it is entirely possible that the treasure still exists, somewhere in Mexico, where it has remained hidden for centuries. Only comparatively recently – in the 1980s – was the Templo Major, the central ceremonial pyramid of Tenochtitlan, discovered in the very centre of Mexico City. Workers had been digging a tunnel for a new metro stop when they discovered this architectural treasure. There may be much more than this still waiting to be discovered, buried in the foundations of one of the world's largest cities. The Aztecs may even have buried some of the gold in an effort to hide it from the invaders, either in the city or up in the mountains.

There is also the possibility that the conquistadors did discover a large amount of gold, but concealed its true quantity in order to avoid handing it over to their king. Alternatively, in their greed, they may have miscalculated and found there was just not as much gold in existence as they had originally believed. There is a very real likelihood that this last explanation has some basis in truth, given the avaricious behaviour of the Spaniards and the lengths they went to in order to secure the gold.

Time passed and the Spaniards had renewed success in their invasion efforts, while they continued to search for further riches. Their conquest extended south into South America, where they continued the orgy of greed and destruction against the Incas. It seems likely that they were spurred on by the stories they had heard about the riches of Mexico.

Although history maintains that the Spaniards never actually found the ultimate hoard of the Aztecs, it remains unclear as to whether this is actually the truth. However much gold they found, it is unlikely that they would ever have been satisfied. What is certain is that Aztec gold did exist, as quantities of it have been recovered today, but whether there is a huge hoard still waiting to be discovered remains shrouded in mystery.

THE DINOSAURS

In the long history of life on earth, countless species have become extinct. Of these, perhaps the best known and certainly the most intriguing has been the disappearance of the dinosaurs. For millions of years, these huge beasts were the unquestionable masters of the planet, living on every continent of the world with nothing to challenge their supremacy.

However, there came a point, around 65 million years ago, when the reign of one of the most successful life forms ever to exist came to an end. Just why this happened is an enduring mystery, and although a number of theories have been put forward over the years, they have yet to be proven.

The theories are based upon what slim evidence still exists from the period. By examining rock and fossil formations, some vital information can be gleaned about what may have happened in the past. From these studies experts have established that at the time of the disappearance of the dinosaurs there was great upheaval in progress on earth.

For millions of years, these huge beasts were the unquestionable masters of the planet, living on every continent of the world with nothing to challenge their supremacy.

Examination of the natural history of the planet has enabled scientists to draw a line between the age of the dinosaurs and the age of the mammals which followed. This boundary between two different periods of life on earth separates the older Mesozoic era (the time of the dinosaurs) from the later Cenozoic era (the time of the mammals, which we, as humans, inhabit). Geologists refer to the former age as 'K', and to the latter as 'T' – thus the mass disappearance of the dinosaurs has become known as the 'K-T extinctions'. It was not only the dinosaurs that went into extinction at this time, however. In fact, as much as half of all life on earth ceased.

Geologists have established that the huge disturbances that occurred on the planet were climatic in nature. It seems that conditions altered dramatically and earth ceased to be the relatively temperate and stable planet that it had been throughout the Mesozoic era. Instead, it became the cooler and more changeable world that we know today and, as time went on, a number of ice ages occurred. The speed at which these changes took place at the time of the K-T boundary is a source of great mystery. What could have caused such a rapid change?

Two main theories have been put forward to explain what happened. Some people believe that the change was as a result of a gradual process originating from the activity of the earth itself. Others are of the opinion that there was some kind of massive cataclysmic event, such as a meteor strike on the planet. Both arguments have a substantial amount of evidence to support them.

Those who support the idea of a more gradual climate change believe that it may have been caused by sustained massive volcanic eruptions over a long period of time. This would have

A meteor entering the earth's atmosphere in 2002.

caused a 'greenhouse' effect and altered the global climate dramatically. This theory is lent credence by the fact that geologists are certain that there was indeed a time of increased volcanic activity towards the end of the Cretaceous period.

However, just as there is convincing evidence for the idea of volcanic activity, there is also a very plausible argument to support the notion of a meteor impact. Indeed, it is even possible that perhaps both even took place. Researchers discovered iridium dust, trapped in the layers of rock that correspond to the time of around 65 million years ago. This unusual substance was present in sufficient quantities to indicate that it could only have come from one of two places. Either it had originated from space, in which case the dust could have been released into the atmosphere as a result of a meteor impact, or its source was the molten mantle of the earth which is comparatively rich in iridium.

It seems that a large portion of the Gulf of Mexico is actually an enormous crater.

In addition to looking within earth's structure, scientists have also examined its external appearance, in an effort to try to understand what happened. One of the major problems they have faced, however, is that the planet looks radically different today from how it would have appeared 65 million years ago. This makes it extremely difficult to locate any evidence of either volcanic eruptions or a meteor crater. In 1980, however, a discovery was made that was thought to provide the proof that scientists were looking for.

It seems that a large portion of the Gulf of Mexico is actually an enormous crater. Known as the Chicxulub Crater, it forms the edge of part of the Yucatan Peninsula. The rock formations in the area contain large amounts of shocked quartz, which is formed by violent tremors such as those that occur as a result of an impact. It was estimated that, in order to create such a crater, the meteor would have had to be at least 10 km in diameter. A collision of this magnitude is large enough to have had a truly global effect.

If such a meteor had hit earth, enormous volcanic eruptions would have thrown large amounts of soot into the air and released noxious gases. These would have caused acid rain, which would have poisoned the water supply and destroyed plant life. The quantity of particles in the atmosphere would also have led to a cooling of the earth, as less sunlight would have been able to penetrate the atmosphere. The effect of this would have been similar to that of a nuclear winter.

Bearing in mind that dinosaurs are believed to have been cold-blooded animals, the effect of this global cooling would have been catastrophic. Many animals would have been reduced to torpor, as their metabolisms would have slowed down due to the extreme cold. Food supplies would also have dwindled, as disruptions at the lower end of the food chain, caused by the loss of plant life, affected the carnivores at the upper end. Most must have died of malnutrition.

As time progressed, the climate would have been dragged in the opposite direction. After the initial cooling down of the earth, the increased number of greenhouse gases would have caused it gradually to warm up again – eventually becoming even warmer than it had been originally. Most creatures can only live within certain set parameters of temperature, and those with the capacity to survive the original cooling may then have expired when the subsequent warming took place.

Such extremes would have had a less notable effect on small mammalian creatures since their warm blood would have given them greater protection against these sharp changes. Thus it is to these mammals that some people look in order to explain the demise of the dinosaurs.

One theory is that the survival of the mammals was not merely a question of them out-evolving the dinosaurs and being better adapted to survive the changing environment. After all, it seems that the dinosaurs had reached a new peak of their evolutionary scale shortly before they became extinct, with giant carnivores such as tyrannosaurus rex evolving relatively shortly before the end. Rather, it has been postulated that the mammals simply ate all of the dinosaurs' eggs and thus reduced their numbers. However, this is an extremely difficult hypothesis to prove either way.

The focus upon the eggs is interesting for another reason. Many modern reptile eggs are very sensitive to changes in temperature while they are incubating and any fluctuations can affect the sex of the creature when it hatches. A sustained period of climate change could have led to a huge imbalance in the numbers of males and females, and so had a disastrous effect on their breeding potential and survival rates.

Although the dinosaurs are the most highly publicized species to have suddenly become extinct, they are certainly not the only ones. To date, science has recorded five mass extinctions on earth, of which the end of the dinosaurs was by no means the worst. At the end of the Permian era (290–248 million years ago), for example, more than 90 per cent of all life on the planet was wiped out. Why?

Some scientists have stipulated that there is an element of regularity in these extinctions and that, aside from the asteroid impact theory, there may be another cosmic cause. Perhaps there is a comet or cloud of debris in space that only comes into contact with earth every 25 million years or so. To date, this idea remains to be proven and generally receives far less support than the other theories examined so far.

The science involved in determining the causes of mass extinctions is of great relevance to us today. Human beings have become arguably the most potent force to act upon the world and we have a degree of ability to shape and control our environment. However, this sense of power can be deceptive and we should be prepared to expect the unexpected.

The dinosaurs, too, were the dominant species and yet their reign was brought to an abrupt end. Whether this was due to a single event such as a meteor, or as a result of a slower process of volcanic and tectonic activity, we cannot be certain. It could just as easily have been a combination of the two factors, or it could even have been caused by another factor altogether that has not survived, such as a plague or parasite.

> Human beings have become arguably the most potent force to act upon the world and we have a degree of ability to shape and control our environment.

An unforeseen cataclysmic event, such as a meteor strike, could potentially annihilate our planet and, for all our presumed power, we are just as vulnerable as the dinosaurs. This fear has been reflected in the large amount of popular entertainment which depicts huge apocalyptic disasters befalling the planet, with mankind being powerless to resist, despite all its scientific advances. Only now is it being considered that

A drawing of two of the major species of dinosaur – triceratops and the infamous tyrannosaurus rex.

such a horror, in the form of global climate change, may actually be caused by mankind.

Perhaps we, as human beings, should look at the fate of the dinosaurs and take heed. Many people believe that the rapid progression of technology in the last century or so may be causing the drastic changes in our weather patterns which have been notable for both their frequency and ferocity. The fact that the dinosaurs were most likely killed by such climate change should give us food for thought and send a shiver down our spines.

The changes to our present climate are believed to be responsible for a rate of species extinction that is easily comparable to any of the great mass extinctions of the past. This alarming information has led many scientists to believe that we may potentially be teetering on the threshold of another such extinction.

This can only give us greater impetus to understand the reason why the dinosaurs disappeared. By unravelling the mystery of their extinction, perhaps we will stand a better chance of preventing our own.

THE ROANOKE SETTLERS

The early history of the USA is shrouded in mystery, and the identity of those who discovered the North American continent is still in dispute. Supporters of St Brendan, the Danes, the Chinese and the earliest inhabitants of Asia all lay claim to the discovery. Another enigma is the fate of the Roanoke settlers who, some ninety years after Columbus breached the American shores, vanished without a trace.

Roanoke is an island off the North Carolina coast measuring about 19 km by 3 km. In the sixteenth century, the island would have been covered with untamed vegetation. In 1584, an initial expedition to Roanoke Island was dispatched from England, funded by Sir Walter Raleigh. The explorer and adventurer had been awarded colonial rights by Queen Elizabeth I of England as a special prize for his ocean-going exploits against the Spanish as a privateer, or 'authorized pirate'. The expedition represented a marvellous opportunity to cash in on nature's riches. But rewards were not to be so easily won.

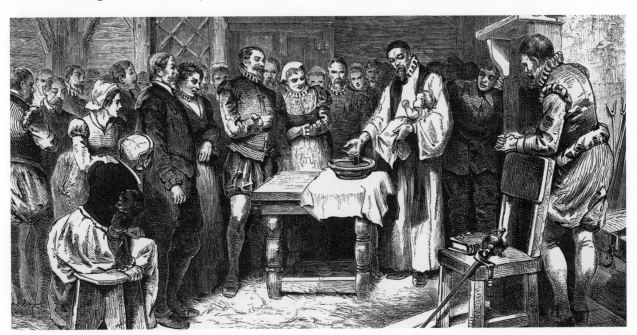

The Roanoke settlers celebrate the baptism of Virginia Dare, the first European child to be born in the American colony.

On arrival at Roanoke this first expedition, under the leadership of Sir Richard Grenville, did not get off to a promising start. Their most pressing concerns were a lack of food (since their supplies had been ruined by seawater) and the presence of local tribes in the vicinity. Even though they were strangers in a strange land, and dependent on the Native Americans for food, water and information, the English chose a heavy-handed approach and antagonism between the settlers and the indigenous population soon accelerated to acts of murder.

Antagonism between the settlers and the indigenous population soon accelerated to acts of murder.

Grenville decided to report back to England, leaving Ralph Lane and about a hundred other men who were painstakingly hacking a settlement out of the wild landscape of Roanoke. He pledged to return in April 1586 with ships and supplies.

Short of food and water, Lane further threatened the locals to secure their co-operation. Unsurprisingly, it was a policy that largely failed. Grenville did not turn up in April 1586 as promised. When Sir Francis Drake stopped at Roanoke in June, a ragged band of Englishmen boarded his ship and headed for home with him. Grenville turned up a few weeks later at the empty site. He deposited fifteen men there before he too returned to England.

In 1587 another pioneering group set off comprising ninety-one men, seventeen women and nine children. Their leader John White, who was a veteran of the first voyage, was told to pick up the fifteen men from Roanoke and head on to Chesapeake Bay to found a new settlement, grandly entitled the 'Cittie of Ralegh'.

When they landed at Roanoke on 22 July 1587, they found the skeleton of just one of the men left there by Grenville, a poor omen for what lay ahead. But the expedition navigator Simon Fernandes claimed he could not go on to Chesapeake for fear of autumn storms. So the colonials were compelled to stay at Roanoke and establish their settlement there.

Everything began on a note of optimism. Within a month White's daughter gave birth to a girl and little Virginia Dare was the first English child born in the American colony. Furthermore, White was hopeful of repairing relations with local Native Americans and he struck up an understanding with the Croatan tribe. However, his attempts at cordiality with other tribes were rebuffed. Hostilities became as tense as before and one man, George Howe, was killed.

When it became clear to White that the long-term viability of the colony looked doubtful, he decided to go back to Britain for extra assistance. He left 117 people at Roanoke, including his daughter, granddaughter and another newborn.

Now international events played their part in the fate of the settlers. As White attempted to rally a return expedition, the Spanish sent its Armada against England. Every high capacity vessel was needed for the defence of the realm, and White found himself reduced to two small ships.

Unfortunately the captains of these vessels were more interested in picking up booty from enemy ships they encountered on the voyage to America than in reaching the stranded settlers. Eventually they were attacked themselves and the supplies earmarked for Roanoke were stolen. White and the ships returned to port in England with nothing.

It was a further two years before White finally returned to Roanoke, landing on 18 August 1590 for what he imagined would be a happy reunion with his granddaughter on her third birthday. He found no one. The settlers had quite simply vanished, and a search of the area confirmed there was no trace of them to be found. But they had left just one clue. The name 'Croatoan' was carved into one of the posts in the Roanoke fort where the settlers had lived, while the letters 'CRO' were found on a tree. In an era when spelling was imprecise, Croatoan or Croatan was the name of both the friendly Native American tribe and of an island. It seemed to White that the settlers had departed, and had indicated their destination as Croatan Island. He pondered why the signal did not include a Maltese cross, which would have indicated that group members considered themselves in danger. But there were no signs of attack at the Roanoke site and White was confident that they must be in a safe haven.

However, White's attempts to reach Croatan were repeatedly thwarted by bad weather, as though the elements were in league against him. Eventually, defeated, he returned at the bidding of his crew to England, leaving the mystery of the missing settlers unsolved.

To this day, there has been no proven explanation for the disappearance of all 117 people. It is possible that they were wiped out in an attack by hostile Native Americans or perhaps even by Spanish forces keen to colonize the region themselves. Captain John Smith, who landed at Jamestown in 1607, was certainly convinced that they had been horribly massacred. Unfortunately, there is no way of finding out the exact location of the Roanoke settlement, so archaeological probes are out of the question.

One current opinion is that a terrible drought paralysed the area at the time. Lack of food and fresh water could have driven the settlers to another site where they later died, perhaps after turning to cannibalism. Alternatively, they might have resorted to boat construction in a desperate

> The settlers had quite simply vanished, and a search of the area confirmed there was no trace of them to be found.

bid to return to England and perished at sea. In support of this theory, it was found that a pinnace or small ship left by White was missing.

Another theory maintains that the Elizabethan political subtext may have a direct bearing on the incident. While Raleigh had an admirer in Queen Elizabeth, he also had a host of enemies at court, who probably envied his success in the colonies and his colonial rights. Modern day investigation has suggested the second Roanoke expedition was sabotaged, primarily to put Raleigh in the shade. Not for the failure of the Roanoke colony but for other overseas misdemeanors, Raleigh was finally put to death at the Tower of London in 1616 by King James I.

So the quest to uncover the truth about the vanished settlers goes on. The prevailing theory is that they were not killed, but were absorbed amongst the Croatan Native Americans. The exact history of the native tribe between the Roanoke settlement and the wholesale colonization of North America is indistinct. However, we do know that following lethal smallpox epidemics, the Croatans joined with the remnants of other tribes. The new group became known as the Lumbee tribe, and evidence has emerged over the years to suggest that the members of this tribe have mixed blood. Indeed, in 1719, white hunters visited Robinson County, North Carolina, just 160 km inland from Roanoke, where they found a tribe of unusually fair-skinned Native Americans who spoke English. A 1790 census of the Robinson County Indians revealed that 54 of the 95 family names mirrored those of the lost colonists. Surely this was more than just coincidence...

An engraving of one of the chieftains of Roanoke island. Could the settlers have become absorbed into the indigenous tribes?

THE VANISHED BATTALION

When a person disappears, a range of possible reasons for what has happened spring to mind. Did the missing person suffer some kind of mental breakdown? Did they take their own life? Or could they even have been kidnapped? These are the most obvious explanations. When, however, a large number of people vanish together, without trace, the usual assumptions become less valid.

When a group of people disappears on land, rather than in the air or at sea, the occurrence becomes even more perplexing. The sea will always hold a certain mystique and is easily capable of hiding the evidence if lives have been lost there. This is much harder to do on land, however, and it is thus truly remarkable that, in 1915, no fewer than 250 soldiers and 16 officers simply disappeared from a battlefield in the Dardanelles region of France.

Although well known for its scrupulous record keeping, the military was and is unable to shed any light on what might have happened. Furthermore, the strong adherence to the laws that prevent desertion would seem to preclude the idea of these men trying to escape their duties. It is very unlikely that more than a few of the officers spoke French, and anyone captured deserting would have been shot as an example to others. In addition to this, the men who disappeared were formed from the staff of the king's Sandringham estate. Undoubtedly, this would have been a source of great honour to them and not something that they would have discarded lightly.

The men in question had formed E company of the Fifth Territorial Battalion of the Royal Norfolk Regiment, which had been formed in 1908 at the personal behest of King Edward VII. More informally, however, the soldiers were known as 'The Sandringhams'. These men would all have known each other well, both through their work on the estate and due to the fact that they had all grown up together in the same area.

The Sandringham estate, from which the battalion obtained its nickname.

Prior to the outbreak of war, the company consisted of just over a hundred part-time territorial soldiers, but after hostilities began more men from the area joined up voluntarily. In those days, military rank would have been decided by social class rather than on any martial merit, with the members of the local gentry forming the ranks of officers. The middle-ranking soldiers, the non-commissioned officers (NCOs), would have been chosen from workers such as the butlers, foremen and gamekeepers, while the rank and file of the troops would have consisted of the labourers and servants from the royal estate.

Despite their lack of experience, the men were keen to engage with the enemy and, after their initial training, they were taken to Turkey to

The last sighting of the missing men occurred on 12 August 1915, just two days after they had arrived at the conflict.

participate in the battle at Gallipoli. They were led into this first engagement by their commanding officer, Colonel Horace Proctor Beauchamp, who would have been eager for his company to make its name on the battlefield.

The last sighting of the missing men occurred on 12 August 1915, just two days after they had arrived at the conflict. They had been given the order to advance on a position that was held by the Turks about 2 km away. The position was well defended and they had to attack in broad daylight with little in the way of cover. As the troops

advanced, Colonel Beauchamp led from the front and harried his men to press the assault. The soldiers are believed to have driven ahead further than the rest of the main assault and may have become cut off from them. They were last sighted entering some woods near the Turkish position, in disarray, and obscured by smoke and clouds.

When the battle was over it was realized that the entire group of men was missing. Despite the horrendous rate of casualties in the First World War, it was unusual for there to be no survivors at all. Enquiries were made to ascertain whether any of them were being held in Turkish prisoner-of-war camps, but this was proven not to be the case. How, then, could this many men have simply disappeared, literally, in a cloud of smoke?

Is it possible that the reason behind the battalion's disappearance lies within the realms of the paranormal? In 1965, on the fiftieth anniversary of the fateful Gallipoli landings, a former New Zealand sapper, Frederick Reichardt, claimed that he had witnessed a strange event that could explain what had happened, and his account was supported by three other veterans.

Reichardt stated that he and his fellow soldiers had witnessed the Sandringhams' heroic charge into the woods, whereupon they seemed to rush headlong into a peculiar formation of about eight loaf-shaped clouds which were lying at ground level over the area. The soldiers were seen to enter the clouds, but never appeared again. Reichardt states that, after about an hour, the clouds rose up into the sky, leaving no trace of the soldiers of the Norfolk battalion.

Whether this explanation has any basis in reality is open to speculation. There are some

Allied troops gather on the beaches in the Dardanelles.

who would argue that perhaps some kind of religious intervention had taken place.

Others view the story of the clouds as evidence of an extraterrestrial abduction. This seems to tie in with some of the descriptions given when ships and aircraft disappear, as they often vanish into cloudy skies. It should be remembered, however, that heavy clouds are an indication of poor weather conditions, which could explain the disappearances.

A third suggestion is that the clouds seen on the battlefield were not due to atmospheric conditions at all, but were in fact palls of smoke emanating from the intense fire and bombardment of the battlefield. As such, then, the soldiers had not disappeared at all, but had simply been killed. This seems unlikely, however, as there are very few military engagements in which there are no survivors whatsoever.

A fourth and final possibility is believed by many historians to be the most likely explanation, although perhaps this is because they are unwilling to countenance some of the other, more unusual, theories. The suggestion put forward is linked to the brutal reputation of the battalion's Turkish opponents, who were renowned for taking no prisoners. If they did happen to hold any soldiers captive, it was usually only for a very brief period, before they then executed them en masse. In support of this theory, a large number of corpses was found buried on the battlefield in the following years, with execution-style gunshot wounds to the head. Could the peculiar disappearance of all these men be attributed simply to a mass murder?

Although the disappearance of these men is shrouded in mystery, it is certainly not the only occasion on which soldiers of the Great War have gone missing in action. What sets this mystery apart from others, however, is the fact that all the men vanished together, never to be seen again.

THE *MARY CELESTE*

A ship bobbing on the open seas, its crew inexplicably missing, sails flapping aimlessly in the wind. A search aboard reveals no trace of life, and few clues as to what might have occurred. The story of the *Mary Celeste* is one of history's most intriguing mysteries.

On 7 November 1872, Captain Benjamin Spooner Briggs sailed out of New York. He was

Theories about the possible fate of those aboard have abounded.

bound for Genoa, Italy on what should have been a workaday voyage. With him was his wife Sarah, 30, their 2-year-old daughter Sophia Matilda, and a capable crew of two Americans, one Dane, one German and three Dutchmen. In the hold of the half-brig *Mary Celeste* was a cargo of 1,700 barrels of alcohol intended for wine fortification.

After she left New York there were no further reports of her progress until 5 December, when the ship *Dei Gratia*, loaded with petroleum, spotted her between the Azores and the Portuguese coast. As it happened, the captain of the *Dei Gratia*, David Morehouse, was one of Briggs' personal friends, and the pair had dined together shortly before Briggs left New York.

Morehouse noted the erratic progress of the *Mary Celeste* and tried to make contact for some time before dispatching a boarding party.

Led by Chief Mater Oliver Deveau, the merchant seamen climbed aboard the erring ship. But it quickly became clear that the *Mary Celeste* was completely deserted, and there were few clues as to why. The chronometer and sextant were missing but the log book was in its place. Hatches were open but the crew's oilskins were still there. The lifeboat was gone, although food and water supplies were intact, as were the barrels. The galley stove had been dislodged. Belongings aboard the ship were soaked and there was water sloshing about in the hold where one pump was not working. But the ship was, to all intents and purposes, still seaworthy. Ignoring the sinister atmosphere aboard the mystery ship, some hardy members of the crew from the *Dei Gratia* sailed her into Gibraltar.

Reading the last entry in the ship's log, Morehouse learnt that the *Mary Celeste* had passed 10 km from St Mary's in the Azores at 8 am on 25 November, some ten days earlier. Just what happened between that day and the discovery of the empty ship may never be discovered.

Theories about the possible fate of those aboard have abounded. Suspicions that it was

The *Mary Celeste* was found floating, empty but undamaged, in the sea between the Azores and the Portuguese coast.

some manner of insurance scam have been dispelled. Briggs was a devout man with a solid reputation. Likewise, there is nothing to indicate a mutiny among the crew, who were all experienced men well used to short commercial voyages such as these.

Abel Fosdyk claimed that during a swimming race, some members of the crew were attacked by sharks. When the others rushed to see what was happening, they fell overboard and met the same fate...

Some have speculated that Briggs and his crew members became drunk on the liquor they were carrying. But their cargo was lethal industrial alcohol rather than regular tipple – and the scenario would have required a sea-change in personality by the teetotaller Briggs – it seems wholly unlikely.

What about the possibility of an attack by pirates? But surely if pirates had boarded the vessel there would be some sign of a desperate struggle? Besides, the $35,000 cargo had not been stolen, nor had the ship's supplies.

A freak wave caused by an undersea earthquake has also been ruled out, as there are no records of such cataclysmic events occurring at the time. And although a sudden waterspout might explain why the ship was sodden, it could not account for the disappearance of those on board.

At a British Board of Inquiry in Gibraltar, Morehouse had to defend himself against charges of conspiring both with Briggs and against him to coin the salvage value of the ship. But ultimately the inquiry proved nothing, other than to assert that there was no sign of blood on the ship.

One man, having examined the calamity in depth, felt he had touched on the correct explanation. Charles Edey Fay made a detailed study of the oddities surrounding the discovery of the *Mary Celeste*. He concluded that Briggs had probably taken advantage of unexpectedly calm conditions to ventilate the cargo. In fact, nine barrels of the alcohol had leaked, causing noxious fumes to pour out of the hold. In the chaos that ensued, perhaps it seemed as if an explosion was imminent or that the ship was sinking.

Briggs, who had never carried alcohol before, may well have given the order to abandon ship and take to the lifeboat. His best option was to maintain contact with the ship through the halyard, a weighty rope. Once they felt the danger had passed, those in the lifeboat would have clambered back aboard the ship and resumed their voyage. What they had not anticipated was a change in the weather. Fay's theory is that they were surprised by a squall, and the halyard was severed, leaving the lifeboat adrift in the open. The lifeboat would then either have sunk, or drifted in a south-easterly direction away from the land and the shipping route. Either way, its hapless occupants were doomed either to drown or to die of thirst, starvation or exposure.

A letter from the Servico Meteorolgico dos Acores confirmed that a period of calm gave way to gale force winds during that fateful night of 25 November 1872. The halyard upon which the lives of those in the lifeboat depended was found frayed over the side of the ship.

Fay's findings are outlined in *The Story of the Mary Celeste*, which he had published in 1942. His account, rooted in fact, was very different from many of the more fanciful stories inspired by the empty ship. One fictional account, published in 1883, was written by a certain Arthur Conan Doyle. He changed the name of the ship to *Marie Celeste* and asserted that everyone aboard the fated vessel came to a violent end.

The waters were further muddied by the claims of Abel Fosdyk. He claimed to have been a stowaway aboard the *Mary Celeste*, and recounted how he had watched the captain and some crew members being eaten by sharks during a swimming race. As the others rushed to witness the tragedy they all fell overboard and met the same end. Fosdyk said he clung to driftwood until being washed up on African shores. But Fosdyk wrongly identified the nationalities of all the crew, so it seems his account was also made up.

Fictional though their accounts may be, Conan Doyle and Fosdyk both helped to keep the memory of the *Mary Celeste* alive. Intriguingly, she was not the only ship found abandoned at sea. In 1849, the Dutch Schooner *Hermania* was discovered dismasted and deserted. Six years later, the *Marathon* was found in a similar state, yet neither of these ships became household names.

Arthur Conan Doyle changed the name of the ship to Marie Celeste and asserted that everyone aboard the fated vessel came to a violent end.

The infamous ship was built in Nova Scotia in 1860, and was to have a brief but dramatic existence. Some accounts allude to her being an unlucky ship prior to 1872, although there are no details to support this notion. But, as the sole survivor of the 1872 disaster, she was not destined for a long life. Just a dozen years after limping into Gibraltar, she was wrecked on the rocks at Haiti. Her captain on that occasion was later punished for attempting insurance fraud.

In 2001, the coral-covered wreck of the *Mary Celeste* was located. The discovery caused ripples of excitement worldwide, but the ship's skeleton gave up no secrets, and eventually the hype subsided. The mystery of the *Mary Celeste* proved as impenetrable as it was 130 years ago.

DR LEON THEREMIN

The peculiar disappearance of the scientist and inventor Dr Leon Theremin is thought to have more to do with the shady world of international espionage than with any other possible cause. It seems likely that Theremin vanished in order to work for the Kremlin and thus further the Soviet cause, but whether this was of his own choosing, or whether he was coerced into doing so, is a matter for speculation.

Dr Theremin arrived in the USA in 1927, bearing his original Russian name, Lev Segeivitch Terman. His particular area of expertise was radio electronics, and it did not take him long to put these skills to commercial use. After spending some time working on a revolutionary musical instrument, he successfully obtained a patent for it, and it became known as the 'Theremin'. The way in which this strange instrument is played is totally unprecedented, since sounds are created by moving the hands around two radio antennae rather than by any physical contact with the machine.

The eerie notes emitted by this instrument resulted in its use in a number of films of the time, including those of Alfred Hitchcock, in which the sounds were used to create suspense. The effect of this was to raise Dr Theremin's public profile and he began to enjoy a kind of celebrity status in the USA. This fame, however, may have proved to be a double-edged sword, as whilst Theremin enjoyed the fruits of his success, those with sinister intentions became aware of how this talented scientist could assist them in their schemes and plans.

It was Theremin's experiments in the field of radio waves and frequencies, and subsequent creation of the first radio surveillance 'bug', which are thought to have sealed his fate. In 1938 the inventor went missing, and after a while he was presumed to be dead.

It eventually transpired that Theremin had left his

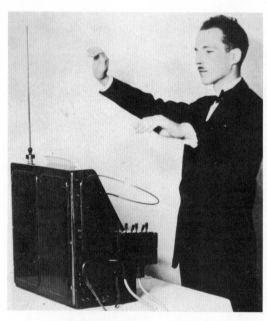

Leon Theremin playing his revolutionary musical instrument.

house in 1938 in the company of several Soviet agents, who accompanied him back to his homeland. Here, he was thought to have worked for the Soviets on espionage devices and security systems. It is unclear whether or not he was in fact kidnapped, but it seems unlikely that he would have voluntarily exchanged his successful life in New York for the Siberian labour camp in which he ended up.

Many questions about this intelligent man remain unanswered. Was Theremin really interested in using his skills to further the demands of the Cold War powers? This seems unlikely and, although trained in the field of science, when given the choice, Theremin applied himself instead to the peaceful development of music.

Theremin's unexplained disappearance was one of the many curious incidents that have been attributed to the Soviet authorities during the Cold War.

Theremin's unexplained disappearance was one of the many curious incidents that have since been attributed to the Soviet authorities during the Cold War. The incredible paranoia and secrecy of that period has left many lasting mysteries. Only now, years after the era ended, are we finding even small clues as to the truth of what actually went on at that time.

LORD LUCAN

The disappearance of Lord Lucan has perplexed the nation and confounded the law for decades. There are many unanswered questions concerning the crimes from which he fled and, thirty years later, the mystery is no nearer to being solved.

Until the time of his vanishing, Lord Lucan lived the life of a typical English aristocrat. After leaving boarding school, he embarked upon a short career in the armed forces. This was followed by a brief stint in merchant banking before he turned his hand to his main passion in life – gambling. In this, he displayed an obvious affinity with risk-taking. In fact, he enjoyed such success that he earned himself the nickname of 'Lucky', and, to the consternation of his wife, took up gambling as a profession.

However, as time went on, Lucan's luck appeared to change and he accrued a large tally of gambling debts that threatened the financial security of his children. It was this, together with other factors, which led to the breakdown of his marriage and the ensuing bitter custody battle.

On 7 November 1974 matters went from bad to worse. In Lucan's family home in London, two crimes took place – the murder of the children's nanny, Sandra Rivett, and the attempted murder of his wife. Accounts of the events which took place on this night vary as much as the many theories that attempt to explain what happened. However, the identity of the prime suspect for both of these crimes is something upon which all seemed to agree – Lord Lucan himself.

After the crimes took place, Lucan gave his own personal account to friends. He stated that an assailant had entered the house and brutally attacked his wife, leaving her hysterical and bleeding profusely. Lucan had interrupted the assault and wrestled with the attacker, slipping during the struggle in the blood that covered the floor. Realizing that he had thus unwittingly implicated himself in the attack, he reasoned that he would have difficulty in proving his innocence, and decided to flee.

In opposition to this is the report given by Lady Lucan, which was supported by an inquiry. In this, she claimed that Lucan had intended to murder her that night, but that the attempt had gone wrong and he had killed the nanny by mistake. Lady Lucan stated that she herself had fought with her ex-husband, and had been lucky to escape with her life. Her injuries appeared to support this story, but was her assailant actually her husband?

A third theory that has been put forward is that Lucan had hired a hit man to kill his wife, but that the supposed assassin had mistakenly murdered Sandra Rivett instead, as the two women were of a similar build. Lucan then attempted to dispose of Rivett's body, but on being disturbed by his wife had tried to murder her, in line with the original plan.

Many believe that the fact that Lucan fled the scene of the crime and abandoned his distressed wife is proof of his culpability. Since Lucan's disappearance, there have been many unofficial reported sightings of this elusive fugitive all over the world. This has served only to deepen the sense of mystery surrounding this particular case, and it seems likely that unless he surfaces, the truth of the crime and how he managed to vanish without trace may never be known.

Lord Lucan on his wedding day in 1963.

AGATHA CHRISTIE

It is somehow fitting that Agatha Christie, the undisputed queen of mystery writing, should have been involved in her own mysterious event – her sudden, unexplained disappearance.

Christie disappeared on the evening of Friday 3 December 1926. When asked by the police to provide an alibi, her husband Archie was forced to admit that he had spent the weekend with his mistress. This information led police to suspect that Archie may have had a motive for murder, or that she may have taken her own life.

A wide-ranging search began immediately and, the next day, her abandoned car was discovered, strewn with her clothes and belongings. The vehicle was located near both a quarry and a lake, fuelling suspicion that Christie may have committed suicide. Coincidentally, the lake had actually featured in one of her crime novels as the site of a drowning. In light of these factors, the police had it dredged, but they found nothing.

The search was then widened to the surrounding countryside, with thousands of volunteers drafted in. This also proved fruitless. Then, after a few days of press publicity, Christie was identified as being alive and well in a health spa in Yorkshire, where she was staying under an assumed name.

The official explanation was that Christie had been suffering from amnesia, brought on by the death of her mother. This, however, sounded more like a fabrication than anything grounded in reality, and the public remained mystified.

Over the years, there has been much speculation about what happened. Could it have been an act of revenge on Christie's adulterous husband, or even a cleverly constructed publicity stunt? Christie never revealed her actions or motives to anyone, and as she died in 1976, it is unlikely that the truth of her mysterious disappearance will ever be revealed.

HOUNDS SEARCH FOR NOVELIST

Beagles were used yesterday in the renewed hunt around Newlands Corner for Mrs. Agatha Christie, the vanished novelist, the latest portrait of whom appears above. On the right is Rosalind, her seven-year-old daughter, photographed in the grounds of her home at Sunningdale.

A newspaper clipping from the period in which the famous authoress went missing.

FLIGHT 19

One of the most intriguing disappearances of all time was the loss of an entire squadron of aircraft, which vanished without trace, leaving no clue as to what had happened. The occurrence engendered much controversy, not only because there were conflicting views on the exact circumstances behind the event, but also because it kick-started the mythical reputation surrounding the area of the disappearance, the now infamous Bermuda Triangle in the Atlantic Ocean.

The squadron's compasses were not working and the pilots believed themselves to be lost.

All kinds of explanations have been put forward in an attempt to understand the puzzle. Some blame freak weather conditions, whilst others, more bizarrely, believe that the squadron may even have been kidnapped by aliens. This theory was popularized by Stephen Spielberg in his film *Close Encounters of the Third Kind*, in which the pilots of Flight 19 were shown being returned to earth in an alien spacecraft.

This intriguing case poses many questions. How was it possible that not one, but all five planes in a squadron, with several experts on board, could vanish so inexplicably? Even more bewildering was the fact that the search and rescue plane that was sent after them was also lost, for reasons that are still unknown.

Flight 19 – consisting of five Naval Avenger torpedo-bombers – departed Fort Lauderdale on a training flight on 5 December 1945. Each of the five planes was supposed to have had three men on board, but on the day in question, one had failed to appear, so that this flight consisted of fourteen airmen in total. Of these, thirteen were in the final stages of their training, although all of them were more than capable of handling their aircraft. The exercise was being led by Lt Charles Taylor, a highly experienced pilot, who had acquired much expertise in flying over the Florida Keys.

Their flight plan was to conduct a practice bombing run over an area known as the 'Hen and Chickens Shoals' that lay to the east of the Florida Keys. The squadron was then to continue to fly east over the ocean until it was around 190 km from the shore, before turning north for another 113 km. It would then turn south-west and return to base. This triangular course would take the aircraft over the Bahamas, and would steer them almost continuously through the Bermuda Triangle.

US Navy 'Avenger' torpedo bombers flying in formation.

The flight took off at 2.10 pm in good weather, although conditions looked as if they might take a marked turn for the worse towards the evening. After less than two hours, just before 4.00 pm, Fort Lauderdale received a radio transmission in which Lt Taylor stated that the squadron's compasses were not working and the pilots believed themselves to be lost. It is now known that the Bermuda Triangle is one of two areas of the world – the other being the Devil's Triangle in Asia – in which there is an unusual level of magnetic interference which can adversely affect compass readings. Could this be the reason behind the loss of so many ships and aircraft in the region?

Lt Taylor reported over the radio that he believed that the squadron was flying over the Florida Keys. He was advised that, if he was certain of this, he should direct the aircraft north towards Miami and the mainland.

If, as is thought today, Lt Taylor was mistaken and he was in fact over the Bahamas, then by flying north, Flight 19 would have taken itself further out into the Atlantic Ocean and away from safety.

No-one had any reason to suspect that this was the case, however, and the squadron continued northwards. To complicate matters further, atmospheric interference from the approaching storm, coupled with the radio waves from commercial radio broadcasts in nearby Cuba, were hampering efforts to communicate with the flight. Taylor was urged to switch to the emergency frequency, which would have facilitated radio communication, but he refused. One of the aircraft was encountering problems with its radio, and Taylor feared that by changing frequencies he might lose contact with it altogether.

As time passed, the sense of urgency at the Fort Lauderdale base increased. As it was winter, the sun was due to set at around 5.30 pm, and bad weather conditions were moving down from the north.

At 5.15 pm, radio contact was briefly re-established, and Taylor informed the base that the flight was now heading west. He was heard advising the squadron to remain close together. The plan was that when the first aircraft ran out of fuel the remaining bombers would all ditch in the sea, thus increasing the likelihood of everyone surviving.

A seaplane, the first of several rescue aircraft, was launched shortly after 6.00 pm, but it rapidly lost contact with the shore. This was attributed to the bad weather, which had caused an antenna to become iced over. Nevertheless, it seemed that the base had lost another of its machines. A further aircraft, a Martin Mariner, was then sent after the seaplane, but, once more, radio contact was lost. Shortly after the Mariner had failed to appear at the scheduled rendezvous, the crew of a nearby ship reported sighting an aircraft that exploded. They were unable to attempt any kind of rescue, as by now the conditions at sea were atrocious.

What is so baffling about this disappearance is that no survivors, bodies or debris from the lost squadron were ever found. Although the poor weather may have had a large role to play, no-one could be sure of exactly what had happened, and a US Navy inquest attributed the disaster to 'causes or reasons unknown'. To this day, it is a complete mystery how an entire squadron of aircraft could simply disappear when it was so close to its home coastline.

GLENN MILLER

Glenn Miller not only enjoyed great acclaim as a musician and entertainer, but also served as an officer in the US Air Force during the Second World War. His successful combination of the two roles earned him great respect and he played a large part in boosting the morale of the Allied troops during the conflict.

So it was a huge shock to the world, when, having boarded an aircraft in England on 15 December 1944, he disappeared into oblivion. He had been on his way to Paris to conclude arrangements with his band for the Christmas Day concert for Allied troops, but he never reached his destination. The true reason for his disappearance remains unknown to this day, although there has been much speculation as to what happened to the famous performer.

It was not unusual during the 1930s and 1940s for aircraft to vanish inexplicably. Such losses were not confined to the Bermuda Triangle but occurred all over the world. While no-one could be sure of the reasons for these disappearances, the most probable explanation was that it was mechanical failure because of the fledgling nature of the aviation industry at that time.

Aside from this possibility, two main theories (one from each opposing side of the war) have been put forward to explain what happened to Miller. The German tabloid newspaper *Bild* claimed that Miller had died from a cardiac arrest while in the company of a prostitute. It was suggested that these facts had been covered up by

the British and Americans in order to protect the troops' morale. No evidence has ever come to light to support this claim and the Allies dismissed it as mere propaganda.

The Allies maintained that Miller's light aircraft, a Norseman UC-64, had encountered bad weather which had caused it to ditch in the English Channel. It is certainly true that Miller's flight had been delayed for several days by stormy conditions, so there might be some truth behind this theory.

Recently, however, fresh evidence has come to light that may suggest a completely different explanation and might, indeed, reveal elements of a cover-up on the part of the Allies. This new information is contained in the logbook of an RAF navigator, Fred Shaw, and may hold the key to the disappearance. In fact, the revelations within its pages have been described by the Ministry of Defence as 'the most likely solution to the mystery'.

During the war, Shaw carried out bombing raids in an Avro Lancaster, and his records show that, on the day in question, his bomber had been recalled from a raid over Germany due to bad weather. It was usual in these cases for bombers to jettison their load over the sea as a precaution before landing. For this purpose there were specially marked jettison areas which all aircraft were advised to avoid.

It is entirely possible that either Miller's aircraft strayed into this no-go zone, or else the bomber dropped its load outside the defined boundaries. Whatever the case, the crew of the bomber reported seeing a small aircraft hit the water after being thrown off track by the bombs.

Whether or not these facts were known to the Allied command at the time is another mystery in itself. It is unlikely, however, that they would have run the risk of damaging public morale during the war. Sixty years later, the truth of the matter may finally be coming to light.

Glenn Miller and his band performing in 1943.

AMELIA EARHART

Even as a child, Amelia Earhart set herself apart from her peers. Growing up in Atchison, Kansas, she spent her spare time shooting rats with a rifle, climbing trees and riding. After completing her schooling she worked as a nurse's aide in a Canadian military hospital before beginning a career in aviation. Thrilled at the prospect of a newly emerging civilian aircraft industry, she persuaded her father to pay for a first flying lesson on 28 December 1920. A year later she bought an aircraft of her own, a bright yellow bi-plane nicknamed 'Canary'. Before long she was achieving aviation records.

In 1922 she was the first woman to reach 4,270 m. In 1928 she became the first woman to cross the Atlantic. She made this audacious flight with two men in a Fokker F7, which departed from Trepassey Harbour in Newfoundland and arrived at Burry Port in Wales some 21 hours later.

Four years after this, she became the first woman to fly solo across the Atlantic. Bad conditions meant she had to put down in Londonderry, Northern Ireland, rather than Paris as planned. Nevertheless she was hailed a national hero, becoming the first woman to be awarded the 'Distinguished Flying Cross'. An international celebrity, she rubbed shoulders with royalty, received roses from Italian dictator Mussolini and had an audience with the pope. The public was enthralled by her continuing adventures, like the solo flight across the Pacific from Honolulu to Oakland, California, in 1935.

In 1931 she married publisher and publicist George Putnam who managed her career. Although Earhart had already satisfied her dearest ambition – to prove that women were equal to men in jobs that required 'intelligence, co-ordination, speed, coolness and willpower' – she yearned to undertake one more spectacular exploit. As her fortieth birthday loomed, she determined to fly around the world.

She yearned to undertake one more spectacular exploit. As her fortieth birthday loomed, she determined to fly around the world.

In 1937, a first attempt at a round-the-world flight was aborted after Earhart's aircraft crashed on take-off in Hawaii. But when she took off from Miami on 1 June that year, accompanied by navigator Fred Noonan, all went according to plan. The two commenced their 46,670 km odyssey in favourable conditions.

By the end of the month, all but 11,265 km of the marathon had been completed. However, the hardest leg lay ahead. Earhart had to fly from Papua New Guinea to a tiny, uninhabited atoll called Howland Island in the middle of the ocean.

A runway was constructed especially for the event, and the US Navy Coast Guard cutter *Itasca* was standing by to provide radio guidance. Despite all the preparations made for the tricky journey, it ended in disaster. Radio contact

The spirited aviatrix had achieved everything she wanted in life, but she yearned to take on one more big challenge.

between Earhart and *Itasca* was at first patchy and then became non-existent.

On 2 July 1937, the *Itasca* headed north-west in a bid to find the missing aircraft. There were distorted radio signals, and wild speculation that the missing pair was marooned on any one of numerous deserted islands in the region. However, some sixteen days later, the huge search and rescue operation was called off, having drawn a blank.

Before long there were a host of conspiracy theories about the disappearance. Even with the passing of time, these have not abated.

A 1943 film called *Flight for Freedom* suggested Earhart had been employed by the US government on a spying mission over Japanese-held territory. Although the fateful flight was prior to the Second World War, tensions were already running high in the Pacific as Japan, having invaded China, sought to strengthen its grip on the region. This theory might have been dismissed as Hollywood hype were it not for a series of perplexing events that occurred during the ensuing world conflict.

In 1944, after the Americans captured Saipan from the Japanese, soldiers found a photograph album containing pictures of Earhart. There were reports by the Saipanese of sightings of a white woman on the island. Could it mean that the missing aviatrix was on Saipan? An army sergeant claimed to have seen US marines on the island guarding a hangar housing Earhart's plane, which was later burned, according to him.

On the adjoining island, Tinian, a marine gunner from the US believes he was shown the graves of Earhart and Noonan in 1944. He was told they had been executed as spies.

The collective implication of these accounts is that Earhart was indeed a US government spy, who was captured by the Japanese and killed. Rather than admit the truth and risk the embarrassment of causing the death of this popular figure, US authorities decided to cover up the scandal.

The implication of these accounts is that Earhart was a US government spy, who was captured by the Japanese and killed.

However, this is not the only theory about Earhart's disappearance. Another says that, with the plane running short of fuel, she and Noonan landed on or near the uninhabited island of Nikumaroro, where they ultimately perished.

If this was indeed the case, then they might have discovered a stash of supplies on Nikumaroro, left by a ship's captain and some of his crew who were shipwrecked there in 1929. After being rescued, Captain Daniel Hamer explained: 'Before leaving camp, all provisions etc. were placed in the shelter but I sincerely hope that no one will ever be so unfortunate as to need them.'

When the island was searched in 1940, there was evidence of recent habitation. But there was a marked absence of plane wreckage and, indeed, bodies. Skeleton parts discovered on the island were later said to be that of a man, possibly one of the victims of the SS *Norwich City* shipwreck. The analysis could have been incorrect, but unfortunately re-examination is now impossible since the bones are missing. Nevertheless, one devoted group, The International Group for Historic Aircraft Recovery, felt the evidence for Earhart on Nikumaroro was so compelling that it mounted a series of expeditions to search for clues. Nothing it has found to date puts the theory beyond doubt. But expedition members have discovered the remains of a shoe that might have fitted the aviatrix and some items that possibly came from the plane. Although it still favours the Nikumaroro theory, TIGHAR investigators have been to other islands in pursuit of the truth about Amelia Earhart.

Yet another theory in existence is that Earhart was kept prisoner throughout the war and released when her prison camp was liberated, returning incognito to live under an assumed name in America. Unfortunately, the proof to support this notion is sparse indeed.

Science will almost certainly answer the Earhart mystery after appropriate evidence is brought forth. But at the moment that remains elusive and the hunt for clues continues.

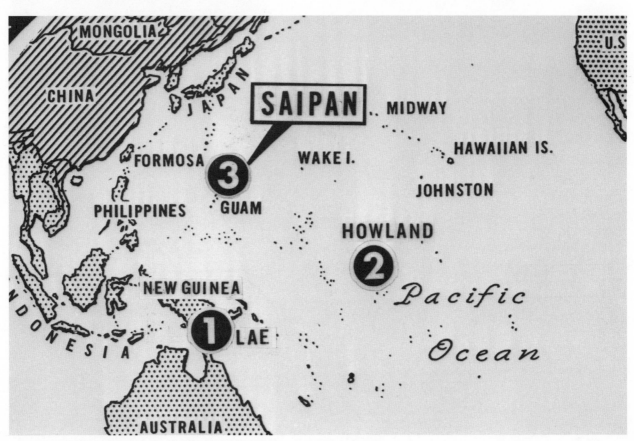

A map of Earhart's route shows how she may have ended up on the island of Saipan. Could she have been a US agent, spying on the Japanese?

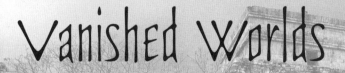

Vanished Worlds

Throughout the history of mankind, cities and states have sprung up all over the world, achieved their age of greatness and then subsided back into the dust from which they came. Some of these lost worlds leave written evidence of their great achievements encrypted in a forgotten language, such as the Egyptian hieroglyph or the Mayan codex. Others may leave behind little more than a puzzling legacy of monuments or even just the legends of their existence.

ATLANTIS

When it comes to discussing the mystery of Atlantis, there are two opposing views. One view holds that it was a great civilization from long ago, known and discussed among the ancients. The other insists it is a long-standing fabrication, a fictional island that represents a lost Eden.

The most significant account of Atlantis is by the ancient philosopher Plato (427–347BC) in two stories called *Critias* and *Tinnaeus*. The sceptics claim that the entire account is a metaphor, and that Plato is using Atlantis to

So just what does Plato say about this utopian Atlantis?

illustrate the disastrous fate of corrupt regimes. Yet significantly Plato says more than once that the stories he recites are true. Nowhere else in his work does he claim allegorical events to be real.

So just what does Plato say about this utopian Atlantis? Well, it was big – larger than Asia and Libya combined. Its people were virtuous, its soldiers skilful, its kings wise. There were fertile plains backed by mountains, hot and cold springs, horse racing and elephants. A central temple was adorned with golden statues. A system of deep-water canals enabled shipping to enter the city and irrigation kept crops green and abundant.

Curiously, Plato makes much of a precious metal called orichalcum that was mined in Atlantis and was a familiar decoration of the buildings there. It was, he says, second only to gold in value. But even by Plato's time, this prized commodity had vanished. No one knows precisely what type of metal orichalcum is, although it is mentioned years later by the Roman commentator Josephus in relation to Solomon's Temple. But here too, evidence is scarce, and there is little archaeological data to confirm the materials used in that great temple. Whatever the physical properties of orichalcum, it seems certain that it was of great value to ancient cultures, and that Atlantis was rich in it.

According to Plato, Atlantis was an island once ruled by Poseidon, god of the sea. Poseidon fell in love with a native of Atlantis and she bore him five sets of twins. Admittedly, this part of his story does not seem to be anchored in reality, and the date is implausible. Plato dates the era of Atlantis to 9,000 years before his own day. Today, we have no knowledge of sophisticated civilizations existing so early in human history. It would have been a shining jewel in a Stone Age world.

But if Atlantis did exist, it was doomed to destruction. Plato's account tells how, within a single day and night, a natural disaster eradicated the entire civilization. This is entirely credible, since we know how powerful and ruthless nature can be. The island apparently disappeared into the depths of the sea, leaving only a shoal of mud that barred shipping from the area thereafter. Presumably an earthquake was to blame for the wholesale destruction, which would have extinguished the lives of countless thousands.

Initially it might sound like Plato was recycling some favourite myths that have cropped up through the ages. Atlantis bears some resemblance to a Garden of Eden, while its destruction might be likened to a great flood similar the one in the Bible and in numerous other beliefs. But why then did Plato go into such historical detail about the civilization and the metal they mined? What if Atlantis was simply the ancient name for another culture that had been wiped out, one that we have evidence of today?

For a long time it seemed as if Plato must have been referring to the Minoan civilization on Crete. This was named only relatively recently by an archaeologist, and no one knows what Plato's contemporaries would have called it. The Minoans had glorious palaces, paved roads and running water. A colossal volcanic eruption on the island of Thera, 100 km away from Crete, caused wholesale destruction in the region, but it did not obliterate the Minoans immediately. Archaeological evidence indicates they survived the tsunamis and the noxious sulphur clouds that must have followed the volcanic explosion, but fared poorly in the face of the ensuing climate change. By 1450BC the Minoan civilization had burnt out, succumbing either to starvation, insurrection or invaders.

Perhaps it was to the Minoans that Plato was referring? However, he confidently dates Atlantis to an era far earlier than that of the Minoan civilization on Crete. It leads one to speculate where the Minoans might have lived before migrating to the island.

What if Atlantis was simply the ancient name for another culture that had been wiped out, one that we have evidence of today?

Other sites for Atlantis have been put forward, and these have been as far flung as Spain, South America, the Caribbean, Cyprus and the South China Seas. The evidence for Spain has been supported by satellite photographs, which appear to show concentric circles like those described by Plato. Although the size of the circles does not exactly match the philospher's description, this might be accounted for by a mistake in translating his unit of measurement, the stade, to present day measurements. The proposed site lies in salt marshes near Cadiz.

Ancient writings contain accounts of attacks on Egypt and the eastern Mediterranean by 'the Sea People'. One theory is that the Sea People, the Atlanteans and the Iron Age residents of southern Spain, the Tartessos, were one and the same.

Tiahuanaco in the Bolivian Andes of South America has been earmarked as a possible Atlantis. Satellite photography has revealed it boasted hundreds of miles of inland canals. The residents are believed to have been of the Aymara tribe, a

This seventeenth-century woodcut shows a supposed location of Atlantis. One more recent theory is that the civilization was in fact that of the Minoan people on Crete.

pre-Inca civilization. Such an investment in waterways implies they were a seafaring race who probably traded with Europeans and Africans. Generally, Tiahuanaco is thought to have dated from the middle of the first millennium (c. AD500) but one researcher, Arthur Broznansky, was certain it was significantly older.

Elusive in place and time, it seems impossible, even using modern technology, to pin down Atlantis to one geographical location.

Nevertheless, many beliefs have sprung from the possible existence of Atlantis. Many people believed it to be the single root of all civilization. The odd coincidences of ancient history, like the way pyramids were built on both sides of the Atlantic and that various races chose to write in hieroglyphics, might have been explained by the existence of the great Atlantis. But there is no evidence of a linking civilization, and science has largely dismissed such claims.

The Nazis believed the Atlanteans were a superior race and the ancestors of the Ayrans, those favoured by the unsavoury fanatics for peopling the earth. Hitler's henchman Heinrich Himmler was particularly taken with the theory and invested much in a fruitless search.

There have even been claims that the Atlanteans were in fact highly advanced aliens, although evidence has been hard to come by. Edgar Cayce, the famous American psychic and healer, maintained that Atlantean existence focused on a giant crystal. This was used not only for healing but in a psychic sense for communication and teleportation. Disaster struck when the crystal exploded. Although they seem bizarre, Cayce's theories are backed by thousands of people today. He remains the inspiration behind the Association for Research and Enlightenment, based in America but present in sixty different countries.

If the mystery of Atlantis has retained its grip on human imagination for so long, it is because it remains a powerful symbol of the nature of human civilization, reminding us that however wealthy and powerful nations become, the forces of time and nature will eventually overcome them.

CIUDAD BLANCA

Hidden somewhere in the vast, impenetrable jungle of the Central American coast is the legendary 'Ciudad Blanca', or 'White City'. The city is said to have contained incredible wealth and yet was abandoned hundreds of years ago for unknown reasons. Although a number of international expeditions have endeavoured to uncover its secret location and sophisticated satellite technology has been used, the density of the jungle spanning Nicaragua and Honduras is so great that, to date, the task has been impossible.

The first recorded mention of the 'Ciudad Blanca' dates back to 1526, when it was referred to by Hernando Cortes – the Spanish conqueror of Mexico – by the twin names of Xucutaco and Hueitapalan. It is unsurprising that the Spanish were interested in the city as it was said that its riches rivalled those of Tenochtitlan, the wealthy Aztec capital. Inspired by such a notion, Cortes sent many of his followers in search of the lost kingdom, but the treacherous nature of the Mosquito Coast prevented the conquistadors from finding it and they soon abandoned their search.

It is thought however that, even by the time of the conquistadors, the 'Ciudad Blanca' was in decline. At that time the area was inhabited by the Pech people, who are believed to have

A contemporary portrait of Hernando Cortes.

originated from South America. Many skirmishes are recorded as having taken place between the Pech and the Spanish, as well as with the neighbouring tribes.

So what happened to this city, and how did it come to be abandoned? One possible theory is that it may just have exceeded its natural limits of expansion and was thus abandoned. Or perhaps, already shrinking, it was ultimately unable to survive the arrival of the conquistadors on the continent, since the Spanish invaders altered the balance of an entire way of life and had a damaging effect on many of the formerly advanced and prosperous civilizations of Meso-America.

The speed at which the jungle of the Mosquito Coast could devour an empty city is remarkable, especially as, prior to the arrival of the Spanish, it had been an incredibly populous area of the world. The 'Ciudad Blanca' is only one of the many undiscovered cities that are hidden in Central America, but for modern Honduras it would be a national and cultural treasure, should it ever be recovered.

THE MAYA AND THE AZTEC

The Mayan and Aztec civilizations are both fascinating examples of advanced cultures in Central America, developed long before the arrival of the Spanish invaders. Although the Mayans preceded the Aztecs, the two peoples shared a number of common belief systems, particularly in matters such as astronomy, religion and ritual sacrifice and both built large observatories, temples and pyramids in which to conduct these practices.

The Mayan culture reached its height between AD900 and AD1200. During this period their influence spread across a huge area of Central America and they were trading with nations as far away as Peru in the south of the continent. One of their great strengths was the quality of their architecture and construction, which was so advanced that, even today, there are examples of buried temples and pyramids to be found all over the Yucatan Peninsula of Mexico.

Concepts of space and time were extraordinarily significant to the Maya. They used a highly complex system to mark the passage of time, establishing a calendar that gave each day its own specific name, in line with precise astronomical calculations. As the cycle progressed, any cosmic event, such as a planetary transit, was treated with great reverence.

Central to the Mayan religious and cosmic beliefs was ritual human sacrifice. Such bloodshed was deemed to be particularly necessary at the time of the solar eclipse, in order to meet the needs of the gods.

When a full revolution had been made through the possible sequences of calendar days, the system would then start again, giving rise to an inbuilt cycle of rebirth and regeneration. Each time this happened, great events were predicted to take place. Interestingly, this is expected to happen next in 2012, giving the modern world an opportunity to assess the accuracy of Mayan prophecy.

It is believed that conditions such as drought or disease, together with warfare, drove the Maya into decline and by AD1300 they were building constructions that were of markedly inferior quality. By the time of the Spanish conquest of Mexico in the early 1500s, many of the great ruins of the Maya that one can visit today in Mexico were already lost or abandoned.

As the Mayan civilization collapsed, a number of other cultures in the region were in the ascendant, most notable of which were the Aztecs. When the Spaniards first came into contact with these people, they were astonished by what they saw. Large indigenous populations lived in elegant cities based around vast pyramids and ceremonial centres. The riches and splendour of the ruling class seemed incomparable, and there was a high standard of social development. Yet the Spanish were shocked when they discovered the huge extent of

A Mayan head carved on a small piece of bone.

ritual human sacrifice being performed in these temples and pyramids.

The Aztecs practised the same form of sacrifice as the Maya, although perhaps with even greater fervour. Their sacrificial victims would be the captured warriors of opposing tribes, or slaves taken from subject peoples. Slaughter was often performed on a huge scale in order to sanctify newly-built temples, consecrated in honour of the Gods – excavations of the larger Mexican pyramids have revealed the existence of hundreds of kneeling skeletons buried deep within the foundations. Images of skulls and skeletons would appear on the architecture of the buildings that were constructed specifically for the purposes of human sacrifice.

Some of the rituals almost defy understanding. Some victims faced having their beating hearts cut out with a stone blade by the high priests. The hearts would then be placed on a special altar as an offering while corpses were cast down the steps of the pyramid and sometimes cannibalized.

Some victims faced having their beating hearts cut out with a stone blade by the high priests.

Other rituals, performed at a significant turning point in the astral calendar, would involve the flaying of victims' skin from their bodies while they were still alive. A priest would then take the skin and wear it for an entire month. This type of ritual symbolized rebirth, the loss of human skin being akin to the process of renewal inherent in the shedding of the skin of the serpent, a creature revered by the Aztecs.

Over time, this people's appetite for blood increased, and later temples are generally found to have larger quantities of human remains lying beneath them. It seems that once the cycle of bloodshed had begun, it could only get greater and that demands for sacrifice grew in line with the Aztecs' prosperity. One particularly gruesome tale is that recorded by the Spanish conquistadors, which states that on their arrival in the Aztec capital of Tenochtitlan – the centre of what is now Mexico City – they observed a monument constructed entirely of human skulls.

A rough estimate deemed that this structure comprised 125,000 skulls, arranged in a precise geometrical pattern.

This mystical fascination with death seems cruel and alien to us today, yet it was an integral part of the culture of these ancient civilizations, where ways of life had developed over several thousand years in isolation from what was thought of as the 'known world'. The destruction of the Aztecs, although an incredible military feat by the conquistador leader Cortes, was ultimately the annihilation of a highly developed culture.

It seems strange that the conquistadors were initially granted so much leeway on their arrival in Mexico since the Aztec king, Montezuma, was quite capable of defeating the invaders. In fact, his restraint was due to an ancient prediction which spoke of the future arrival in the land of the god Quetzalcoatl, who would then use his great power and wisdom to help the Aztec and Mexican peoples to achieve greater glory. Also known as the 'feathered serpent', this most revered of beings was described in terms that matched the armoured and bearded newcomers who then arrived from the east – the direction of the rising sun.

Although this prophecy appears to be accurate regarding the arrival of the Spanish, the result was, of course, quite the reverse of what had been predicted. With the arrival of the Spanish invaders, the Aztec culture was destroyed forever, as the conquistadors saw it as their duty to eliminate every trace of this once mighty people. Thus another of the world's ancient cultures had disappeared forever.

THE AGE OF THE PHARAOHS

There are perhaps no monuments more immediately associated with the concept of mystery than the great pyramids of Egypt. Although such structures are present all over the world, it is the Egyptian examples that are both the most ancient and spectacular and thus have the power to capture our imagination.

The precision of the line is such that some Egyptologists believe it may have been intended as a conduit for the Ka, or spirit of the Pharaoh.

The most evocative pyramid of all is the largest, which marks the tomb of King Khufu at Giza in Egypt. King Khufu, the son of Sneferu and Queen Hetepheres I, was the second Pharaoh of the fourth dynasty. Inheriting the throne while still in his twenties, he nevertheless immediately began the planning and construction of his tomb. He became the first Pharaoh to build a pyramid at Giza and in so doing began a period of monument building that was to span the ages. The clues offered by the great pyramid offer a tantalizing insight into the exact purpose of this kind of structure.

The great pyramid took well over twenty years to complete, using around 2.3 million individual blocks of stone, weighing up to 2.5 tonnes each. The sheer size of the tomb may well have reflected the great power and respect enjoyed by this particular pharaoh. The entire process of mummification, monument building and ritual burial are aimed at the concept of granting the king a passport to the afterlife. In preparation for this, vast chambers were built within the tomb and filled with an immense variety of riches.

On further examining this pyramid, a number of factors have led many to suspect that there may be some hidden meaning contained within the structure. First, Khufu's personal burial chamber is larger than that of any other pyramid in the world and its construction is of the highest standard. In fact it is so intricate that it contains a small shaft, running all the way from the burial chamber up to the sky in a completely straight line.

The precision of the line is such that some Egyptologists believe it may have been intended as a conduit for the Ka, or spirit of the Pharaoh. It has also been suggested that the line of the

The pyramids at Giza, Egypt, which were built by King Khufu during a thirty-year period around 2,550BC.

shaft from the burial chamber would have aligned with the constellation of Orion at the time of the king's burial and, furthermore, that this pyramid and the two others built at Giza may actually form a representation on earth of this particular constellation. Support for this theory is provided by the fact that Orion had particular importance for the Egyptians in terms of the afterlife.

There has also been much discussion about the supposed mathematical perfection of the pyramid's dimensions and position. Considering the religious importance of these factors to the Egyptians, these points may be worth considering. Each face of the pyramid is hyper-accurately oriented towards each of the cardinal compass points. The Egyptians used precise geographical North, which is aligned with the spin axis of earth, rather than magnetic North. This fact demonstrates the Egyptians' advanced understanding of the world and suggests that

they were aware that earth was a sphere that rotated. The position of the great pyramid exactly straddles the 30th parallel latitude, setting it precisely one-third of the way between the North Pole and the equator.

Just as there seems to be a very precise positioning involved in the construction of the pyramid at Giza, so too can a curious alignment be seen in the temple of Amen-Ra at Karnak. Here, doorways to the monument have been built so that they line up exactly along the bearing 26° south of East, to 26° north of West, over the distance of almost 1 km. This coincides exactly with the position of the rising and setting suns on the days of the spring and winter solstices.

Such factors could be coincidental, but taken together they begin to suggest that perhaps the edifices of ancient Egypt contain some greater significance in their structure. The deliberately huge scale of the pyramids would moreover ensure that they defied the ravages of time and

thus carry this message into subsequent millennia. Certainly, many Egyptian monuments would seem to demonstrate the importance to this ancient people of certain times of the year, such as the solstices. The Egyptian calendar also followed a kind of cyclical zodiac that applied a particular cosmic importance to each particular day. This is in its essence very similar to the ideas expressed in astrology today in cultures all over the world.

The pyramids are a potent symbol of mysticism and inspire great curiosity all over the world. Their true meaning and purpose can only be guessed at, and we will probably never know the real answers. Perhaps what is most important, though, is that the pyramids prompt us to ask the right questions, questions about the power and wisdom of the ancients, the nature of civilization and the mysteries of the universe.

THE ANASAZI

Little known today, the Anasazi civilization existed for almost one thousand years in the area of the USA now called Arizona and New Mexico. At their cultural peak, in around AD1050, the Anasazi were a thriving community, who built huge structures in which to live. Palaces, some containing up to 500 rooms, were cut into the cliffs and many displayed a considerable complexity of construction. However, by the middle of the twelfth century, the society had collapsed and its population had scattered. By AD1300 the tribe had disappeared altogether. The reasons why are unknown to this day.

Early explorers and relic collectors were amazed by what they found of this tribe, uncovering a remarkable abundance of abandoned pottery and artefacts. Initially, the discoveries were credited to the distant Aztecs as it was believed that the indigenous people living in this region would be incapable of constructing such an organized community. Only later did it become apparent that another civilization altogether may have been responsible.

Is it conceivable that such a sophisticated community could just vanish?

The greatest development of structures built by the Anasazi was discovered at Chaco Canyon, New Mexico, and was believed to have been the hub of a community of outlying farms and settlements. Several huge palaces were located here and it is thought that trading, spiritual ceremonies and astronomy were all practised in this central area. Is it conceivable that such a sophisticated community could just vanish?

It has not been unknown over the course of history for civilizations to decline or disappear. Some peoples – such as the residents of Pompeii or the Minoans of Crete – are known to have been wiped out as a result of natural disaster, but the fate of other civilizations remains a cause for speculation. What we do know is that there are numerous factors that could bring about the demise of a civilized society, such as drought, famine or war. At some sites, such as those where burned dwellings have been found, the sad fate of the inhabitants is all too apparent.

The rise and fall of some cities or states has been well documented over time, giving us the opportunity to learn from the mistakes and misfortunes of the past. It is true to say that, at any time, our hold on the status quo is only ever a precarious one, and if we can avoid repeating some of the errors made by our forebears, perhaps we can really be said to have made progress.

The remains of Mesa Verde in Arizona – a typical structure, carved from the cliffside, which was erroneously attributed to the Aztecs.

THE MOCHE

The Moche people formed the first great civilization of Peru, preceding both the Chimu and the Incas. Although it is known that the Moche lived for about 1,000 years – from around 100BC until about AD900 – their origins are uncertain. Were they indigenous South American people, or was there any truth in local legends that spoke of the tribe arriving by raft, under the leadership of a heroic figure known as 'Naymlap'?

Equally mysterious is why the Moche culture ultimately faded from the continent. One theory is that it might have been as a result of war, as surviving cultural treasures, such as art and pottery, dating from the latter part of their era seem to reflect a growing preoccupation with militarism.

The Moche were a particularly progressive people for their time, especially in the fields of architecture and engineering. Their vast and durable buildings – some of which are still standing today – were constructed out of adobe bricks, made from mud and then baked in the sun. Some of these buildings are estimated to contain as many as 100 million bricks.

One of their notable achievements was the building of

The tomb of a Moche warrior priest.

Chan Chan, the largest pre-Columbian city in America, and this, like all their cities, served a largely religious function. Most of the buildings and pyramids were used for the purposes of worship and astronomy. Two of the largest surviving pyramids are known as 'Huacas del Sol y de la Luna', or 'Temples of the Sun and the Moon', indicating their religious preoccupation with the stars and the motion of the heavens.

Another sign of the Moche's sophistication can be found in their unparalleled systems of irrigation, which are used to this day by local farmers. The Moche created hundreds of miles of irrigation channels and canals, a system which allowed them to gather water from high in the Andes and increase their crop yields. At the height of their success, the region was more highly cultivated and productive than it is today.

Unfortunately, the Moche did not possess a system of writing, so we are limited in what we can learn about them. Many questions about the Moche, these highly advanced progenitors of Peruvian culture, will remain unanswered.

THE DOGON

The people of the Dogon tribe, in Mali, west Africa, live in small villages miles from any civilization other than the famously remote Timbuktu. Despite their apparent geographical and cultural isolation, this remote tribe have been in possession of astronomical knowledge that, although now overtaken, was for hundreds of years far in advance of Western understanding.

The first Western scientists to make contact with the Dogon were two French anthropologists – Dr Marcel Griale and Dr Germaine Dieterien –

A Dogon tribesman with his daughter in southern Mali.

who reached the tribe in 1931. Astonished by what they found there, they remained in Mali to research this people for more than thirty years. During this time, they gained access to the Dogon's religious and cultural traditions, and eventually came to earn their trust.

The secret tribal lore of the Dogon revealed fascinating information. Long before Galileo made his revolutionary discoveries in Europe, the Dogon seem to have had knowledge of the rings of Saturn. They were also aware of the existence of the four major moons of Jupiter and knew that the earth is a planet, and that all planets orbit the sun.

The tribe also had an extensive understanding of the Sirius binary star system, which was unknown to the West until 1862, when it was spotted from the world's most powerful telescope. The Dogon were fully aware that Sirius actually comprises two stars, Sirius A and Sirius B, which orbit each other in a fifty-year cycle with the result that, for a large part of this cycle, only one of the two stars is ever visible.

Sirius A – a bright star that we refer to as the 'Dog Star' – was to the Dogon the most important star in the sky, as they believed that it was here that life originated. Sirius B – which is 100,000 times less visible than its twin, and which we class as a 'White Dwarf' star – was known to the Dogon as the second star of this system.

Such ideas are relatively recent in modern astronomy yet the Dogon were aware of this information long before instruments such as telescopes were invented. The mystery deepens still further when we consider the tribe's own explanation of how they acquired their detailed astronomical knowledge. According to tribal lore, they were given this information by a race of godlike extraterrestrials, the Nommo, who originated from the Sirius star system.

Dogon legend tells how the Nommo arrived on a type of spaceship, accompanied by fire and thunder. These aliens were terrifying in their appearance, being fish-like and bearing similarities to the amphibious gods of some other ancient religions such as the Egyptian Isis and the Babylonian Oannes. According to tribal lore, these aquatic beings released huge quantities of water onto the earth in which to live.

The Dogon referred to Sirius B as 'the Nommo star', and also spoke of a mystical third star, Sirius C, which, to date, has not been recognized by modern science. The tribe called this star the 'Sun of Women', and predicted that it would re-appear in the sky when the Nommo chose to reveal themselves to earth once again.

The Dogon, therefore, have their own explanation behind their remarkable knowledge. But what does the wider world think? Three main theories have been put forward.

Firstly, it has been suggested that the Dogon may have learned about Sirius through an undocumented contact with the outside world. However, this argument would seem to be invalidated by the fact that the tribe's knowledge of Sirius was documented on cuneiform tablets many years before modern science even became aware of the star system.

Secondly, it is possible that one of the great ancient civilizations, such as Egypt or Persia, was itself in possession of this astronomical knowledge and had passed it on to a member of the Dogon, perhaps a wandering tribal nomad. This theory seems unlikely, however, since by nature the Dogon people choose to live a life of isolation away from the rest of the world.

The third possible explanation is that perhaps an ancient visionary priest or psychic prophesied this information to the tribe and it became woven into Dogon mythology. However, this seems almost as remarkable an idea as the tribe's own explanation. Perhaps it is the Dogon's own account that we should, after all, take as being

> According to tribal lore, they were given information by a race of godlike extraterrestrials, the Nommo, who originated from the Sirius star system.

the correct one. After all, they have been proved right on numerous counts already. Their isolation and ignorance of wider theories of alien life beings lends their explanation further credence. How could they describe an extraterrestrial unless they had actually encountered one?

The mystery remains, but what seems likely is that supposedly 'primitive' tribes such as the Dogon were, in fact, far more advanced than was thought possible.

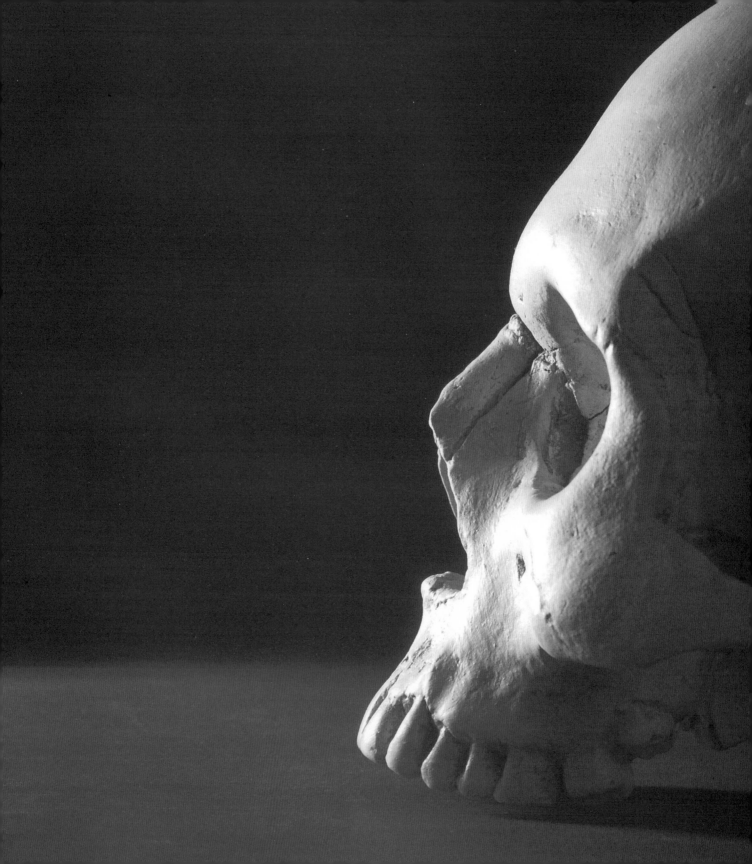

Medical Marvels

Throughout history, humans have battled against disease and some have lived with unique deformities and bizarre syndromes. With the advance of medical science, many hitherto little-understood conditions can now be treated and often cured. Nevertheless, some disorders are so strange and so rare they cannot be fully explained. Although the human body is wonderfully complex, it cannot compare with the intricate nature of the human mind. As our understanding of disease processes improves, we hope to better understand the mysterious complexities of the human brain.

EXTREME PHYSICAL ABNORMALITIES

Throughout history, there have been individuals who have stood out from the rest of mankind as a result of their extreme physical abnormalities. Although in previous times, society has often ridiculed and mistreated those who look so out of the ordinary, today such treatment is frowned upon.

The world's endless appetite for the strange and unusual has, however, brought many such people into the spotlight, and even turned some of them into celebrities in their own right – the case of the so-called 'elephant man' is one example. History has produced some extraordinary characters, whose very existence is a total mystery.

One such individual, Pasqual Pinon, achieved a degree of fame in the early years of the twentieth century. For three years he was a star performer in the Sells-Floto Circus sideshow due entirely to the fact that he possessed two heads, a condition known as craniopagus parasite. Rather than having two necks, the second of his heads protruded from the top of his skull, and was about half the size of his main head.

Pinon claimed that his second head could behave independently of the other head and had functioning senses of sight and smell. He also alleged that, up until the age of 20, he was able to speak through the mouth of the second head. At this age, however, he suffered a debilitating stroke, which left the head in a state of atrophy.

Medical science has been suspicious of this claim, as it differs markedly from anything seen before or since. Although there have been other recorded cases of people being born with two heads, they have never been known to exist before in this kind of physical formation. On the very

> Pinon claimed that his second head could behave independently of the other head and had functioning senses of sight and smell.

rare occasions it has happened, the second head has always sat upside down on top of the main head, so that the tops of the two skulls are joined together. An example of this 'mirror image' effect can be seen in the miraculous 'Two-Headed Boy of Bengal', and more recently in a girl born in the Dominican Republic, Rebeca Martinez.

Scientists have therefore concluded that Pinon was either a remarkable new case, or that he was in some way faking his abnormality. One possibility is that the protrusion from the top of his skull may have been not a second head at all, but an unusual type of tumour. He might then have attached a waxen face to the front of this large lump, and invented the curious story of his youth.

If Pinon was guilty of enhancing his deformity to increase his earning potential, then he would not have been the first person to act in this way. Another star of the sideshow was William Durks, who claimed to have not two heads, but two faces. In reality, however, Durks had a cleft mouth and a split nose. Although only one of his eyes functioned properly, he would add a false third eye to the middle of his face, thus creating the effect of having two faces.

Certain individuals have required no such adjustment of their physical appearance to mystify their audiences. Siamese (conjoined) twins are a rare natural abnormality, occurring as a result of an incomplete separation in the womb of a single fertilized egg. The term originates from the first widely publicized case of such twins, Chang and Eng, who were born in Siam and went on to become celebrities in their own right, performing throughout the nineteenth century. The twins lived for more than 60 years, and both eventually married, fathering 21 children between them.

The most famous European from this period of history with such a condition was Jean Libbera. Born in Rome in 1884, Libbera performed under the title of 'The Man with Two Bodies'. In certain cases of conjoined twins, the incomplete division of the egg in the womb results in only one normal sized person, the other twin failing to develop fully into an individual.

The Siamese twins, Chang and Eng.

This was the essence of Libbera's condition, for he had an almost fully formed body attached to his own, from the shoulders down. His vestigial twin was attached to Libbera's torso by the neck and shoulders, with a small semi-formed skull actually located within Libbera's body itself.

Medical science termed the second twin an 'epigastric parasite' as, although it was formed of living tissue, it survived by feeding from Libbera's system.

There is still a great deal to be understood about the functions and workings of the human body, which is a machine so complex as to be incomprehensible at times. For centuries, mankind has been fascinated by mysteries that lie within our own bodies and, of all the world's great unknowns, perhaps it is this that is the most remarkable.

THE FALLON CANCER CLUSTER

Fallon, a small agricultural town in Nevada, is similar in many ways to hundreds of other towns across the USA. One fact, however, sets it apart. Despite its population of just 7,500, Fallon has one of the largest proportions of cancer sufferers in the USA. Moreover, almost all of those affected have been children, diagnosed with leukaemia.

> It seemed that the only link between the cancer patients was the fact that they lived, or had once lived, in Fallon.

It took some time before doctors realized that such a pattern was forming within the community, and they were mystified as to how this could have occurred, as leukaemia is not a contagious disease. They started a desperate search for a common denominator between the cases – if this factor were to be found, then it could be investigated in depth, but without it, the task would be enormous.

Accordingly, each affected family was interviewed at length, and asked detailed questions about anything that might have had an impact on their health. Doctors even noted all the cleaning products and chemicals that were kept in their homes. However, the search proved inconclusive – it seemed that the only link between the cancer patients was the fact that they lived, or had once lived, in Fallon.

This immediately led doctors to believe that there must be something about the town that was causing such an incidence of illness among its inhabitants. Their investigation of the area revealed several possible causes, although none of these has ever been proved conclusively, and of course there is always the chance that a combination of factors could be to blame.

One of the favoured theories about the Fallon cancer cluster is that the town might have been subjected to some form of contamination from the huge naval air base that is located only 16 km away. Large numbers of military personnel pass through the air base in order to undertake fighter jet training over the Nevada Desert. Thus, contamination could occur in one of two ways: firstly, the huge flow of people through the air base could introduce a wide variety of viruses or illnesses into the small community; and secondly, the vast quantities of aviation fuel used by the base could pollute the environment to such an extent that serious illness could have resulted.

Although research on cats and cows has shown that viral infections can cause leukaemia in animals, no test has ever shown that this is possible in humans. It might be, however, that there has to be an element of genetic susceptibility present before such a situation can arise. European research studies have proved that the health of residents of small towns can be adversely affected by large influxes of people, as their immune systems have not become acclimatized to the wide variety of illnesses introduced to the community. It is possible, therefore, that an unusual virus found its way into Fallon via the air base, and then went on to have a disastrous effect on the vulnerable population.

The second, more likely, possibility is based upon the notion that some type of environmental pollution could have taken place. The air base, home to the US Navy's 'Top Gun' school that was made famous in the film of the same name, uses a reported 155 million litres of fuel every year. The exhaust emissions from this quantity of fuel are undoubtedly significant. In addition to this, all of the aviation fuel used flows through a pipeline travelling directly under the town of Fallon. Although no leak in this pipeline has ever been suspected or found, the likelihood cannot be ruled out completely.

When further investigations into military activity in the area were carried out, however, the theory of fuel contamination actually paled into insignificance next to something altogether more sinister.

Back in 1963, the American military conducted 'Project Shoal', the trial detonation of a 13 kiloton nuclear bomb, in an underground test site in the Sand Mountain range, less than 50 km from Fallon. It is well known that previous nuclear explosions, such as those at Hiroshima and Chernobyl, have led to an increased incidence of cancer among the population.

> It is well known that previous nuclear explosions, such as those at Hiroshima and Chernobyl, have led to an increased incidence of cancer among the population.

Official reports, however, state that no radiation from this experiment should ever have endangered Fallon for, among other factors, the depth at which the test was carried out would have prevented any possible contamination from radioactive fall-out.

Nevertheless, the fact still remains that a nuclear test was performed very close to the town and, although more than 40 years have passed, it will be many thousands of years before the radioactive contamination completely fades from the site.

It has also been established that, of all the towns in the USA, Fallon has some of the highest levels of naturally occurring arsenic in its water supply. Having said that, the authorities maintain that the arsenic is still not present in sufficient quantities to endanger health, and it should also be remembered that prior to the

Scientific research has shown that viral infections can cause leukaemia in cattle such as these.

Further tests upon the natural environment around Fallon have revealed the presence of mercury – a highly toxic heavy metal – in a nearby lake and irrigation canals.

Similarly threatening are some of the fertilizers and pesticides that would have been used in large quantities in the mainly agricultural community of Fallon.

Over a period of several generations, trace elements of these toxins could have built up to such an extent in the food chain that they posed a threat to human health.

To date, there has been no official explanation for the cancer cluster at Fallon. With so many harmful substances present in the area, however, the possibility that the cases have arisen due to contamination of the local environment seems quite likely. Moreover, it is even possible that further, secret, contamination might have taken place here.

In addition to 'Project Shoal', the US military could have carried out other tests in this remote area of Nevada. Due to the inherent need for military secrecy, especially throughout the Cold War, it would be highly unlikely that the results of such tests would be revealed to the public.

Alternatively, as some scientists have suggested, such cancer clusters may just exist naturally and perhaps there is nothing unusual about the situation in Fallon, other than the level of misfortune for those concerned.

With no definitive explanation offered by science, the case remains a mystery. Perhaps time will provide an answer – in the meantime, it can only be hoped that the tragic fate that befell the town of Fallon will not be repeated elsewhere.

discovery of the cancer cluster the water had been drunk by several generations of residents without any recorded ill effects. Nevertheless, it has been suggested that the problem might only have become evident after sufficient time had passed to allow the traces of arsenic to build up to a level that might cause harm.

TREPANNING

The practice of trepanning – the cutting or drilling of a hole through a patient's skull – can be traced back to the days of our ancient ancestors and is still performed in a limited way today. Although its purpose is primarily medical, trepanning could be said to straddle both the scientific and mystical spectrums as it also has a spiritual application.

Some of the earliest examples of trepanning can be traced back as far as 4,000 years ago, when it was performed by early Peruvian tribes from the Inca and pre-Inca societies. When the first skulls containing holes were discovered, it was initially thought that these were as a result of fatal head wounds acquired in conflict. On closer inspection, however, archaeologists realized that some of the skull holes had been cut with great precision and many of them showed signs of bone regeneration, meaning that the person involved had survived the procedure.

Archaeologists realized that a type of surgery must have been performed on these people, although quite how primitive man managed to achieve this with tools made from rock and flint, and no form of antiseptic, is nothing short of remarkable.

The fact that skulls bearing the tell-tale holes of trepanning have been discovered on almost every continent of the world indicates not only how widespread this incredibly dangerous practice was, but also that man must have become very skilled at it, with so many patients obviously surviving surgery.

Archaeologists realized that some of the skull holes had been cut with great precision.

By the early 1900s, when trepanning was practised quite frequently, the technique had advanced so much that precise tools were being crafted specifically for the task. Scalpels and circular drill-saws were regularly used to reduce the likelihood of splintering bone or damaging the brain during the operation.

Throughout the ages trepanning has been performed for a number of reasons, some of which are still behind the practice today. Firstly, there were purely medical forms of trepanation, which would have been carried out to relieve pressure on the brain and so save the person's life. A warrior with head wounds, for example, might have been treated in this way. This type of surgery, still practised as an emergency procedure today, indicates the remarkable level of understanding of anatomy and medicine possessed by primitive man.

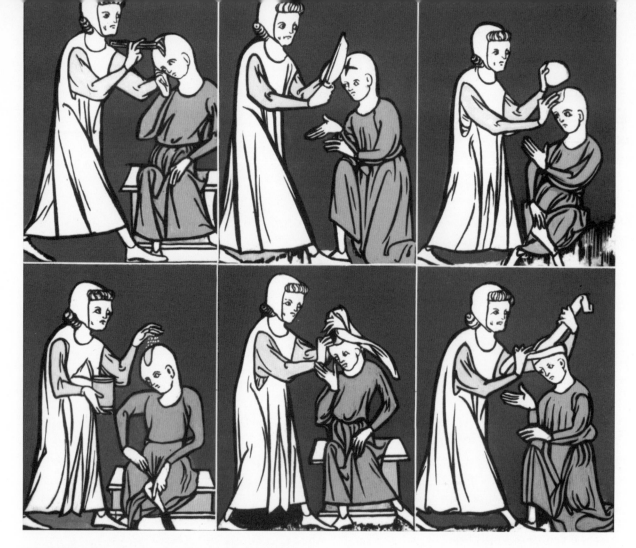

A thirteenth-century illustration of the practice of trepanning.

Secondly, some trepanations were performed in an attempt to cure head-related maladies such as migraine, epilepsy or mental illness. The practice was not carried out with a genuine understanding of the ailment itself, but rather in an attempt to expel demons or evil spirits that were thought to dwell inside the head of the sufferer. This has a resonance with what is known of primitive man's ideas of possession by demons, and it is believed that the operation actually continued for these

reasons as late as the Middle Ages in Europe. It may even still be carried out by remote civilizations in some parts of the world.

Thirdly, there is somewhat grim evidence to show that trepanning was performed for purposes such as the creation of jewellery or magical implements and could have been inflicted on unwilling subjects such as prisoners. Talismans have been recovered from Bolivia and Peru consisting of several discs of human skull, polished and perforated and then strung on a necklace, which was supposedly imbued with the power to protect the wearer.

Finally, trepanning has also been carried out for quasi-religious reasons, as part of an exercise in expanding consciousness in order perhaps to acquire mystical powers. It is known that our ancestors, with their interest in shamanism and sacrifice, had a particularly strong sense of the supernatural and it is likely that trepanning would have been performed as part of a ritual for the purposes of entering an altered state of mind.

There has been a limited resurgence of interest in this last application today, with some people successfully performing self-trepanation in order to achieve a state of enlightenment similar to that sought by primitive man. There are several documented cases of such practices, some even cutting holes into their heads with electric drills. Although the procedure is criticized by the medical profession – as it puts the person at risk of blood poisoning, cerebral meningitis, lobotomy or even death – enthusiasts speak highly of it, claiming that it has, in fact, enhanced their level of consciousness.

A prime devotee of self-trepanation is a Dutchman named Bart Hughes, the founder of the New World Trepanation Movement. He managed to successfully conduct a self-trepanation as far back as the 1960s, after forming his own theory about the functions of the brain. Like many spiritually inclined people before and after him, Hughes was seeking to discover a higher level of awareness, which he associated with the mindset of childhood. He believed that children have greater powers of

imagination and perception, and this stems from the nature of their skulls.

When a child is born, its skull is formed of several plates that expand through childhood to allow growth. Only once a person reaches adulthood does the skull harden and solidify. Hughes maintained that this ossification of the skull inhibits cerebral processes by restricting the flow of blood and oxygen to the brain. He believed that through self-trepanation he had liberated his brain and his consciousness from his restrictive skull and claimed to feel immediate benefits, saying that he felt as a child once more, his brain having the room to pulse with his heartbeat.

It is likely that trepanning would have been performed as part of a ritual for the purposes of entering an altered state of mind.

Hughes was so enamoured with his discovery that he expounded its benefits to the world at a press conference. This concerned the authorities, and they subsequently placed Hughes in a mental asylum for observation. This did not, however, prevent a number of people from following his teachings and from repeating the experiment at home on themselves.

Although the medical establishment dismisses the alleged spiritual benefits of trepanation as being due to nothing more than the power of faith healing, perhaps it really can enhance an individual's consciousness, concentration and intelligence, as has been claimed.

SUPERHUMAN POWERS

There can hardly be a person alive who has not dreamed of possessing superhuman powers at some point in their lives. What is truly amazing is the fact that these abilities have actually been shown to exist outside the world of fiction, and are in evidence even today.

They were said to head into battle without armour or even chain mail, and to fight like raging beasts.

Throughout history, certain groups of warriors have earned themselves fearsome reputations for their incredible strength and martial invulnerability. There is no doubt that these warriors revelled in this image of themselves, and benefited from a psychological advantage on the battlefield. In many cases, however, their reputation would be based on genuinely extraordinary powers.

The Berserkers were among the most terrifying groups of warriors ever to wage war on Europe – it is from their very ferocity that the word 'berserk' is derived. Originating from Scandinavia, the Berserkers essentially became the elite fighting force of the Vikings, renowned for their immunity to weapons. To demonstrate this invulnerability, they were said to head into battle without armour or even chain mail, and to fight like raging beasts.

There is little doubt that, to a large extent, the status enjoyed by the Berserkers could be attributed simply to their unparalleled ferocity in battle. A warrior who ignored his wounds, no matter how grave, and continued to fight would have been a terrifying adversary. It is entirely possible, however, that these warriors did not actually feel their wounds, having been worked up into such a state of bloodlust that they were able to overlook their injuries until the battle was over and they had calmed down from their furious state.

Alternatively, the Berserkers' invulnerability in battle could have been achieved by the performing of spells or rituals prior to engaging the enemy. This might have induced in them an altered, trance-like state in which they could avoid the sensations of pain, or at least postpone them until they were ready. Whatever the means by which they achieved their remarkable powers, it was highly effective, as the accounts of their vanquished foes attest.

The Berserkers were not the only group of warriors to be known for their immunity to pain, and invulnerability to weapons. The Rufa Dervishes were feared and respected by friend and foe alike, and it is testament to their reputation that they are immortalized in a phrase ('whirling dervish') that describes their ferocity and aggression.

These words also hint at the root of their powers, which, according to reliable reports, were induced at religious rituals in which the warriors would work themselves into a state of religious delirium or ecstatic trance, known as Halah. In a frantic celebration of their ability to deny pain, the Dervishes would carry out the widespread self-infliction of wounds throughout the group. They might grasp hold of white-hot irons or place hot coals in their mouths that would glow as the men breathed and were even said to pierce themselves with special spikes. Following this ecstatic frenzy, a healing ritual would take place, with the Shiakh of the group breathing upon each man's wounds and praying. Within a day, even the most life-threatening of the injuries would have healed.

The Dervishes entered battle as supremely confident warriors, with a strong belief in their own invulnerability. This would be particularly advantageous when the fighting was at its height, since the warriors held any injury in contempt and so earned a reputation for outstanding bravery.

The battlefield is not the only arena where such superhuman powers have been displayed, however – sometimes, they can be applied in a much more peaceful way. Spiritual figures such as Tibetan monks and Indian yogis are able to control their bodies in ways that seem utterly beyond comprehension. Onlookers have been captivated by their remarkable ability to stay alive in the most inhospitable environments, or

A young Dervish during the early twentieth century.

by their displays of amazing physical prowess.

Some of the monks of the Tibetan Himalayas seem able to defy the extreme cold of their environment. In a system known as 'tummo' (inner fire), they undertake extensive training in the form of numerous hours of meditation every day, focusing intently on the flame of warmth within their own bodies. When they are deemed to have mastered this ability, the monks face a dangerous test that, if they are not sufficiently prepared, may prove fatal.

Although this test involves nothing more than sitting in silent meditation, it is its location that is the real challenge. The monks meditate outside in the bitter cold of the mountains, wearing only a thin tunic that has been soaked in freezing water. The test requires the monk to render the tunic completely dry using just the heat from his body.

Only when the monk has performed this seemingly impossible feat three times in one sitting is he considered to have passed the test. He will then wear nothing more than just the

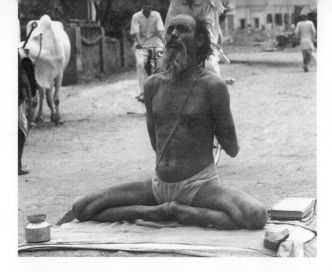

A yogi in Rajasthan, practising physical control.

incredible control over the microscopic functions of his own body that he could also dramatically alter its temperature. In a stunning display, he was able to make one side of his palm overheat, while the other would grow grey with cold. In effect, he had induced a temperature differential in this hand of 12°C.

Another, perhaps, even more famous example of the abilities of the yogis was publicised in a 1974 photograph, which depicted a yogi who was apparently still alive even though his head was buried beneath sand. According to witnesses, he had stopped breathing completely and had reduced his heartbeat to just two beats a minute. In this condition, he could survive with his head buried for days at a time.

This minute and precise control of reflex actions was not believed possible until the mid-twentieth century, when science at last provided an explanation. The yogis are able to achieve these feats through the power of meditation alone, which enables them to lower their metabolism, control their body temperature, heartbeat and even the electrical activity in their brains. It has been reported that certain yogis are also capable of levitation.

Such dramatic displays of control demonstrate the mysterious power of the human brain, which is accessible to some of those who have dedicated their lives to the achievement of an advanced meditative state. This superhuman ability offers a tantalizing glimpse to the rest of humanity of the amazing potential that lurks within the furthest reaches of human consciousness which, for now, lies out of the reach of the majority of humankind.

thin tunic, having demonstrated that he has no need for any warmer clothing. The fact that human beings can accomplish such tasks is truly incredible and yet the practice is about much more than the simple generation of warmth.

The entire system is an ideology in itself. The monks believe that, in releasing the heat from their bodies, they are burning away spiritual impurities such as envy or ignorance and refreshing their spirit. They maintain that a healthy mind will lead to a healthy body, and in many respects they have been proved right. Notwithstanding the deeper meaning behind this exercise, the fact remains that these holy men have completely shifted the boundaries of what is considered possible for a human being.

Much of the most unusual evidence of supernormal powers comes from the yogis of India. In the 1950s, researchers at the Menninger Foundation in Kansas, USA, came across one yogi who could produce a voluntary heart fibrillation that was measured at 306 beats per minute. Such speeds are rarely recorded in humans at their peak of adrenalized exertion. The same yogi had such

'WALKING CORPSE' SYNDROME

Cotard's syndrome is a particularly dangerous and unpleasant disorder. Also known as 'Walking Corpse' syndrome, it is usually associated with a serious depressive state, and frequently involves psychosis. The main symptom of the condition is the patient's absolute conviction that he or she is dead.

The condition takes its name from the French doctor, Jules Cotard, who first diagnosed the condition in 1880, calling it '*délire des négations*' (delusion of negation). It is possible, however, that the syndrome was discovered almost a century prior to this. In 1788 a man named Charles Bonnet spoke of a case in which a woman was so convinced of her own death that she lay in a coffin, dressed in a shroud. She even requested that she be buried, but no one would consent to this. She refused to move from the coffin, remaining there for several weeks until she actually was dead.

An actor dressed up as a zombie at the DVD release party of *House of 1000 Corpses* – just one of the many popular films about the living dead.

It seems likely that this woman did suffer from Cotard's syndrome because of the nature of her delusions, although these can be many and varied. Patients might believe that only part of their body is dead or perhaps that just their spirit has departed. They might feel as if their body is no more than a shell, or that they have turned to stone. Or, even more bizarrely, the hallucinatory convictions might be so powerful that sufferers actually describe the smell of their own rotting flesh, or the sensation of worms crawling through their skin. Treatment of patients with this bizarre condition is a complex and challenging process.

Although, in many cases, sufferers otherwise function normally and rationally, the delusions over their mortality can place them, and those around them, in serious danger. Some individuals have committed suicide, or tried to do so, in an attempt to prove that they are genuinely dead.

Others remain totally convinced of their own invulnerability, believing that, as they are dead, they can come to no harm.

Most patients with this disorder will, in physical terms at least, be perfectly healthy. However, in a prime example of the power of the human mind, the nature of the condition can often have a serious effect on bodily health – patients have been known to starve themselves, believing food unnecessary for them, or even attempt to amputate their own limbs.

Although the preoccupation with mortality that is a hallmark of this condition can be found in other areas of severe mental illness, the fact remains that Cotard's syndrome is rare. Treatment today still focuses more on containment than on cure, but it is hoped that the growing pace of medical discovery will one day offer real hope to those affected by this curious disorder.

'JUMPING FRENCHMAN OF MAINE' SYNDROME

'Jumping Frenchman of Maine' syndrome is a peculiar condition in which the patient displays an exaggerated reflex reaction as a result of the alarm or panic arising from even the smallest of

> The patient displays an exaggerated reflex reaction as a result of the alarm or panic arising from even the smallest of shocks.

shocks. A typical response involves leaping, shrieking and waving the arms and, in some cases, the patient adopts the foetal position.

All of these reactions are generally grossly disproportionate to the actual shock involved.

The condition was first diagnosed in 1878 by an American physician, Dr Beard, who recorded his discoveries in a dispatch to the American Neurological Association. He based his diagnosis on studies of a small number of French-Canadian lumberjacks from the Moosehead Lake area of Maine, USA – it is from here that part of the name originates.

Dr Beard also noted another strange response in many of these patients – the involuntary reflexive obedience to sudden or sharp commands. For instance, the order to strike someone would be immediately obeyed without a conscious thought for the consequences of this action, even if it were carried out against a friend or family member. Patients who suffered from this particular trait would often echo the words that had been uttered. Some would even do this when they were spoken to in another language, repeating the phrase immediately without understanding its meaning.

It was found that, for the vast majority of sufferers, the onset of symptoms began soon after they had started working as a lumberjack, suggesting that the logging work might have induced the condition in some way.

Investigations into this apparent link attempted to discover some kind of neurotoxin in the flora and fungi of the forest, or perhaps an insect, that might be the cause of the unusual behaviour. However, to date, nothing has been discovered to prove a connection, although it remains a potential explanation.

Doctors now believe that the syndrome is not actually neurological in its origins, but is, in fact, a psychological condition. In the early days of research, it was thought to be allied to Tourette's syndrome, but although there are certain similarities between the two disorders, 'Jumping Frenchman of Maine' syndrome is a distinctive condition in its own right.

Extreme stress has been suggested as a cause of the condition, after comparisons were made between its symptoms and those of First World War soldiers suffering from 'shell shock', in whom loud noises prompted a similar response. This was rejected, however, because there was apparently nothing in the loggers' environment that could bring about such levels of stress.

The tranquil waters of Moosehead Lake, in Maine, USA.

It is more likely that the syndrome is genetic in origin, as the majority of sufferers seem to have come from small, isolated communities in which there may have been some inbreeding within families, such as the loggers of Maine and, most recently, among men living in the Beauce region of Quebec.

Until more cases of this rare condition are uncovered and studied, it is unlikely that the true explanation for such an unusual affliction will be revealed.

For now, the cause of the disorder remains as much of a mystery as the identity of the original 'jumping Frenchman of Maine'.

'ALICE IN WONDERLAND' SYNDROME

The peculiar condition known as 'Alice in Wonderland' syndrome drastically affects the visual and mental perception of the sufferer. Characteristic of the syndrome is a completely distorted sense of time, distance, size and space, that can leave the patient totally disorientated and in a state of serious distress. Little is understood about the cause of the condition, although doctors believe that it can be linked in some way to better known afflictions.

> Could it be possible that Carroll actually suffered from this condition himself, and that his own symptoms provided him with the inspiration for his classic novel?

The syndrome was first diagnosed in 1955 by an English psychiatrist, John Todd. Finding the symptoms of the illness amazingly far-fetched, he named it after Lewis Carroll's famous book, although the condition has also been termed 'Lilliputian hallucination', after the tiny characters of Robert Swift's book *Gulliver's Travels*. The fact that both terms are borrowed from fantasy fiction is testament to the bizarre nature of the illness.

A patient with 'Alice in Wonderland' syndrome will typically also be a sufferer of migraine headaches, which are believed to be linked in some way to the condition. Strangely, it is recorded that Lewis Carroll himself actually suffered from severe migraines for most of his life. Could it be possible that Carroll actually suffered from this condition himself, and that his own symptoms provided him with the inspiration for his classic novel?

It seems likely, as a number of the condition's symptoms are mirrored in the story of what happens to Alice. Just as, after eating and drinking two separate magical concoctions, Alice becomes first tiny, and then larger than a house, so those with this syndrome may experience similar distortions – a form of visual and sensory hallucination can make them feel as if their entire body, or sometimes just parts of it, have grown or shrunk in scale. Problems that result from this, such as feelings of invulnerability or paranoia, can place a patient in serious danger.

To date, no thorough explanation of this condition has been offered, although the theory regarding its link with migraine headaches is believed to be sound.

In common with other strange medical phenomena, one of the obstacles to research is the scarcity of cases. So few people with this syndrome have existed that it is very difficult to compare and contrast different cases. Without doubt, this is one of the most unusual conditions ever to test the powers of medical science. Will scientists, in the years ahead, be able to solve it?

An illustration by Sir John Tenniel for the first edition of Lewis Carroll's *Alice in Wonderland*.

INDEX